Mastering ZeroMQ
Advanced Techniques for High-Performance Messaging Systems

Nova Trex

© 2024 by Wang Press. All rights reserved.

No part of this publication may be reproduced, distributed, or transmitted in any form or by any means, including photocopying, recording, or other electronic or mechanical methods, without the prior written permission of the publisher, except in the case of brief quotations embodied in critical reviews and certain other noncommercial uses permitted by copyright law.

Published by Wang Press

For permissions and other inquiries, write to:
P.O. Box 3132, Framingham, MA 01701, USA

Contents

1 Introduction to ZeroMQ: Basics and Architecture   9
   1.1 Understanding the Need for Messaging in Modern Applications 10
   1.2 The Basics of Messaging Protocols 13
   1.3 ZeroMQ Architecture and Design Principles 18
   1.4 How ZeroMQ Works 23
   1.5 Key Features and Benefits of Using ZeroMQ 27

2 Setting Up a ZeroMQ Environment   33
   2.1 Choosing the Right Development Environment 34
   2.2 Installing ZeroMQ on Various Platforms 37
   2.3 Configuring Your Development Environment 40
   2.4 Basic Configuration Testing 45
   2.5 Troubleshooting Common Installation Issues 49

3 The ZeroMQ Messaging Patterns   55
   3.1 Exploring Messaging Patterns 56
   3.2 Request-Reply Pattern 60
   3.3 Publish-Subscribe Pattern 64
   3.4 Push-Pull Pattern 68

3.5　Dealer-Router Pattern 72

　　3.6　Advanced Pattern Combinations 75

4　Working with Sockets in ZeroMQ　　**81**

　　4.1　ZeroMQ Socket Types 81

　　4.2　Socket Lifecycle: Creation to Termination 86

　　4.3　Binding and Connecting Sockets 89

　　4.4　Asynchronous I/O with ZeroMQ 93

　　4.5　Managing Socket Options and Contexts 97

　　4.6　Handling Socket Errors and Exceptions 102

5　Advanced Patterns and Use Cases　　**107**

　　5.1　Combining Patterns for Complex Workflows 108

　　5.2　Scalable Architectures with ZeroMQ 111

　　5.3　Building Microservices with ZeroMQ 115

　　5.4　High-Performance Computing Applications 120

　　5.5　Real-time Data Processing Use Cases 125

　　5.6　Case Studies of ZeroMQ in Industry 130

6　Integrating ZeroMQ with Various Programming Languages　　**137**

　　6.1　ZeroMQ Language Bindings Overview 138

　　6.2　Using ZeroMQ with Python 142

　　6.3　ZeroMQ in C/C++ Applications 147

　　6.4　Integrating ZeroMQ with Java 152

　　6.5　ZeroMQ with JavaScript and Node.js 158

　　6.6　Cross-language Messaging with ZeroMQ 162

7　Security and Error Handling in ZeroMQ　　**169**

7.1 Understanding ZeroMQ's Security Model 170
7.2 Encryption and Authentication in ZeroMQ 175
7.3 Implementing CurveZMQ for Secure Communications 180
7.4 Error Detection and Management Techniques 185
7.5 Handling Timeouts and Message Failures 190
7.6 Debugging and Logging in ZeroMQ 196

8 Performance Tuning and Best Practices 203
8.1 Optimizing ZeroMQ Configuration 203
8.2 Efficient Message Handling 207
8.3 Network Considerations for High Performance 210
8.4 Improving Scalability with ZeroMQ 214
8.5 Monitoring and Profiling ZeroMQ Applications 219
8.6 Best Practices for Robust ZeroMQ Solutions 222

9 ZeroMQ with Distributed Systems 227
9.1 Role of ZeroMQ in Distributed Architectures 227
9.2 Implementing Fault Tolerance with ZeroMQ 232
9.3 ZeroMQ for Real-time Data Pipelines 237
9.4 Synchronizing Distributed Components 242
9.5 ZeroMQ in Multicloud and Hybrid Environments . . . 247
9.6 Case Studies: ZeroMQ in Large-Scale Systems 252

10 Exploring Real-world Applications of ZeroMQ 259
10.1 Financial Services and Trading Platforms 260
10.2 ZeroMQ in IoT and Sensor Networks 264
10.3 Media and Content Delivery Networks 268
10.4 Healthcare Information Systems 272
10.5 Telecommunications and Messaging Systems 277

10.6 Collaborative and Distributed Software Development . 281

Introduction

In the realm of distributed systems and messaging frameworks, ZeroMQ emerges as a premier choice for developers and architects aiming to build high-performance and resilient communication infrastructures. Characterized by its lean and efficient design, ZeroMQ is more than just a conventional messaging protocol; it stands as a versatile library that equips you with the means to design and deploy sophisticated network architectures with unparalleled ease and agility. ZeroMQ's extensive applicability spans numerous sectors—from high-frequency trading environments demanding ultra-low latency to Internet of Things (IoT) ecosystems and scalable cloud-native microservices.

At its core, ZeroMQ embodies a minimalist philosophy that emphasizes performance and simplicity. This is reflected in its elemental building blocks—the diverse socket types and foundational messaging patterns—which facilitate a gamut of communication paradigms including asynchronous messaging, publish-subscribe, and request-reply models. The library cleverly abstracts the inherent complexities of message transport, routing, and topology management, thereby freeing developers to concentrate on crafting incisive application logic without being bogged down by intricate networking code.

ZeroMQ's flexibility is further exemplified by its compatibility across a multitude of programming languages and platforms. With robust language bindings for major languages such as C++, Python, Java, and JavaScript, ZeroMQ seamlessly integrates into diverse development ecosystems, thereby harmonizing disparate software stacks and delivering a unified communication strategy irrespective of the platform.

Security stands as a cornerstone in the design of ZeroMQ, which is vital as cybersecurity becomes a mounting concern across all fields. ZeroMQ incorporates advanced encryption and authentication protocols, like CurveZMQ, to ensure message integrity and confidentiality. This provides developers with the confidence to deploy ZeroMQ in environments that demand stringent security, without sacrificing the performance benefits ingrained in its design.

Performance tuning and adherence to best practices are critical when deploying ZeroMQ in practical, production scenarios. This involves fine-tuning network configurations, leveraging ZeroMQ's asynchronous capabilities, managing socket behaviors, and optimizing parallel processing to maximize throughput and minimize latency.

This book, "Mastering ZeroMQ: Advanced Techniques for High-Performance Messaging Systems," is dedicated to offering a comprehensive, in-depth exploration of ZeroMQ. It serves both as a beginner's introduction and as an advanced guide to mastering ZeroMQ—from grasping the essential concepts and foundational setups to delving into advanced configurations and performance optimization strategies. By exploring ZeroMQ's core features, tuning techniques, and real-world applications through detailed explanations, pragmatic examples, and strategic insights, this book aspires to empower developers to leverage ZeroMQ in creating high-performance, scalable messaging solutions that meet the complex demands of modern distributed systems. Whether you are a novice developer or a seasoned technology professional, this book is structured to illuminate the potential of ZeroMQ in crafting cutting-edge, robust messaging architectures.

Chapter 1

Introduction to ZeroMQ: Basics and Architecture

ZeroMQ is a high-performance asynchronous messaging library that serves as a fundamental building block for crafting scalable distributed applications. It is designed to handle complex communication patterns with minimal overhead, differentiating itself from traditional messaging solutions. The library provides various messaging protocols, enabling efficient and flexible data exchange between systems. ZeroMQ's architecture emphasizes simplicity and speed, making it suitable for applications requiring low-latency and high-throughput messaging. Understanding the need for messaging in modern applications and the unique design principles of ZeroMQ is essential for leveraging its capabilities effectively in real-world scenarios. This chapter lays the groundwork for comprehending ZeroMQ's role in the evolving landscape of networked systems.

1.1 Understanding the Need for Messaging in Modern Applications

In distributed computing, the ability to effectively share and communicate information between different parts of a system is paramount. The rise of messaging as a fundamental element in modern applications stems largely from this necessity. Contemporary software development increasingly requires scalable, fault-tolerant, and responsive systems capable of handling various types of data exchanges across distributed components. This requirement has given rise to solutions that rely on asynchronous, non-blocking communication techniques, making messaging an indispensable tool in the current technological landscape.

The essence of messaging lies in its capability to decouple different parts of a system. In a distributed architecture, components often run on separate machines and may need to communicate over a network. Direct communication methods, such as remote procedure calls (RPC), can become challenging due to network latency, the need for continuous availability, and the tight coupling of services. Messaging resolves these issues by providing a means for asynchronous communication, allowing components to function independently and exchange data or commands as needed without waiting for one another to respond immediately.

Decoupling Through Asynchronous Messaging

Asynchronous messaging is pivotal in achieving decoupling, where a software system's components operate independently without persistent connections. This approach allows components to send messages to a queue, which can be processed by another component at a later time. Asynchronous messaging systems leverage message queues to store and forward messages, ensuring that even if the receiving component is unavailable, the messages are retained and delivered once it reconnects. This feature is particularly beneficial for systems requiring high availability and resilience.

To illustrate, consider a microservice architecture where a payment processing service needs to communicate with an inventory service. Implementing a synchronous communication model would lead to service dependencies that could degrade system responsiveness if one service experienced downtime or slow processing. Instead, employing asynchronous messaging, the payment service can send a message to a queue handled by the inventory service. This decoupling enables continued operation, as the payment service need not await an immediate response.

Another benefit is load leveling or smoothing, where workloads are distributed across time. A surge in user demand may lead to a sudden spike in message production. The system can handle such spikes through message queues by processing them incrementally, matching the processing ability of the consumer services, thus avoiding bottlenecks.

```
import zmq

# Setting up a ZeroMQ context and socket
context = zmq.Context()
socket = context.socket(zmq.PUSH)
socket.bind("tcp://*:5555")

# Simulating a producer that sends a set of tasks
for task in range(10):
    socket.send_string(f"Task {task}")
```

In Listing **??**, a producer sends tasks asynchronously using ZeroMQ's PUSH socket, showcasing a basic form of message queue where tasks are produced and added to a processing queue.

Facilitating Scalability and Distribution

Messaging also plays a vital role in scaling applications vertically and horizontally. Vertical scaling involves enhancing a single node's performance capabilities, while horizontal scaling refers to adding more nodes or instances to distribute a system's workload. Messaging allows systems to scale horizontally with relative ease. Adding more consumers to handle messages from a queue can increase a system's throughput, adapting efficiently to higher levels of demand without causing significant re-engineering of systems.

In cloud-based environments, this scalability is even more pronounced. Cloud architectures benefit from messaging by allowing independent deployment and scaling of microservices. Consider an e-commerce platform with distinct services for orders, billing, and shipping. Each service can scale dynamically according to its specific load requirements, aided by a messaging backbone that facilitates inter-service communication despite varying traffic pressures.

Ensuring Reliability and Fault Tolerance

The resilience of communication systems is crucial, particularly in mission-critical applications where downtime or message loss could have severe consequences. Messaging solutions enhance reliability through various mechanisms such as message acknowledgment, persistent message queues, and retry policies.

For instance, when a message is sent, the sending module can be assured of its eventual delivery through a confirmation process implemented by the messaging system. Moreover, if a consumer node fails or becomes unavailable, the messaging system can re-route or reallocate messages to other available nodes, ensuring minimal service disruption. These features make messaging systems suitable for environments requiring strict uptime guarantees and robustness against errors or failures.

```
import zmq
import time

context = zmq.Context()
receiver = context.socket(zmq.PULL)
receiver.connect("tcp://localhost:5555")

while True:
    message = receiver.recv_string()
    print(f"Received: {message}")
    time.sleep(1) # Simulate message processing time
    # Acknowledge the message processing completion
    print(f"Acknowledged: {message}")
```

In Listing **??**, an example consumer receives and processes messages with simulated acknowledgment, highlighting how messaging frameworks can confirm message handling.

Enhancing Cross-Language and Cross-Platform Interactions

Another critical dimension of messaging systems is their ability to foster interoperability across different technology stacks. Many organizations face heterogeneity in their technology environment, using systems developed in various programming languages and runtime environments. Messaging protocols, being language-agnostic and standardized, enable seamless communication and data exchange between components developed using these disparate technologies.

By adhering to standard protocols like AMQP, STOMP, or leveraging libraries like ZeroMQ, developers can facilitate seamless interaction between Java, Python, or C++ applications without the intricacies of cross-language bindings.

Conclusion of Distributed Interaction Needs

Messaging in modern applications is an essential mechanism that addresses the intricate demands of distributed systems. By enabling asynchronous communication, enhancing scalability, ensuring reliability, and fostering cross-platform interoperability, messaging solutions form the backbone of robust, responsive, and resilient software infrastructures. Understanding these aspects is critical for developers and system architects aiming to design systems that can withstand the dynamic and often unpredictable nature of production environments.

1.2 The Basics of Messaging Protocols

Messaging protocols are integral to the functioning of distributed systems, providing the rules and conventions that define how data is exchanged over networks. They enable communication between disparate components, ensuring that messages are formatted, transmitted, and interpreted correctly. Understanding the fundamentals of these protocols is essential for any software engineer or system architect involved in designing or maintaining distributed systems.

Messaging protocols can be classified broadly into two categories: text-based protocols and binary protocols. Text-based protocols, such as HTTP and SMTP, are generally human-readable and easier to debug. In contrast, binary protocols like AMQP and MQTT are more compact and typically offer better performance, especially in terms of bandwidth efficiency.

Text-Based Messaging Protocols

Text-based protocols are characterized by their use of human-readable text for message payloads and headers. Their simplicity and ease of understanding make them popular for many applications, particularly those interfacing closely with web technologies.

HTTP (HyperText Transfer Protocol)

HTTP is the foundation of data communication on the World Wide Web, providing a simple, stateless communication mechanism suitable for a wide range of applications. It's a request-response protocol where clients, usually web browsers, send HTTP requests to a server, which returns HTTP responses containing documents and metadata.

```
# HTTP Request
GET /index.html HTTP/1.1
Host: example.com
Accept: text/html

# HTTP Response
HTTP/1.1 200 OK
Content-Type: text/html

<html>
  <body>Hello, World!</body>
</html>
```

Listing ?? illustrates a simple HTTP GET request and the corresponding server response. While HTTP is not a messaging protocol in the strict sense, it serves a similar purpose in facilitating communication between clients and servers on the internet.

SMTP (Simple Mail Transfer Protocol)

SMTP is a protocol for sending email messages between servers, playing a crucial role in the email domain. Despite its primary role in sending emails, SMTP supports a command/response structure that can be adapted for broader messaging tasks.

```
# Client connects to the SMTP server
220 smtp.example.com ESMTP Postfix

# Client initiates communication
HELO client.example.com
250 smtp.example.com

# Start mail transaction
MAIL FROM:<sender@example.com>
250 Ok

# Specify recipient
RCPT TO:<receiver@example.com>
250 Ok

# Send message body
DATA
354 End data with <CR><LF>.<CR><LF>
Subject: Test Email
```

1.2. THE BASICS OF MESSAGING PROTOCOLS

```
Hello, this is a test email.
.
250 Ok: queued as 12345
# Close communication
QUIT
221 Bye
```

Listing **??** details a typical SMTP session, highlighting its command-oriented nature, where each command is followed by a response from the mail server.

Binary Messaging Protocols

Binary protocols are designed to optimize the encoding and transmission of message data for improved performance, commonly used in high-throughput systems or situations where bandwidth is constrained.

AMQP (Advanced Message Queuing Protocol)

AMQP is an open standard for passing messages between applications or organizations. Its primary application is in message-oriented middleware environments, facilitating message brokerage with strong reliability and security mechanisms.

AMQP ensures message delivery at three levels:

- At-most-once delivery: No retry guarantees, useful in high-speed scenarios.

- At-least-once delivery: Ensures messages are re-delivered until acknowledged, preventing message loss.

- Exactly-once delivery: Guarantees each message is processed only once, even if re-sent.

AMQP organizes messages into exchanges and queues, with exchanges determining how messages are routed to one or more queues.

```
import pika

# Establish connection with RabbitMQ server
connection = pika.BlockingConnection(pika.ConnectionParameters('localhost'))
channel = connection.channel()
```

```
# Declare a queue
channel.queue_declare(queue='task_queue', durable=True)

# Define message properties
properties = pika.BasicProperties(delivery_mode=2)  # make message persistent

# Publish a message to the queue
channel.basic_publish(exchange='',
                      routing_key='task_queue',
                      body='Task data...',
                      properties=properties)
connection.close()
```

Listing **??** demonstrates the use of AMQP via the RabbitMQ implementation to send messages reliably using message persistency features.

MQTT (Message Queuing Telemetry Transport)

MQTT is a lightweight messaging protocol widely used in the Internet of Things (IoT) domain due to its efficiency and ease of use on resource-constrained devices. It follows a publish-subscribe pattern, enabling decoupled and dynamic communication relationships.

MQTT allows various Quality of Service (QoS) levels to balance between message delivery reliability versus performance needs:

- QoS 0: At most once delivery.

- QoS 1: At least once delivery, ensuring messages reach at least one recipient.

- QoS 2: Exactly once delivery, ensuring the message arrives exactly once.

```
import paho.mqtt.client as mqtt

# Define callbacks for connection and message reception
def on_connect(client, userdata, flags, rc):
    print("Connected with result code "+str(rc))
    client.subscribe("test/topic")

def on_message(client, userdata, msg):
    print(f"Message received: {msg.payload}")

# Creating MQTT client
client = mqtt.Client()
client.on_connect = on_connect
client.on_message = on_message

client.connect("broker.hivemq.com", 1883, 60)
```

```
# Publish a message
client.publish("test/topic", "Hello MQTT!")
client.loop_forever()
```

Listing **??** shows a simplistic MQTT client that subscribes to a topic and publishes a message using Paho, a Python MQTT client library. It highlights the protocol's ease of use and lightweight nature.

Comparison and Selection of Messaging Protocols

The decision to choose between messaging protocols depends on the specific requirements of an application. Key considerations include:

- Performance Requirements: In systems requiring low-latency, high-throughput communication, binary protocols like AMQP or MQTT are typically preferred due to their efficient message encoding.

- Scalability Needs: Protocols supporting publish-subscribe patterns, such as MQTT, are suitable for applications where horizontal scaling is essential.

- Reliability and Acknowledgment: Applications needing guaranteed delivery should consider protocols offering strong acknowledgment mechanisms, such as AMQP's various delivery guarantees.

- Resource Constraints: In environments where devices have limited computational power or bandwidth, lightweight protocols like MQTT ensure minimal resource consumption while maintaining effective communication.

The Role of ZeroMQ in the Protocol Landscape

ZeroMQ does not stand as a protocol itself but as a library providing sockets that carry atomic messages. It is designed to bypass the complexity of traditional protocols, allowing developers to focus on message patterns without delving into low-level networking details. ZeroMQ sockets manage message flow seamlessly, thus fitting into various networking architectures as a flexible, versatile solution that simplifies the integration of messaging into applications.

Through native support for multiple messaging patterns such as publish-subscribe, request-reply, and push-pull, ZeroMQ accommodates numerous complex communication scenarios with ease, making it a preferred choice for custom network implementations that require high efficiency and low overhead.

Messaging protocols form the backbone of modern networked applications, providing critical infrastructure for scalable, reliable, and efficient communication. By understanding these protocols' core concepts and applications, developers and architects can design systems that are robust and tailored to their specific communication needs.

1.3 ZeroMQ Architecture and Design Principles

ZeroMQ is a high-performance asynchronous messaging library, not a mere messaging protocol, that is fundamental in simplifying task communication over a network. It is designed to efficiently handle complex communication patterns with minimal overhead, making it distinct from traditional messaging systems. Understanding the architecture and design principles of ZeroMQ is crucial for leveraging its capabilities effectively in distributed applications.

The architecture of ZeroMQ is structured around the concept of sockets, which are surprisingly more than what the name suggests in traditional networking terms. These sockets facilitate various messaging patterns such as request-reply, publish-subscribe, and push-pull, abstracting the complexity of network programming under a simple API. ZeroMQ's design philosophy emphasizes simplicity, speed, and flexibility, with thoughtful consideration towards real-world messaging needs like high-throughput and low-latency requirements.

Core Architectural Components

At the heart of ZeroMQ's architecture are its unique socket types that support different messaging patterns. Unlike conventional sockets, ZeroMQ sockets operate asynchronously, allowing the continuous sending and receiving of multiple messages without blocking. This feature lays the foundation for building highly scalable and responsive appli-

1.3. ZEROMQ ARCHITECTURE AND DESIGN PRINCIPLES

cations.

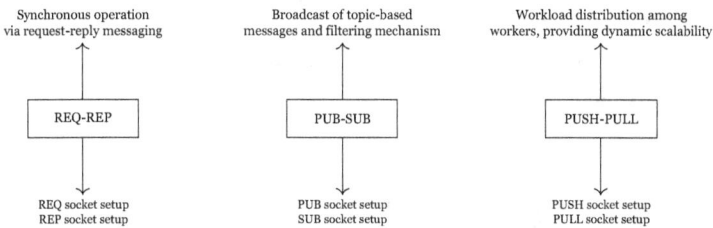

ZeroMQ Sockets

ZeroMQ provides several socket types, each designed for specific message flow patterns, enabling developers to create sophisticated and efficient messaging topologies.

- **REQ-REP (Request-Reply)**: This pattern involves paired sockets where the client sends a request and waits for a reply from the server. It is essential for service query models where synchronous communication mirrors traditional client-server architecture.

```
import zmq

# REQ socket setup
def req_client():
    context = zmq.Context()
    socket = context.socket(zmq.REQ)
    socket.connect("tcp://localhost:5555")

    for request in range(10):
        socket.send_string(f"Hello {request}")
        message = socket.recv_string()
        print(f"Received reply {request}: {message}")

# REP socket setup
def rep_server():
    context = zmq.Context()
    socket = context.socket(zmq.REP)
    socket.bind("tcp://*:5555")

    while True:
        message = socket.recv_string()
        print(f"Received request: {message}")
        socket.send_string("World")
```

Listing **??** exhibits the REQ-REP pattern in ZeroMQ, demonstrating synchronous operation via request-reply messaging.

- **PUB-SUB (Publish-Subscribe)**: This pattern disseminates messages to multiple subscribers based on topic filters. Publishers broadcast messages, and subscribers receive them only if they have subscribed to the relevant topics.

```
import zmq

# PUB socket setup
def pub_server():
    context = zmq.Context()
    socket = context.socket(zmq.PUB)
    socket.bind("tcp://*:5556")

    while True:
        topic = "topic1"
        message = "Information update"
        socket.send_string(f"{topic} {message}")

# SUB socket setup
def sub_client():
    context = zmq.Context()
    socket = context.socket(zmq.SUB)
    socket.connect("tcp://localhost:5556")
    socket.setsockopt_string(zmq.SUBSCRIBE, "topic1")

    while True:
        message = socket.recv_string()
        print(f"Received message: {message}")
```

Listing ?? illustrates the PUB-SUB pattern, showcasing the broadcast of topic-based messages and the filtering mechanism inherent to subscribers.

- **PUSH-PULL (Pipeline)**: This pattern is used primarily for parallel task distribution, where a PUSH socket distributes messages among multiple PULL sockets, enabling load balancing implicitly.

```
import zmq

# PUSH socket setup
def push_producer():
    context = zmq.Context()
    socket = context.socket(zmq.PUSH)
    socket.bind("tcp://*:5557")

    for task_nbr in range(10):
        message = f"Task {task_nbr}"
        socket.send_string(message)
        print(f"Sent: {message}")

# PULL socket setup
def pull_worker():
```

1.3. ZEROMQ ARCHITECTURE AND DESIGN PRINCIPLES

```
context = zmq.Context()
socket = context.socket(zmq.PULL)
socket.connect("tcp://localhost:5557")

while True:
    message = socket.recv_string()
    print(f"Received: {message}")
```

Listing ?? details the PUSH-PULL pattern for distributing workload amongst available workers, providing seamless dynamic scalability.

Design Principles of ZeroMQ

ZeroMQ embraces several core design principles that reflect in its lightweight, scalable, and adaptable nature:

Asynchronous I/O

One of the cornerstones of ZeroMQ's design is its support for asynchronous I/O operations. By allowing non-blocking send and receive operations, ZeroMQ permits applications to handle messages efficiently without being stalled by network delays, thereby enhancing overall system throughput.

Scalability by Design

The socket abstraction in ZeroMQ enables natural distribution and parallelism. By configuring multiple socket types, developers can design systems that scale out easily, accommodating growing loads without overhauling infrastructure.

Cross-Platform and Language Support

ZeroMQ's portability across platforms and its availability in numerous programming languages make it a versatile tool for diverse technological ecosystems. This cross-language support facilitates communication in heterogeneous environments, providing a consistent API regardless of the underlying language.

Efficient Memory Usage

ZeroMQ manages memory efficiently through zero-copy mechanisms, minimizing performance overhead when transferring messages between contexts or threads. This design choice is paramount for high-frequency messaging tasks prevalent in real-time systems.

Automatic Message Queuing

Internally, ZeroMQ effectively queues messages automatically, buffering them as needed until the consumer is ready to process them. This queuing mechanism aids traffic flow management and enhances the robustness of message transmission even under fluctuating conditions.

Integration and Implementation Considerations

Designers and developers using ZeroMQ should consider specific architectural nuances:

- **Message Frames**: ZeroMQ messages can consist of one or more frames, akin to frames in a streaming protocol, allowing for the transmission of complex data structures segmented into manageable parts.

- **Context Management**: ZeroMQ sockets require a context, which serves as a container for all transport state. Proper management of this context is crucial for ensuring resource optimization and avoiding leaks.

- **Topology Design**: Choosing the appropriate messaging pattern is critical. Patterns dictate the flow of data and the overall system throughput and reliability. Balancing between them based on application requirements can drastically reduce latency and optimize resource use.

ZeroMQ: A Practical Approach

ZeroMQ's simplicity and efficiency make it well-suited to a broad array of applications, including high-frequency trading systems, real-time analytics, and cloud-based service architectures. Its flexibility allows it to operate seamlessly within microservices and distributed system frameworks, enhancing maintainability and scalability of communication interfaces.

Through its rich set of features and architectural elegance, ZeroMQ stands as a uniquely powerful messaging library, bridging the gap between high-level message passing and low-level socket operations. For developers aiming to build responsive, dynamic, and scalable distributed applications, ZeroMQ offers the tools and abstractions needed to excel in modern, complex networked environments.

1.4 How ZeroMQ Works

To fully comprehend ZeroMQ's potent functionality as a messaging library, a detailed exploration of its working mechanics is essential. ZeroMQ abstracts the complexities underlying network communication through its sophisticated socket-based architecture, enabling effective message-passing in distributed systems. It leverages a set of transport protocols and socket patterns to provide flexible, high-performance messaging capabilities.

The core operations of ZeroMQ involve its ingenious handling of sockets, contexts, and message queues, along with its mechanisms for message framing and transmission. These components function together to deliver a library that excels in providing asynchronous communication, thus supporting applications needing low-latency and reliable data transfer.

ZeroMQ Sockets and Communication Patterns

ZeroMQ sockets diverge from traditional Berkeley-style sockets by offering a higher-level abstraction. These sockets are tailored to distinct messaging patterns, each addressing specific communication needs. Understanding these patterns is crucial for leveraging ZeroMQ in various application scenarios.

Request-Reply Pattern

The request-reply (REQ-REP) pattern enables synchronous communication, where a client sends a request to a server and expects a reply back. This is similar to RPCs (Remote Procedure Calls) and is utilized in applications requiring back-and-forth message exchange.

An advanced implementation would involve managing complex sequences of request and response communication ensuring each request correlates accurately to its reply, preserving integrity in multi-threaded environments.

```
import zmq
import time
from threading import import Thread

def req_client():
    context = zmq.Context()
    socket = context.socket(zmq.REQ)
    socket.connect("tcp://localhost:5559")
```

```
    for request in range(5):
        socket.send_string(f"Request {request}")
        message = socket.recv_string()
        print(f"Client received: {message}")

def rep_server():
    context = zmq.Context()
    socket = context.socket(zmq.REP)
    socket.bind("tcp://*:5559")

    while True:
        message = socket.recv_string()
        print(f"Server received: {message}")
        time.sleep(1) # Simulate processing time
        socket.send_string(f"Response to {message}")

Thread(target=rep_server).start()
time.sleep(1)
Thread(target=req_client).start()
```

In Listing **??**, the use of threads illustrates handling simultaneous requests in a multithreaded environment, ensuring messages are appropriately correlated.

Publish-Subscribe Pattern

The publish-subscribe (PUB-SUB) pattern allows for decoupled, one-to-many distribution of messages. This pattern is critical in scenarios like news dissemination or multicast updates where a single publisher must notify multiple subscribers.

ZeroMQ enhances this model with the ability for subscribers to filter messages based on topics, ensuring they receive only relevant data.

```
import zmq
import random

def pub_server():
    context = zmq.Context()
    socket = context.socket(zmq.PUB)
    socket.bind("tcp://*:5560")

    topics = ['sports', 'news', 'weather']
    while True:
        topic = random.choice(topics)
        message = f"{topic} update available"
        socket.send_string(f"{topic} {message}")

def sub_client(topic_filter):
    context = zmq.Context()
    socket = context.socket(zmq.SUB)
    socket.connect("tcp://localhost:5560")
    socket.setsockopt_string(zmq.SUBSCRIBE, topic_filter)
```

1.4. HOW ZEROMQ WORKS

```
    while True:
        message = socket.recv_string()
        print(f"Subscriber received: {message}")

Thread(target=pub_server).start()
time.sleep(1)
Thread(target=sub_client, args=("sports",)).start()
Thread(target=sub_client, args=("weather",)).start()
```

Listing **??** demonstrates topic filtering in ZeroMQ's PUB-SUB pattern, where subscribers selectively receive information.

Pipeline Pattern

The pipeline (PUSH-PULL) pattern supports load distribution by pushing tasks to a set of workers (pullers), ideal for distributing workloads across parallel processing units.

This pattern naturally accommodates dynamic scalability, where task distribution is optimized as workers dynamically join or leave the processing pool.

```
import zmq
import time
import random
from threading import Thread

def push_producer():
    context = zmq.Context()
    socket = context.socket(zmq.PUSH)
    socket.bind("tcp://*:5561")

    task_id = 0
    while True:
        task_id += 1
        work = f"Task {task_id}"
        socket.send_string(work)
        print(f"Sent: {work}")
        time.sleep(random.uniform(0.1, 0.5)) # Simulating variable task frequency

def pull_worker(worker_id):
    context = zmq.Context()
    socket = context.socket(zmq.PULL)
    socket.connect("tcp://localhost:5561")

    while True:
        work = socket.recv_string()
        print(f"Worker {worker_id} received: {work}")
        time.sleep(1) # Simulating task processing time

Thread(target=push_producer).start()
time.sleep(1)
for i in range(3): # Launching multiple workers
```

```
Thread(target=pull_worker, args=(i,)).start()
```

Listing **??** describes how ZeroMQ manages dynamic task distribution efficiently using the pipeline pattern.

Message Framing and Queuing in ZeroMQ

ZeroMQ works by segmenting messages into frames, facilitating the transmission of complex data structures by breaking them into manageable parts. This segmentation reduces overhead, allowing for efficient transmission.

Additionally, ZeroMQ queues messages on both sender and receiver sides, buffering them to handle disparities in processing speed and network latency. This queuing mechanism is critical to maintaining a consistent flow of messages under varying network conditions.

Message Atomicity and Multi-Frame Messages

Atomicity is an essential property of ZeroMQ sockets, preserving message boundaries without interleaving, despite network failures or sudden fluctuations in connections. In particular, multi-part or multi-frame messages can be sent atomically, ensuring that all parts of a message are received contiguously and completely.

```
import zmq

def send_multi_frame_message():
    context = zmq.Context()
    socket = context.socket(zmq.PAIR)
    socket.bind("tcp://*:5562")

    # Sending a multi-part message
    socket.send_multipart([b"frame1", b"frame2", b"frame3"])
    print("Sent multi-frame message")

def receive_multi_frame_message():
    context = zmq.Context()
    socket = context.socket(zmq.PAIR)
    socket.connect("tcp://localhost:5562")

    # Receiving multi-part message
    frames = socket.recv_multipart()
    print("Received multi-frame message:")
    for frame in frames:
        print(frame.decode())

Thread(target=send_multi_frame_message).start()
time.sleep(1)
Thread(target=receive_multi_frame_message).start()
```

As seen in Listing **??**, ZeroMQ efficiently handles multi-frame messages, preserving message structure and boundaries.

Transport Layer Independence

ZeroMQ abstracts the transport layer, allowing developers to use different protocols (e.g., TCP, PGM, or in-process) without altering code logic. This feature provides flexibility in adapting to different network conditions and infrastructure setups without significant refactoring.

Security Considerations and Implementations

While ZeroMQ itself is lightweight, it provides mechanisms to ensure secure messaging. Encryption can be layered atop ZeroMQ channels using libraries like CurveZMQ, which implement modern cryptographic protocols over ZeroMQ's transportation framework for secure communication.

```
# Example illustrating CurveZMQ-based secure channels
# Details of implementation would include key exchange and encryption setup
```

By adopting necessary security practices, ZeroMQ can become suitable for environments demanding secure data transmission while maintaining its performance advantages.

Understanding these operational principles and leveraging ZeroMQ's robust feature set allows developers to architect highly efficient, responsive, and scalable messaging systems, pivotal in today's fast-paced data-driven landscape.

1.5 Key Features and Benefits of Using ZeroMQ

ZeroMQ, often heralded as a revolutionary messaging library, is lauded for its unique blend of simplicity, performance, and flexibility. It is specifically designed to address the demanding needs of modern distributed applications through an architecture that supports fast and easy message passing between applications or among components within an application. This section delves into the key features of ZeroMQ, underscoring the benefits that make it a preferred choice among developers working on high-performance computing, scalable systems, and real-time applications.

High-Performance Messaging

ZeroMQ is optimized for high throughput and low latency, enabling it to handle millions of messages per second on a single machine. Its efficient memory management and zero-copy architecture substantially reduce the overhead associated with message passing, making it suitable for latency-sensitive applications such as financial trading platforms and real-time data analysis systems.

The core of ZeroMQ's performance lies in its use of asynchronous I/O and messaging queuing. Messages can be sent and received without blocking the main execution flow, allowing applications to remain responsive even under high load.

Asynchronous Messaging and Non-blocking I/O

ZeroMQ supports asynchronous messaging, which facilitates non-blocking communication between components. In asynchronous messaging, the sender continues executing subsequent tasks immediately after dispatching a message, without waiting for the receiver to acknowledge receipt. This design pattern is pivotal for applications requiring high concurrency and parallel processing.

```python
import zmq
import time

def non_blocking_client():
    context = zmq.Context()
    socket = context.socket(zmq.REQ)
    socket.connect("tcp://localhost:5570")

    # Send a request async while performing other operations
    socket.send_string("Request data")
    time.sleep(2) # Simulate doing other work
    if socket.poll(timeout=1000): # Check if a response is ready
        response = socket.recv_string(zmq.NOBLOCK)
        print(f"Received: {response}")

# Socket setup for server
def non_blocking_server():
    context = zmq.Context()
    socket = context.socket(zmq.REP)
    socket.bind("tcp://*:5570")

    while True:
        time.sleep(1) # Simulate doing some work
        if socket.poll(timeout=1000): # Check if there's a request
            request = socket.recv_string(zmq.NOBLOCK)
            print(f"Received request: {request}")
```

1.5. KEY FEATURES AND BENEFITS OF USING ZEROMQ

```
socket.send_string("Response data")
```

In Listing ??, we illustrate a non-blocking implementation using the REQ-REP pattern, demonstrating ZeroMQ's capacity for handling asynchronous I/O efficiently.

Multiple Communication Patterns

ZeroMQ provides various socket communication patterns, each tailored to suit different types of distributed application designs:

- **Request-Reply (REQ-REP)**: Facilitates point-to-point communication with synchronous request and response operations.

- **Publish-Subscribe (PUB-SUB)**: Supports disseminating messages to multiple subscribers with topic-based filtering.

- **Push-Pull (Pipeline)**: Utilizes parallel task distribution across multiple workers.

- **Exclusive Pair**: A two-way exclusive communication pattern used for peer-to-peer messaging.

```
import zmq

def exclusive_pair_peer1():
    context = zmq.Context()
    socket = context.socket(zmq.PAIR)
    socket.bind("tcp://*:5571")

    while True:
        socket.send_string("Message from Peer1")
        msg = socket.recv_string()
        print(f"Peer1 received: {msg}")

def exclusive_pair_peer2():
    context = zmq.Context()
    socket = context.socket(zmq.PAIR)
    socket.connect("tcp://localhost:5571")

    while True:
        msg = socket.recv_string()
        print(f"Peer2 received: {msg}")
        socket.send_string("Reply from Peer2")
```

Listing ?? exhibits ZeroMQ's exclusive PAIR pattern, which can be used in situations where a direct connection between two applications is required.

Seamless Scalability

ZeroMQ sockets abstract the complexities of network programming and automatically handle message queuing and distribution, which aids in building scalable systems. Its ability to effortlessly scale across multiple machines or within clustered environments is one of its most celebrated features.

Dynamic scaling with ZeroMQ can be easily achieved by adding more workers or nodes without altering the core application logic. For instance, in a distributed processing architecture using the PUSH-PULL pattern, additional worker nodes can be incorporated to handle increased message load seamlessly.

Cross-platform and Language Independence

ZeroMQ supports a multitude of programming languages including, but not limited to, C++, Python, Java, and .NET, making it incredibly versatile and adaptable to almost any software stack. This language independence ensures consistency and ease of use in multi-language environments, enabling teams to integrate different components developed using disparate technologies without the need for intricate binding logic.

Message Framing and Multipart Messages

ZeroMQ excels in efficiently handling complex multipart messages, crucial for applications needing to break down large data payloads into manageable sections. Multipart message support ensures entire data structures are sent atomically and received in their entirety, maintaining message integrity and context.

```
import zmq

def send_multipart():
    context = zmq.Context()
    socket = context.socket(zmq.PUB)
    socket.bind("tcp://*:5572")

    # Send a multipart message comprising three parts
    socket.send_multipart([b"part1", b"part2", b"part3"])

def receive_multipart():
    context = zmq.Context()
    socket = context.socket(zmq.SUB)
    socket.connect("tcp://localhost:5572")
    socket.setsockopt_string(zmq.SUBSCRIBE, '')
```

1.5. KEY FEATURES AND BENEFITS OF USING ZEROMQ

```
multipart_msg = socket.recv_multipart()
for part in multipart_msg:
    print(f"Received: {part.decode()}")
```

Listing ?? captures ZeroMQ's ability to handle multipart messages, making it ideal for applications requiring structured data transmission.

Portable Across Networks

The architecture of ZeroMQ is designed to function seamlessly over various network protocols, allowing for flexible deployment across different infrastructure. With ZeroMQ, developers can switch between in-process communication, TCP, and inter-process communication without substantial code modifications. This flexibility is particularly advantageous in environments where the networking infrastructure may vary between deployments.

Advantages in Microservices Architecture

In microservices architectures, where small, self-contained services require reliable communication, ZeroMQ shines through its lightweight nature and capability to integrate effortlessly. It offers fast inter-service communication, crucial in environments where ms-level latencies can significantly impact system performance.

ZeroMQ's support for different patterns simplifies service orchestration and scaling in microservices, making it suitable for complex application ecosystems.

Conclusion

ZeroMQ provides a versatile, efficient, and feature-rich framework for handling messaging in distributed systems. By utilizing its advanced socket patterns, asynchronous I/O capabilities, and support for seamless scalability, developers can design applications that are not only high-performing but also adaptable to dynamic network requirements. Its cross-platform support and ability to handle complex messaging requirements make it an invaluable tool in modern software development, facilitating the creation of robust and scalable communication architectures.

Chapter 2

Setting Up a ZeroMQ Environment

To effectively develop applications using ZeroMQ, it is imperative to set up a suitable development environment. This process involves selecting the appropriate operating system and integrated development environment (IDE), installing ZeroMQ across various platforms, and configuring the necessary libraries and dependencies. Ensuring the environment is configured correctly is crucial for optimal functionality, which includes conducting basic configuration tests to validate the setup. Proficiency in troubleshooting common installation issues is also essential to maintain a smooth development process. This chapter provides comprehensive guidance on these initial steps, establishing a solid foundation for further exploration of ZeroMQ's capabilities.

2.1 Choosing the Right Development Environment

Selecting the appropriate development environment when working with ZeroMQ is a fundamental step that influences the effectiveness and efficiency of application development. As developers embark on this journey, it is crucial to consider both operating systems and integrated development environments (IDEs) that cater to the specific requirements of ZeroMQ, as well as the developer's personal preference and expertise.

The choice of an operating system plays a significant role in the development lifecycle. ZeroMQ is a flexible messaging library compatible with Windows, macOS, and Linux; thus, the decision largely rests on factors like system performance, development workflow, and intended deployment environments. Developers must weigh the pros and cons of each operating system in terms of compatibility, ease of use, and support for development tools.

For Windows users, ZeroMQ provides a stable platform with various IDE options such as Visual Studio and Code::Blocks. Visual Studio is particularly popular due to its comprehensive development suite, debugging capabilities, and integration with a wide range of libraries and frameworks. Below is a minimal example demonstrating the inclusion of ZeroMQ in a Visual Studio project, showcasing the integration within a C++ build environment:

```cpp
#include <zmq.hpp>
#include <iostream>

int main() {
    zmq::context_t context(1);
    zmq::socket_t socket(context, ZMQ_REP);
    socket.bind("tcp://*:5555");

    while (true) {
        zmq::message_t request;
        socket.recv(&request);
        std::cout << "Received Hello" << std::endl;

        zmq::message_t reply(5);
        memcpy(reply.data(), "World", 5);
        socket.send(reply);
    }
    return 0;
}
```

2.1. CHOOSING THE RIGHT DEVELOPMENT ENVIRONMENT

To efficiently manage dependencies and integrations within Visual Studio, developers should ensure all necessary library files are linked correctly and environment variables are set to point to ZeroMQ installations. The IDE's settings can be navigated via *Project Properties*, allowing for the configuration of include directories and additional library directories.

On macOS, developers benefit from a UNIX-based system that supports powerful command-line tools integral to network programming tasks. Apple's Xcode provides a robust development environment, combining a source editor, debugging tools, and an integrated interface for Git version control. Despite its closed ecosystem, one advantage is Xcode's natural integration with macOS development libraries. However, developers often prefer command-line tools coupled with lightweight text editors such as Sublime Text or Visual Studio Code for more control and efficiency in handling ZeroMQ's configurations. Utilizing the Homebrew package manager vastly simplifies ZeroMQ installation and environmental configuration, as demonstrated:

```
brew install zeromq
```

Once installed, developers can compile ZeroMQ applications with GCC or Clang, capitalizing on the libraries included via the brew installations. Setting paths via terminal commands and modifying the $PATH variable ensures system-wide availability of ZeroMQ tools.

Furthermore, Linux users typically experience an edge in developing with ZeroMQ due to the high degree of control afforded by Linux's package management systems and its robustness for server applications—a natural fit for distributed systems frameworks. When configuring ZeroMQ with popular IDEs such as Eclipse CDT or CLion, developers integrate packages using comprehensive package managers like APT (for Debian-based distributions):

```
sudo apt-get install libzmq3-dev
```

Configuring CLion involves using CMake, a cross-platform build system, which simplifies the management of software builds for complex applications. An example CMakeLists.txt file for a ZeroMQ project illustrates this:

```
cmake_minimum_required(VERSION 3.10)
project(ZMQExample)

set(CMAKE_CXX_STANDARD 11)

find_package(PkgConfig)
pkg_check_modules(ZMQ REQUIRED libzmq)

include_directories(${ZMQ_INCLUDE_DIRS})
link_directories(${ZMQ_LIBRARY_DIRS})

add_executable(ZMQExample main.cpp)
target_link_libraries(ZMQExample ${ZMQ_LIBRARIES})
```

The find_package and pkg_check_modules functionalities auto-detect ZeroMQ's installation paths, adding both header and binary files to the build sequence, streamlining the process of creating portable code across Linux environments.

IDEs like Eclipse and CLion also ease debugging through graphical interfaces that offer breakpoints, variable watches, and call stacks visualization, potentially enhancing productivity in detecting and resolving issues within ZeroMQ applications.

Aside from operating systems, the analytical choice of the right IDE is founded on coding requirements, developer preference, and the complexity of the project. IntelliJ IDEA, NetBeans, and others offer Java support, catering to developers leveraging ZeroMQ's Java bindings. However, the availability of plugins and extensions across platforms often makes IDE preferences subjective and largely dependent on individual needs.

Considering cross-platform requirements, VS Code emerges as a potent candidate, balancing a lightweight footprint with substantial extensibility. Featuring extensions like C/C++ and CMake Tools, VS Code inherently supports ZeroMQ projects while giving flexibility in configuring custom build tasks and integrated terminal usage. The capacity to add extensions for language-specific needs and collaborate through shared repositories provides a comprehensive development experience when working with the ZeroMQ ecosystem, where disparate systems and languages frequently converge.

Ultimately, assessing the right development environment for ZeroMQ applications necessitates reflecting on multiple factors: operating system compatibility, development workflow, language requirements, and personal comfort with the chosen tools. As ZeroMQ facilitates distributed and scalable application communication, a well-considered development environment serves as the backbone for seamless integration and efficient scaling, ensuring that developers harness ZeroMQ's full potential in building robust and flexible messaging solutions.

2.2 Installing ZeroMQ on Various Platforms

ZeroMQ is a high-performance asynchronous messaging library designed for use in scalable and distributed systems. Installing ZeroMQ on different platforms entails understanding the specific package management systems and methods pertinent to each operating system. The installation process, although comparable in intent, is subject to varying degrees of complexity depending on whether you are installing on Windows, macOS, or Linux. Below, we delve into detailed instructions for successful setup across these platforms, ensuring a reliable foundation for development.

For Windows users, installing ZeroMQ requires a combination of installer tools and manual configuration. A common approach is to utilize a package manager like vcpkg to handle the complexity of downloading and compiling libraries. First, ensure you have Git and CMake installed for vcpkg's functionality. Begin by cloning the vcpkg repository:

```
git clone https://github.com/microsoft/vcpkg.git
.\vcpkg\bootstrap-vcpkg.bat
```

Upon initializing vcpkg, you must integrate it with Visual Studio. This integration allows you to handle package imports without the manual addition of library files to Visual Studio projects:

```
.\vcpkg integrate install
```

Finally, install ZeroMQ using vcpkg:

```
.\vcpkg install zeromq
```

Proper integration with Visual Studio entails configuring project properties to recognize ZeroMQ's include and library directories automatically, streamlining the process of adding ZeroMQ capabilities to your applications.

On macOS, developers have the advantage of leveraging Homebrew, a popular package manager that simplifies installation processes:

```
brew update
brew install zeromq
```

Homebrew automatically resolves and installs ZeroMQ's dependencies, ensuring the library is ready for use across various projects. It also keeps a stable repository of packages, allowing seamless version control and updates. Post-installation, ZeroMQ is usually readily available in the default library path, easing its inclusion in native macOS development using Xcode or command-line tools.

Command-line usage on macOS often adopts the following execution for ZeroMQ's base functionalities, showcasing environment setup and initial tests using CLI contexts for message passing and connectivity:

```
gcc -o myapp myapp.cpp -lzmq
./myapp
```

Linux provides a slightly different environment for ZeroMQ installation, dependent heavily on the specific distribution. Debian-based systems, such as Ubuntu, facilitate ZeroMQ installation through APT:

```
sudo apt update
sudo apt install libzmq3-dev
```

Alternatively, on Red Hat-based systems like Fedora, usage of DNF or YUM is appropriate, indicated as follows:

```
sudo dnf install zeromq
```

```
sudo yum install zeromq
```

Post-installation, a typical use-case scenario involves verifying the library setup integrity by compiling and executing a basic ZeroMQ workload. Below is a sample C++ program designed to test ZeroMQ's proper installation by establishing a simple client-server connection:

```
// server.cpp
```

2.2. INSTALLING ZEROMQ ON VARIOUS PLATFORMS

```cpp
#include <zmq.hpp>
#include <string>
#include <iostream>

int main () {
    zmq::context_t context(1);
    zmq::socket_t socket(context, ZMQ_REP);
    socket.bind("tcp://*:5555");

    while (true) {
        zmq::message_t request;
        socket.recv(&request);
        std::string reply_data("World");
        socket.send(zmq::buffer(reply_data), zmq::send_flags::none);
    }
    return 0;
}
```

```cpp
// client.cpp
#include <zmq.hpp>
#include <iostream>

int main () {
    zmq::context_t context(1);
    zmq::socket_t socket(context, ZMQ_REQ);
    socket.connect("tcp://localhost:5555");

    zmq::message_t request("Hello", 5);
    for (int i = 0; i < 10; ++i) {
        socket.send(request, zmq::send_flags::none);
        zmq::message_t reply;
        socket.recv(reply);
        std::cout << "Received " << reply.to_string() << std::endl;
    }
    return 0;
}
```

Compile these files using G++ or GCC, ensuring ZeroMQ libraries and headers are in your path:

```
g++ server.cpp -o server -lzmq
g++ client.cpp -o client -lzmq
```

Running these binaries will initiate a test server-client interaction, verifying whether ZeroMQ has been properly installed and is functional.

For scenarios requiring customized builds, ZeroMQ's repository available on GitHub provides access to its source code. Installation from source involves downloading the repository, ensuring build-essential tools like GCC, CMake, and pkg-config are installed, and compiling the source code as follows:

```
git clone https://github.com/zeromq/libzmq.git
cd libzmq
mkdir build && cd build
cmake ..
make
sudo make install
```

Installing from source provides an opportunity to tweak compilation options, including optimization flags suitable for deployment in a specific environment.

Each platform derives its strengths based on developer familiarity and project requirements. Windows benefits from comprehensive development environments integrating ZeroMQ dependencies seamlessly. macOS blends powerful command-line tools with sophisticated IDE options, while Linux offers unparalleled package management flexibility and is well-suited for deploying ZeroMQ in production environments. Ensuring ZeroMQ is appropriately installed establishes a foundation for further exploring the library's extensive features, encouraging efficient development and scalable solutions in distributed applications.

2.3 Configuring Your Development Environment

The configuration of your development environment for ZeroMQ is a pivotal step in enabling seamless development and operation of applications. Configuration involves setting up essential libraries, managing dependencies, and ensuring that integrated development environments (IDEs) efficiently interface with ZeroMQ. Correct setup minimizes development obstacles and facilitates quicker troubleshooting during application execution.

In most scenarios, configuration commences with understanding the toolchain and library dependencies relevant to ZeroMQ. These dependencies vary according to the programming language and environment used in developing ZeroMQ applications. Selecting and configuring an appropriate IDE enhances productivity and aligns the development process with best practices.

Configuring Libraries and Dependencies

2.3. CONFIGURING YOUR DEVELOPMENT ENVIRONMENT

ZeroMQ primarily functions as a C++ library but also supports bindings for other languages such as Python, Java, and .NET. Each language introduces different dependencies:

- **C++:** Link against libzmq. Ensure the compiler includes ZeroMQ headers and links against its libraries.

- **Python:** Utilize the pyzmq package, usually installed via pip.

- **Java:** Employ the JeroMQ, a pure Java implementation of ZeroMQ.

- **.NET:** Use the NetMQ library, which is a .NET-only implementation.

C++ Configuration

Configuration in C++ involves ensuring the include paths and linker settings correctly point to the zeromq library and its header files. An appropriate example in a Makefile for Unix-like systems is as follows:

```
CXX = g++
CXXFLAGS = -std=c++11 -I/usr/local/include
LDFLAGS = -L/usr/local/lib -lzmq

SRC = main.cpp app.cpp
OBJ = $(SRC:.cpp=.o)
EXEC = zmqApp

all: $(EXEC)

$(EXEC): $(OBJ)
    $(CXX) $(CXXFLAGS) $(OBJ) -o $@ $(LDFLAGS)

clean:
    rm -f $(OBJ) $(EXEC)
```

This Makefile ensures the C++ compiler knows where to find ZeroMQ headers and libraries by specifying -I and -L flags.

Python Configuration

For Python, configuration requires the installation of the pyzmq module:

```
pip install pyzmq
```

Ensuring Python properly recognizes the installed module involves testing with a simple script:

```
import zmq

context = zmq.Context()
socket = context.socket(zmq.REP)
socket.bind("tcp://*:5555")

while True:
    message = socket.recv()
    print(f"Received request: {message}")
    socket.send(b"World")
```

The script should execute without errors if pyzmq is correctly installed.

IDE Configuration

Choosing an IDE depends on personal preference, project scope, and language requirements. Robust configuration aids in managing project files, integrating version control, and performing efficient debugging. The following steps cater to some leading IDE configurations:

Visual Studio (Windows)

Begin by creating a new project, ensuring C++ is the selected language. Navigate to Project Properties:

- Under the *C/C++* section, configure *General* settings to include the ZeroMQ headers path in *Additional Include Directories*.

- In the *Linker* section, modify *General* settings to add ZeroMQ library paths.

- Further, ensure zmq.lib is listed under *Input* in *Additional Dependencies*.

Visual Studio facilitates building and debugging C++ applications integrated with ZeroMQ using its configuration interface, providing logical grouping and file tracking, thus improving developer efficiency.

Eclipse CDT (Linux/macOS)

Set up your C++ projects within Eclipse by navigating through:

- System Explorer, identify your project folder, right-click, and click *Properties*.

2.3. CONFIGURING YOUR DEVELOPMENT ENVIRONMENT

- Under *C/C++ Build*, select *Settings*. Add include directories in *GCC C++ Compiler > Includes*.

- Configure library paths under *GCC C++ Linker > Libraries*, and ensure libzmq is listed for linking.

Eclipse CDT comes equipped with a powerful editor and diagnostic tool, which ensures your ZeroMQ-based applications are coherent and adhere to coding standards while offering extensive debugger support.

IntelliJ IDEA (Java)

For Java applications interfaced with ZeroMQ using JeroMQ:

- Integrate JeroMQ by including it in your project's pom.xml if using Maven, or directly through the IDE's package management:

```
<dependency>
    <groupId>org.zeromq</groupId>
    <artifactId>jeromq</artifactId>
    <version>0.5.2</version>
</dependency>
```

- Ensure your project's Project Structure settings under Modules accommodates the necessary source folders and libraries.

- Utilize IntelliJ's built-in terminal and debugger toolsets to navigate through potential issues during development, providing insights into JVM behavior intrinsic to Java applications.

Environment Variables and Paths

Configuring environment variables ensures ZeroMQ's binaries and tools are accessible across different shells and IDE terminals:

- **Windows:** Set system-level environment variables through the *System Properties*. Go to *Environment Variables* and edit the *Path* to include the directory paths to ZeroMQ.

- **macOS/Linux:** Modify the $PATH variable in your .bashrc or .bash_profile with:

```
export PATH="/usr/local/bin:$PATH"
```

These configurations help alleviate path dependency issues and streamline command-line operations, ensuring ZeroMQ executables are promptly invoked.

Code Examples & Testing Libraries

A practical approach to verifying environment configuration involves initiating sample operations using ZeroMQ constructs, such as creating basic message-passing pipelines:

Server

```
// zmq_server.cpp
#include <zmq.hpp>
#include <string>
#include <iostream>

int main() {
    zmq::context_t context(1);
    zmq::socket_t socket(context, zmq::socket_type::rep);
    socket.bind("tcp://*:5555");

    while (true) {
        zmq::message_t request;
        socket.recv(request, zmq::recv_flags::none);
        std::string response = "Data received: " + request.to_string();
        socket.send(zmq::buffer(response), zmq::send_flags::none);
    }
    return 0;
}
```

Client

```
// zmq_client.cpp
#include <zmq.hpp>
#include <iostream>

int main() {
    zmq::context_t context(1);
    zmq::socket_t socket(context, zmq::socket_type::req);
    socket.connect("tcp://localhost:5555");

    for (int request_nbr = 0; request_nbr != 10; ++request_nbr) {
        zmq::message_t request(5);
        memcpy(request.data(), "Hello", 5);
        socket.send(request, zmq::send_flags::none);

        zmq::message_t reply;
        socket.recv(reply, zmq::recv_flags::none);
        std::cout << "Received " << reply.to_string() << std::endl;
    }
    return 0;
}
```

2.4. BASIC CONFIGURATION TESTING

These examples serve both as a test of library configuration and as a template for developing ZeroMQ applications in a production environment.

Effectively configuring your development environment for ZeroMQ not only enhances build efficiency but also fosters a repository of elements integral to producing reliable, scalable systems. By understanding library layouts, IDE integration, and environment synchronization, developers improve their code's portability and robustness, fine-tuning it for deployments across a spectrum of platforms and use cases.

2.4 Basic Configuration Testing

Ensuring that ZeroMQ is correctly configured in a development environment is a critical step that validates all previous setup efforts. Basic configuration testing involves running a series of checks designed to verify that the ZeroMQ library functions properly and integrates seamlessly with your development environment. This section provides a detailed protocol for conducting configuration tests across different platforms and languages, supplemented by illustrative coding examples to facilitate comprehension.

Rationale for Configuration Testing

Testing the configuration serves several key purposes. It verifies that the ZeroMQ library is correctly installed, the dependencies are appropriately managed, and the development environment settings, including compilers, linkers, and interpreters, are rightly aligned. Conducting these tests early in the development process pre-empts potential runtime issues, ensuring the environment is primed for application development.

C++ Testing Protocols

For C++ developers, the testing process begins with employing a simple request-reply pattern, suitable for confirming the basic operability of ZeroMQ.

Server Program:

```
// simple_server.cpp
```

```cpp
#include <zmq.hpp>
#include <iostream>

int main() {
    // Create a ZeroMQ context with a single I/O thread
    zmq::context_t context(1);
    // Create a REP (reply) socket
    zmq::socket_t socket(context, zmq::socket_type::rep);
    // Bind the socket to a TCP address
    socket.bind("tcp://*:5555");

    while (true) {
        zmq::message_t request;
        socket.recv(request, zmq::recv_flags::none);
        // Log the message received
        std::cout << "Received request: " << request.to_string() << std::endl;
        // Prepare the response ("World")
        zmq::message_t reply(5);
        memcpy(reply.data(), "World", 5);
        socket.send(reply, zmq::send_flags::none);
    }
    return 0;
}
```

In this example, the server binds to TCP port 5555 and waits for connections. It logs the received request to standard output and sends a simple "World" response, emulating a basic query-response mechanism. Proper execution without errors confirms the library's server-side capabilities.

Client Program:

```cpp
// simple_client.cpp
#include <zmq.hpp>
#include <iostream>

int main() {
    zmq::context_t context(1);
    zmq::socket_t socket(context, zmq::socket_type::req);
    socket.connect("tcp://localhost:5555");

    zmq::message_t request(5);
    memcpy(request.data(), "Hello", 5);
    socket.send(request, zmq::send_flags::none);

    zmq::message_t reply;
    socket.recv(reply, zmq::recv_flags::none);
    std::cout << "Received reply: " << reply.to_string() << std::endl;
    return 0;
}
```

The client connects to the same address and port, to make a "Hello" request and print the response received from the server. Successful

2.4. BASIC CONFIGURATION TESTING

transmission and receipt signify correct client-server communication and, by extension, a valid ZeroMQ configuration.

Compilation and Execution:

Compile using a command line or makefile configured to incorporate ZeroMQ libraries:

```
g++ -o server simple_server.cpp -lzmq
g++ -o client simple_client.cpp -lzmq

./server &
./client
```

The preceding commands start both programs, affirming ZeroMQ's role in network communications using the defined request-reply paradigm.

Python Configuration Testing

In a Python environment, using 'pyzmq', testing involves a similar procedure, employing interpreted scripts:

Server Script:

```
import zmq

context = zmq.Context()
socket = context.socket(zmq.REP)
socket.bind("tcp://*:5555")

while True:
    # Wait for next request from client
    message = socket.recv_string()
    print(f"Received request: {message}")
    # Send reply back to client
    socket.send_string("World")
```

Client Script:

```
import zmq

context = zmq.Context()
socket = context.socket(zmq.REQ)
socket.connect("tcp://localhost:5555")

# Send a request to the server
socket.send_string("Hello")

# Get the reply
message = socket.recv_string()
print(f"Received reply: {message}")
```

Run these scripts using Python's interpreter:

```
python simple_server.py &
python simple_client.py
```

If no exceptions are thrown, and the expected output occurs, this indicates a successful setup.

Java Configuration Testing with JeroMQ

Java developers typically utilize JeroMQ, a ZeroMQ Java binding, to conduct tests. Here's an example illustrating a simple socket interaction:

Server Class:

```java
import org.zeromq.ZMQ;

public class SimpleServer {
    public static void main(String[] args) throws Exception {
        ZMQ.Context context = ZMQ.context(1);
        ZMQ.Socket socket = context.socket(ZMQ.REP);
        socket.bind("tcp://*:5555");

        while (!Thread.currentThread().isInterrupted()) {
            byte[] reply = socket.recv(0);
            System.out.println("Received request: " + new String(reply, ZMQ.
                CHARSET));
            String response = "World";
            socket.send(response.getBytes(ZMQ.CHARSET), 0);
        }
        socket.close();
        context.close();
    }
}
```

Client Class:

```java
import org.zeromq.ZMQ;

public class SimpleClient {
    public static void main(String[] args) {
        ZMQ.Context context = ZMQ.context(1);
        ZMQ.Socket socket = context.socket(ZMQ.REQ);
        socket.connect("tcp://localhost:5555");

        String request = "Hello";
        socket.send(request.getBytes(ZMQ.CHARSET), 0);
        byte[] reply = socket.recv(0);
        System.out.println("Received reply: " + new String(reply, ZMQ.CHARSET));
        socket.close();
        context.close();
    }
}
```

Compile and run the server and client in separate terminals to test:

```
javac SimpleServer.java SimpleClient.java
java SimpleServer &
java SimpleClient
```

Java-specific ZeroMQ functions spread over multitasking systems trace out potential resource management discrepancies, confirming robustness under load.

Evaluating Test Results

Monitor outputs closely for anomalies or exceptions that could indicate configuration issues or library misuse. Logs and console outputs furnish vital insights into socket behavior, underlying network layers, and response times indicative of system efficiency. Detailed scrutiny enables pinpointing malfunction sources—aids in isolating and resolving configuration problems efficiently.

Conclusion

Testing verifies the congruence of the ecosystem involving libraries, configurations, and the application under operations reflecting real-world scenarios. Fundamentals as basic configuration testing, though seemingly straightforward, mitigate the disruption of development endeavors. The structured approach adopted here provides a scalable framework adaptable to numerous platform setups, nurturing adept proficiency and optimized environment configurations for leveraging ZeroMQ's capabilities fully. Whether for educational purposes or commercial application, a configured environment rooted in these reliable protocols stands as a bastion for expansive ZeroMQ engagement.

2.5 Troubleshooting Common Installation Issues

The process of installing ZeroMQ might encounter several challenges, primarily due to the differences in operating systems, package management, or even the intricacy of library dependencies. This section outlines a structured approach to diagnosing and troubleshooting common installation problems. Understanding these issues in-depth not only affirms a stable development environment but also enhances the learning curve for managing library dependencies and addressing platform-specific anomalies.

Understanding the Installation Process

The initial step in troubleshooting involves a solid understanding of the installation process across different environments. Knowing how ZeroMQ interacts with system libraries and dependencies can help diagnose where issues might arise:

- **Windows:** Installation through vcpkg or manual source buildup tends to reveal path and permissions-related issues.

- **macOS and Linux:** With Homebrew and APT/YUM, dependency resolution and appropriate environmental path settings are critical.

Recognizing how these contexts align with system versioning, compiler settings, and package paths guides the identification of underlying issues.

Common Issues Encountered

Several typical issues arise during ZeroMQ's installation and configuration:

1. **Missing Dependencies:** Often manifests in error messages indicating headers or shared libraries (.so/.dll files) not found during build or compilation.

2. **Environment Path Errors:** Result in executables or libraries being unavailable system-wide, usually following unsuccessful environment variable configuration.

3. **Compatibility Problems:** Stem from mismatched library versions or compiler versioning, incompatible operating systems, or platform-specific features.

4. **Incomplete Package Installation:** Derived from interrupted downloads or corruption during package retrieval, particularly in network-restricted environments.

5. **Configuration File Mistakes:** Errors within IDE setup files such as CMakeLists.txt or makefiles lead to failed build processes, often due to incorrect paths or missing directives.

Addressing these issues requires a systematic diagnostic process tailored to each operating system's strengths and nuances.

Diagnostic Procedures and Solutions

1. **Verifying Dependencies:**

   Ensure all required dependencies for building ZeroMQ are installed. On Unix-like systems, command-line tools like ldd, ldconfig, and pkg-config facilitate dependency checks.

   Example for dependency verification using pkg-config:
   ```
   pkg-config --cflags --libs libzmq
   ```

   If this command returns error messages or empty results, ensure the necessary development packages are installed (e.g., libzmq3-dev on Ubuntu).

2. **Correcting Environment Paths:**

   System variables like PATH, LD_LIBRARY_PATH, and PKG_CONFIG_PATH should include directories for ZeroMQ binaries and configuration files. To incorporate these, update shell configuration files such as .bashrc or .bash_profile:
   ```
   export PATH="/usr/local/bin:$PATH"
   export LD_LIBRARY_PATH="/usr/local/lib:$LD_LIBRARY_PATH"
   ```

   On Windows, adjust the environment variables via *System Properties* to append ZeroMQ paths.

3. **Resolving Compatibility Issues:**

   Check for resource compatibility among ZeroMQ, compiler versions, and external dependencies. Tools like GCC and Clang provide version information useful in aligning precisely matched libraries:
   ```
   g++ --version
   ```

Additionally, reviewing package version documentation guides the adjustment or upgrading of dependencies to supported versions.

4. **Handling Incomplete Installations:**

   Incomplete installations necessitate rerunning package managers with verbose output options to trace and rectify download-specific problems. For instance:

   ```
   brew reinstall zeromq
   sudo apt-get update && sudo apt-get install --reinstall libzmq3-dev
   ```

   These commands seek fresh, complete installations based on the most recent package repositories.

5. **Amending Configuration Files:**

   Errors in configuration files like CMakeLists.txt might signal path inaccuracies or missing flags. Here's a reprised CMakeLists.txt example:

   ```
   cmake_minimum_required(VERSION 3.10)
   project(ZeroMQTest)

   set(CMAKE_CXX_STANDARD 14)

   find_package(PkgConfig REQUIRED)
   pkg_check_modules(ZMQ REQUIRED libzmq)

   include_directories(${ZMQ_INCLUDE_DIRS})
   link_directories(${ZMQ_LIBRARY_DIRS})

   add_executable(testapp main.cpp)
   target_link_libraries(testapp ${ZMQ_LIBRARIES})
   ```

   Ensure find_package and pkg_check_modules are correctly initialized, and directories are absolute paths leading to ZeroMQ library and header locations.

Deeper Analysis and Advanced Troubleshooting

1. **Utilizing Logging and Verbose Output:**

   Most package managers and building tools offer verbose flags (-v or –verbose) that output detailed operation logs, providing insight into configuration and build steps to identify misconfigurations or errors.

2.5. TROUBLESHOOTING COMMON INSTALLATION ISSUES

Example for verbose build:
```
make VERBOSE=1
```

2. **Debugging with GDB:**

   If runtime errors persist post-installation, using a debugger like GDB (GNU Debugger) assists in stepping through execution to pinpoint logical bugs or memory-related issues.

   Example usage:
   ```
   gdb ./test_binary
   (gdb) run
   (gdb) bt # backtrace if there are errors
   ```

3. **Consulting Community Resources:**

   Online forums such as Stack Overflow, GitHub repositories, and ZeroMQ's own mailing lists form a knowledge network where common pitfalls and solutions frequently discussed. Exploring these resources garners both specific fixes and broader understanding.

4. **Reviewing Platform-Specific Documentation:**

   Platforms may entail unique library behaviors or configurations. Reviewing documentation related to your specific OS version may address inherent compatibility challenges.

Engaging Preventive Strategies

- **Comprehensive Documentation Review:** Before installation, closely study ZeroMQ's installation guidelines tailored for your system and use case.

- **Version Control:** Employ tools like git to manage and track changes in configuration files and associated scripts.

- **Sanitizing Build Environments:** Regularly update your build environment tools (e.g., compilers, package managers) to mitigate residual conflicts via newer versions.

- **Rigorous System Checks:** Periodically audit system setups with dependency tools and version checks to stay aligned with ZeroMQ's evolving functionalities.

Installation testing and troubleshooting provide a framework where developers not only gain efficiency but also inculcate a robust technical foundation in managing dependencies and configurations across diverse computing environments. These processes ensure ZeroMQ is aptly integrated, thus optimizing communication frameworks without disruption, promising smoother operation and development experiences.

Chapter 3

The ZeroMQ Messaging Patterns

ZeroMQ offers a variety of messaging patterns that facilitate distinct communication workflows within distributed systems. These patterns, including request-reply, publish-subscribe, push-pull, and dealer-router, are designed to address specific communication needs, enabling both synchronous and asynchronous message exchanges. Each pattern possesses unique characteristics and use cases, which allow developers to tailor their application architecture for optimal performance and scalability. Understanding these patterns is critical for harnessing ZeroMQ's full potential, as they form the core around which robust distributed applications are constructed. This chapter delves into the specifics of each pattern, guiding users in selecting the most appropriate solutions for their messaging requirements.

3.1 Exploring Messaging Patterns

Messaging patterns are fundamental constructs in the design and implementation of distributed applications. They define the protocols for communication between independent processes or systems, thereby ensuring a reliable and structured exchange of information. Within this context, ZeroMQ, a high-performance asynchronous messaging library, offers a repertoire of messaging patterns that underlie robust communication flows across distributed systems. These patterns are integral to managing the complexities inherent in such systems, necessitating a comprehensive understanding for anyone involved in designing or maintaining distributed applications.

ZeroMQ's messaging patterns include Request-Reply, Publish-Subscribe, Push-Pull, and Dealer-Router, each curated to address specific communication paradigms. These patterns enable both synchronous and asynchronous message exchanges, offering developers the flexibility to optimize application architecture for performance and scale. ZeroMQ abstracts many of the complexities associated with traditional socket programming, allowing developers to focus on the design and functionality of their applications.

3.1. EXPLORING MESSAGING PATTERNS

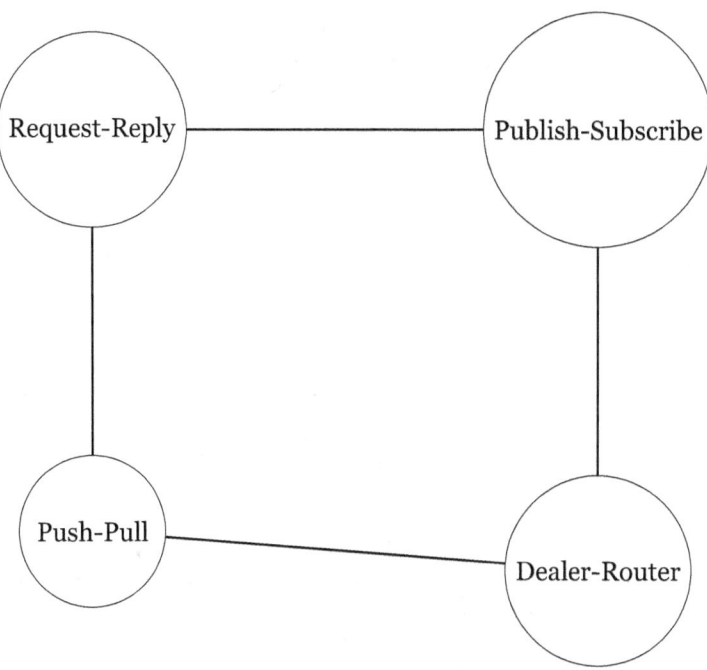

The **Request-Reply** pattern is a synchronous communication model where a client sends a request and waits for a reply from the server. This is akin to a remote procedure call (RPC) where the response is expected for the operation to be considered complete. Conversely, the **Publish-Subscribe** pattern facilitates broadcasting messages from a publisher to multiple subscribers in an asynchronous fashion, improving scalability and distribution capabilities.

ZeroMQ also supports the **Push-Pull** pattern, which is instrumental in distributing tasks among a set of workers for parallel processing, facilitating load balancing and task distribution efficiency. Finally, the **Dealer-Router** pattern represents an advanced configuration of asynchronous request-reply messaging, providing the building blocks for constructing complex workflows and stateful services.

ZeroMQ's abstraction over traditional sockets enables the seamless integration of these patterns. It encapsulates low-level socket operations in an intuitive API, allowing developers to implement sophisticated messaging solutions with minimal code. This capability is further augmented by ZeroMQ's automatic connection management and optimized data serialization processes.

```
#include <zmq.hpp>
int main() {
    zmq::context_t context(1);
    zmq::socket_t socket(context, ZMQ_REQ);

    socket.connect("tcp://localhost:5555");
    return 0;
}
```

In creating robust distributed systems, understanding messaging patterns such as those offered by ZeroMQ is critical. Each pattern brings its own strengths, trade-offs, and implementation details, empowering developers to construct systems that are both efficient and scalable.

To comprehend the full potentials and applications of these patterns, it is beneficial to delve into the specifics of their design and use cases. For instance, the Request-Reply pattern is often deployed in scenarios where confirmation of message receipt and processing is necessary. This pattern can mitigate message loss through retries, although it is inherently bound by the latency of round-trip communication.

```
import zmq

def request_reply_example():
    context = zmq.Context()

    socket = context.socket(zmq.REQ)
    socket.bind("tcp://*:5556")

    for request in range(10):
        print("Sending request %s ..." % request)
        socket.send(b"Hello")

        message = socket.recv()
        print("Received reply %s [ %s ]" % (request, message))

if __name__ == "__main__":
    request_reply_example()
```

The Publish-Subscribe pattern, however, is often utilized in real-time data dissemination applications, where updates need to be broadcasted to multiple endpoints without requiring acknowledgment. This paradigm excels in efficiency and speed, sacrificing guaranteed delivery for higher throughput.

3.1. EXPLORING MESSAGING PATTERNS

Next, consider integration scenarios in which multiple patterns might be necessary. It is not uncommon for systems to require a blend of synchronous and asynchronous messaging. For instance, in a monitoring system, new data might be reported using the Publish-Subscribe pattern, while specific data queries are handled through Request-Reply interactions.

Furthermore, developers must consider the impact of messaging patterns on system architecture. As efficient as these patterns are, they carry inherent latency implications, scaling factors, and reliability considerations. For instance, a poorly designed messaging system using these patterns could inadvertently create bottlenecks or single points of failure.

Another advanced construct is the combination of patterns to address complex business requirements. ZeroMQ allows embedding multiple patterns within the same application, enabling intricate flow controls. Developers can weave together these fundamental building blocks to achieve sophisticated dispatching mechanisms, dynamic load adaptations, and more.

When designing with ZeroMQ patterns, developers must also factor in error handling, which remains a critical aspect of distributed system robustness. Although ZeroMQ simplifies network programming, issues such as lost messages, network partitions, and hardware failures still necessitate thoughtful strategies for error detection and recovery.

The ZeroMQ library provides support for automatic reconnection and kernel-level socket queuing, which helps mitigate temporary disruptions in connectivity. However, additional application-level logic may be required to handle persistent failures or to retry message delivery.

```
import zmq

def simple_error_handling():
    context = zmq.Context()

    try:
        socket = context.socket(zmq.REQ)
        socket.setsockopt(zmq.RCVTIMEO, 5000)  # 5 seconds timeout
        socket.connect("tcp://localhost:5555")

        socket.send_string("Request")
        message = socket.recv_string()
        print("Received response:", message)

    except zmq.error.Again:
```

```
        print("Request timed out, no response received")
    finally:
        socket.close()
        context.term()
if __name__ == "__main__":
    simple_error_handling()
```

Developers should also be cognizant of architectural decisions impacting scalability and throughput. The use of multiple connections, efficient message batching, and fine-tuning high-water mark settings (to control message queuing length) are configurations critical to maintaining optimal performance.

In summary, although ZeroMQ abstracts many complexities of message transport, developers must possess a thorough understanding of the underlying patterns and operational nuances. Armed with this knowledge, they can architect distributed applications that harness the full power and efficiency of ZeroMQ's messaging patterns, paving the way for scalable, resilient, and maintainable systems. As we progress through the subsequent chapters, we will delve deeper into individual patterns, examining their implementation intricacies and real-world applicability.

3.2 Request-Reply Pattern

The Request-Reply pattern is a cornerstone in distributed system architectures, embodying a synchronous communication model that is central to many client-server interactions. In this pattern, a client sends a request to a server and blocks until a reply is received, mirroring the traditional call-and-response mechanism of remote procedure calls (RPC). This model is particularly advantageous when the client requires an explicit acknowledgment or processing result from the server to proceed with subsequent tasks.

In ZeroMQ, the Request-Reply pattern is implemented through the REQ and REP socket types. The REQ socket initiates the communication by sending messages to a REP socket, which processes the message and responds back. This sequence is strictly enforced, with the REQ socket alternating between sending and receiving states, and

3.2. REQUEST-REPLY PATTERN

the REP socket alternating between receiving and sending states. This ensures a well-ordered flow of message exchanges, crucial for maintaining the integrity and coherence of communication in synchronous setups.

```
#include <iostream>
#include <zmq.hpp>

int main() {
    zmq::context_t context(1);
    zmq::socket_t socket(context, ZMQ_REP);
    socket.bind("tcp://*:5555");

    while (true) {
        zmq::message_t request;
        socket.recv(&request);
        std::cout << "Received request: " << request.to_string() << std::endl;

        // Simulate doing some 'work'
        std::this_thread::sleep_for(std::chrono::seconds(1));

        zmq::message_t reply(5);
        memcpy(reply.data(), "World", 5);
        socket.send(reply);
    }
    return 0;
}
```

In the example above, a server is set up using a REP socket to bind to port 5555. The server waits to receive a request, processes it, and then sends back a reply. This illustrates the simplicity of ZeroMQ's API, where communication sockets are managed with ease, promoting rapid development and testing of communication patterns.

Given the synchronous nature of the Request-Reply pattern, it naturally incorporates complexities associated with blocking operations and potential delays. Thus, engineers must diligently consider timeout settings and retries. In high-latency network environments, message acknowledgment can incur significant wait times, impacting the client-side process flow. Configuring appropriate timeouts can mitigate these obstacles, enabling the system to handle transient network failures or server unavailability.

```
import zmq
import time

def request_reply_with_timeout():
    context = zmq.Context()
    socket = context.socket(zmq.REQ)
    socket.connect("tcp://localhost:5555")
```

```
    socket.RCVTIMEO = 5000 # 5 seconds timeout

    for request in range(1, 6):
        print("Sending request {} ...".format(request))
        socket.send(b"Hello")

        try:
            message = socket.recv()
            print("Received reply {} [ {} ]".format(request, message))
        except zmq.error.Again:
            print("No response received, request {} timed out".format(request))

if __name__ == "__main__":
    request_reply_with_timeout()
```

In this Python example, a timeout is set on the socket to allow the client to continue executing if no reply is received within a certain timeframe, providing resilience against temporary disruptions. The zmq.error.Again exception is used to catch scenarios where the server fails to respond within the designated timeout, enabling the application to handle such exceptions appropriately. For applications where message confirmation is imperative, this mechanism provides a viable fallback strategy, supplementing reliability with practical error handling.

Applications of the Request-Reply pattern predominate in scenarios where deterministic operations are essential; that is, an operation does not conclude until a response has been collected. System processes such as database queries, configuration retrievals, file transfers, and microservice interactions commonly exploit this pattern to ensure consistency and integrity of transactions.

Another consideration in the implementation of the Request-Reply pattern is the handling of exception flows and error states. Each request corresponds to a single reply, imposing a strict one-to-one relationship that may inadvertently lead to deadlocks if not correctly managed. One common approach to preventing deadlocks is employing a finite state machine (FSM) to monitor and govern the sequence of send and receive operations, ensuring coherent execution flow.

Scalability within the Request-Reply paradigm is often limited by this inherent need for synchronous fulfillment. In applications where scaling is requisite, load balancing and request distribution strategies are required. ZeroMQ facilitates these demands by allowing multipart messaging, enabling more complex session management and stateful

3.2. REQUEST-REPLY PATTERN

transactions to occur, albeit with an increase in overhead and complexity.

```
#include <zmq.hpp>
#include <iostream>

int main() {
    zmq::context_t context(1);
    zmq::socket_t socket(context, ZMQ_REP);
    socket.bind("tcp://*:5555");

    while (true) {
        zmq::message_t request;
        zmq::message_t client_id;
        socket.recv(&client_id);
        socket.recv(&request);

        std::cout << "Received request: " << request.to_string()
                  << " from client: " << client_id.to_string() << std::endl;

        // Simulate doing some 'work'
        std::this_thread::sleep_for(std::chrono::seconds(1));

        zmq::message_t reply(5);
        memcpy(reply.data(), "World", 5);
        socket.send(client_id, ZMQ_SNDMORE);
        socket.send(reply);
    }
    return 0;
}
```

In the C++ example above, the server employs multipart messaging to handle requests from clients, concurrently allowing the server to track which request pertains to which client. This multipart capability enables robust state management, serving each client individually and maintaining isolation across processes.

An important facet of conversational paradigms like Request-Reply is the need for proper logging and session tracking. This ensures traceability and aids future debugging efforts by documenting request and response metadata. Implementing comprehensive logging not only supports accountability but also enhances the predictability and security of inter-process communications.

In environments where security is paramount, the Request-Reply pattern, like other ZeroMQ patterns, may necessitate additional security layers, such as encryption or authentication protocols. While ZeroMQ itself provides mechanisms like CurveZMQ for managing encryption and authentication, the pattern itself benefits from complementary security practices to ensure integrity and confidentiality in message exchanges.

The benefits of the Request-Reply pattern are offset by their requisite synchronous style, which may inadvertently reduce parallel processing capabilities. To mitigate these constraints, modern systems often blend synchronous patterns with asynchronous counterparts, leveraging the strengths of each to construct high-performing, fault-tolerant ecosystems. Identifying the pattern that resonates best with architectural objectives, while balancing performance, reliability, and maintainability, is core to the engineering of effective communication frameworks.

In summary, while the Request-Reply pattern is synonymous with order and predictability, it requires careful consideration of timeout settings, exception handling, state management, and security measures. By wielding the foundations of this pattern effectively, developers can orchestrate sophisticated communication sequences that imbue distributed systems with resilience and consistency. This pattern forms a pivotal part of the broader ZeroMQ pattern suite, bridging the gap between network transparency and application logic in varied deployment scenarios.

3.3 Publish-Subscribe Pattern

The Publish-Subscribe (Pub-Sub) pattern is a widely employed communication model in distributed systems, known for its efficacy in decoupling message producers (publishers) from message consumers (subscribers). Within this pattern, messages are not sent directly to specific recipients. Instead, they are broadcast on a "logical channel" or topic, allowing multiple subscribers to listen and react to them asynchronously. This architecture facilitates scalable and flexible data distribution across distributed systems, making it particularly suitable for scenarios involving real-time updates, monitoring solutions, and alerting systems.

ZeroMQ's Pub-Sub pattern is implemented using PUB and SUB sockets. A PUB socket acts as a message publisher, broadcasting to one or more SUB sockets. Conversely, a SUB socket subscribes to one or more

3.3. PUBLISH-SUBSCRIBE PATTERN

topics and receives related messages. ZeroMQ efficiently handles the routing of messages from publishers to subscribers, abstracting much of the complexity of message delivery.

An essential characteristic of the Pub-Sub pattern is the one-way communication channel; publishers send messages, and subscribers receive them, with no direct response or acknowledgment required. This unidirectional flow maximizes throughput and minimizes latency, making the Pub-Sub pattern highly efficient for broadcasting data to a large number of consumers.

```python
import zmq
import time

def publisher():
    context = zmq.Context()
    publisher = context.socket(zmq.PUB)
    publisher.bind("tcp://*:5556")

    while True:
        topic = "news"
        message = "Current timestamp is {}".format(time.time())
        publisher.send_string("%s %s" % (topic, message))
        time.sleep(1)

if __name__ == "__main__":
    publisher()
```

In this Python example, a simple publisher is created, which broadcasts a timestamp every second over a network on the topic "news". Subscribers to this topic will receive the timestamp message, showcasing how easily one can structure publisher side logic using ZeroMQ.

A pivotal concept in the Pub-Sub pattern is *topic filtering*, employed on the subscriber side to reduce unnecessary data processing and network load. ZeroMQ allows subscribers to express interest only in specific topics, thereby enabling the selective receipt of messages matching their subscription criteria. Internally, this is achieved using prefix matching on the message topic, significantly enhancing the scalability of the system by minimizing the bandwidth and processing requirements at each subscriber endpoint.

```cpp
#include <iostream>
#include <zmq.hpp>

int main() {
    zmq::context_t context(1);
    zmq::socket_t subscriber(context, ZMQ_SUB);
```

```
subscriber.connect("tcp://localhost:5556");

// Subscribe to "news" topic
const char* filter = "news";
subscriber.setsockopt(ZMQ_SUBSCRIBE, filter, strlen(filter));

while (true) {
    zmq::message_t message;
    subscriber.recv(&message);

    std::string received_message(static_cast<char*>(message.data()), message.size
        ());
    std::cout << "Received message: " << received_message << std::endl;
}
    return 0;
}
```

In the C++ code sample above, the subscriber connects to the same endpoint as the publisher and subscribes to the "news" topic. By using the ZMQ_SUBSCRIBE socket option, subscribers ensure they only receive relevant messages, thereby optimizing resource utilization.

One of the critical advantages of the Publish-Subscribe pattern is *asynchronous communication*. Subscribers can process messages independently and at different rates, offering significant flexibility in distributed systems where local processing speeds and workloads might vary. The absence of acknowledgment overhead typically associated with synchronous patterns, like Request-Reply, means the Pub-Sub pattern provides excellent scalability potential.

However, this scalability advantage comes with trade-offs. In ZeroMQ's implementation, reliability across the Pub-Sub pattern mandates attention; messages are only delivered to subscribers that are connected and have subscribed at the time of broadcast. Thus, any network disturbances or late joins after the publication will result in message loss. This requires applications to carefully consider their resilience strategies and the trade-off between using in-band Pub-Sub mechanisms and alternate out-of-band data synchronization methodologies.

For scenarios where message resilience is crucial, combining the Pub-Sub pattern with other mechanisms that track message state or implement message replay/retry policies might be necessary. These could include checkpointing mechanisms—where applications maintain state or agree on message queue positions—or more complex message storefront methods employed when subscribers reconnect or initially con-

3.3. PUBLISH-SUBSCRIBE PATTERN

nect.

An example of advancing reliability includes architectures where an extra data persistence layer is used—primarily through a logging mechanism that records each broadcast message. Subscribers reconnecting after a disconnection event can then query this data layer to fill in any message gaps resulting from the temporary connection loss.

Security is another aspect that often necessitates consideration. As with other ZeroMQ patterns, the Pub-Sub pattern accommodates the use of CurveZMQ for securing message transfer. Developers must ensure that adequate encryption and access controls are applied where sensitivity of data broadcast is a concern.

While ZeroMQ abstracts a significant portion of socket management and message routing complexities, developers must be conscious of the underlying network behavior. Proper tuning of high-water marks can guard against message overload situations, where the number of undelivered messages exceeds the available buffer capacity.

```
import zmq

def high_water_mark_example():
    context = zmq.Context()
    subscriber = context.socket(zmq.SUB)
    subscriber.connect("tcp://localhost:5556")
    subscriber.setsockopt(zmq.RCVHWM, 10) # Set high-water mark to 10 messages

    filter = "news"
    subscriber.setsockopt(zmq.SUBSCRIBE, filter, len(filter));

    while True:
        message = subscriber.recv_string()
        print(f"Received: {message}")

if __name__ == "__main__":
    high_water_mark_example()
```

In this example, a high-water mark is set on the subscriber socket to 10 messages, which serves as a backpressure mechanism to prevent the subscriber from being inundated with a surplus of messages during high-volume broadcasts.

The Publish-Subscribe pattern's utilization in industry spans across numerous applications, from stock price updates in financial services to synching application state across distributed caches, real-time analytics systems, and collaborative editing platforms. Broadcast efficiency makes it a standout choice for any system where rapid distribution of information to a wide number of recipients is pivotal.

Throughout its implementation, the benefits derived from the Pub-Sub pattern largely depend on the understanding and handling of compensation strategies for its inherent uncertainties. By leveraging ZeroMQ's resilient architecture and flexible API, developers can effectively tune their distribution logic around these patterns, ensuring robust systems characterized by high performance, minimal latency, and maximum efficiency in data distribution.

3.4 Push-Pull Pattern

The Push-Pull pattern, also known as the Pipeline pattern, is a fundamental construct in parallel processing and task distribution within distributed systems. This pattern is characterized by its ability to enable load balancing and task parallelization efficiently. In application scenarios where workloads must be distributed across multiple worker processes, the Push-Pull pattern shines by ensuring that tasks are dynamically allocated and processed as efficiently as possible.

In ZeroMQ, the Push-Pull pattern is implemented with the PUSH and PULL sockets. A PUSH socket sends messages to one or more PULL sockets, which receive them. This communication is inherently one-way, with tasks (messages) being pushed from the producer (pusher) to the consumers (pullers), and proceeds in a round-robin or fair-queuing manner. This mechanism makes the pattern especially useful for scenarios like farm-based parallel processing models, where tasks must be distributed among a set of available workers.

```
import zmq
import time

def task_producer():
    context = zmq.Context()
    producer = context.socket(zmq.PUSH)
    producer.bind("tcp://*:5557")

    for task_nbr in range(100):
        work_message = {'task_id': task_nbr, 'data': 'process_this'}
        producer.send_json(work_message)
        print(f"Sent task {task_nbr}")
        time.sleep(0.1)
```

3.4. PUSH-PULL PATTERN

```
if __name__ == "__main__":
    task_producer()
```

In the Python example above, a task producer sends 100 tasks to the worker pool using a PUSH socket bound to port 5557. Each task comprises a unique identifier and a data payload. The use of JSON for message serialization simplifies both sending and receiving processes, ensuring that complex message structures are efficiently communicated to the workers.

The power of the Push-Pull pattern lies not only in its simplicity but also in its scalability. The pattern abstracts the complexity of task management, enabling dynamic systems that expand or contract based on demand. As more workers (consumers) are introduced into the system, they automatically start receiving tasks, facilitating elasticity.

Key to leveraging the Push-Pull pattern effectively is its fair-queuing mechanism. ZeroMQ implements a non-blocking round-robin delivery strategy: when a worker is ready to receive more tasks, it gets the next available task. This approach ensures that work is evenly distributed across all workers, preventing scenarios where some workers are overloaded while others are idle.

```cpp
#include <iostream>
#include <zmq.hpp>

int main() {
    zmq::context_t context(1);
    zmq::socket_t worker(context, ZMQ_PULL);
    worker.connect("tcp://localhost:5557");

    while (true) {
        zmq::message_t message;
        worker.recv(&message);

        std::string task(static_cast<char*>(message.data()), message.size());
        std::cout << "Processing task: " << task << std::endl;

        // Simulate task processing
        std::this_thread::sleep_for(std::chrono::milliseconds(500));
    }
    return 0;
}
```

In this C++ example, a worker connects to the producer's endpoint and waits to receive tasks. As each task is received, it simulates processing by pausing for half a second, demonstrating the flexibility with which workers can handle tasks at their own pace.

The Push-Pull pattern does not require explicit acknowledgments from the workers to the producers, which enhances throughput by removing superfluous overhead. However, this lack of acknowledgment means that the producer has no confirmation of task completion. For applications that demand guaranteed delivery and completion auditing, supplementary mechanisms, such as out-of-band acknowledgment or worker monitoring systems, may be implemented.

With the Push-Pull pattern's dynamic scaling capabilities, it is well suited for handling varied processing loads, particularly in environments with distributed computations or when resources are heterogeneous. By adopting a plug-and-play strategy, additional worker nodes can be seamlessly incorporated or removed.

Despite its scalability and flexibility, developers using the Push-Pull pattern must be cognizant of the implications of message loss and reliability. Network failures, worker disconnections, or task processing errors might cause undelivered or unprocessed messages. Addressing these issues often involves designing resilient systems with retry mechanisms, state persistence, or redundancy through duplicate message dispatch, ensuring robust handling of these eventualities.

In terms of failure recovery, incorporating strategies such as task checkpointing or using a reliable datastore to persist task states before dispatch can mitigate issues of incomplete processing. Workers can then resume from the last checkpoint, minimizing task redundancy and ensuring greater accuracy.

```
import zmq
import time

def resilient_worker():
    context = zmq.Context()
    worker = context.socket(zmq.PULL)
    worker.connect("tcp://localhost:5557")

    while True:
        try:
            task = worker.recv_json()
        except Exception as e:
            print(f"Failed to receive task: {e}")
            continue

        task_id = task.get('task_id')
        print(f"Processing task {task_id}")
```

3.4. PUSH-PULL PATTERN

```
    try:
        # Simulate processing with potential error
        if task_id % 10 == 0:
            raise ValueError("Simulated error")
        time.sleep(0.5)
    except Exception as e:
        print(f"Error processing task {task_id}: {e}")
        # Log or retry task as necessary
        continue

if __name__ == "__main__":
    resilient_worker()
```

In this example, the worker incorporates basic error handling during task receipt and processing, demonstrating robustness in the face of potential runtime exceptions. By catching exceptions and logging errors, the system can adjust dynamically to unexpected states, increasing resilience.

Task management optimization is another area where nuances of the Push-Pull pattern are realized. Employing worker-specific configurations, such as assigning varying degrees of priority or associating particular task types with specialized nodes, enhances throughput and accuracy.

Security considerations should also be addressed, especially in distributed systems where data integrity and privacy are of prime concern. ZeroMQ supports CurveZMQ, a scalable security framework using elliptic-curve cryptography to secure message transport, which can be integrated to ensure the security of communications within the Push-Pull pattern.

The Push-Pull pattern's simplicity and efficiency make it a preferred choice for numerous applications across various sectors, including image processing pipelines, large-scale simulations, distributed data processing frameworks, and many other systems requiring parallelized workloads. The effectiveness of this pattern enhances not only performance and scalability but also operational efficiency in diversified computing landscapes. With ZeroMQ's flexible and powerful capabilities, implementing the Push-Pull pattern allows developers to construct seamlessly scalable and efficient distributed systems that continue to perform optimally under varying loads.

3.5 Dealer-Router Pattern

The Dealer-Router pattern is one of the most powerful and flexible messaging patterns in ZeroMQ, enabling complex communication scenarios through asynchronous message exchanges. It builds upon the capabilities provided by the base Request-Reply pattern, introducing a versatile and highly customizable mechanism for developing advanced distributed systems. This pattern supports non-blocking operations, message routing, and empowers developers to implement sophisticated communication protocols that can handle high loads and complex interaction flows.

At its core, the Dealer-Router pattern leverages two specific socket types provided by ZeroMQ: DEALER and ROUTER. The DEALER socket acts as an asynchronous version of the REQ socket by not enforcing strict request-reply cycles. This allows for pipelining, where multiple requests can be sent without waiting for replies. On the other hand, the ROUTER socket behaves like a REPLY socket but with additional capabilities, such as routing messages to specific recipients using message envelopes that include identity information. Together, these socket types enable developers to design communication architectures that scale effectively and handle complex routing logic.

One of the key strengths of the Dealer-Router pattern is its ability to decouple message senders and recipients completely. The ROUTER socket can handle messages from multiple DEALER sockets (clients) simultaneously, dispatching responses back to them according to the routing logic defined. This flexibility is particularly beneficial in load-balancing scenarios, stateful communication processes, and it forms the foundation for crafting custom routing algorithms that are adaptable to specific application needs.

```
import zmq
import time

def dealer_client(client_id):
    context = zmq.Context()
    socket = context.socket(zmq.DEALER)
    socket.identity = u"Client-{}".format(client_id).encode('ascii')
    socket.connect("tcp://localhost:5555")

    while True:
        # This client sends a new request to the ROUTER every second
        socket.send_string("Request from client {}".format(client_id))
```

3.5. DEALER-ROUTER PATTERN

```
        # Simulate additional computations
        time.sleep(1)

if ___name___ == "___main___":
    dealer_client(1)
```

In this example, a DEALER socket is used to simulate a client. The identity attribute is set, facilitating the ROUTER socket's ability to track and respond accurately to each client's requests.

The ROUTER socket is the multitasker in this arrangement, capable of dynamically responding to incoming messages from a range of DEALER sockets. This promiscuity allows it to serve as a central message hub, dispatching messages to appropriate clients based on their unique identities. By maintaining rolling but structured message queues, a ROUTER effectively decouples origin and target contexts, ensuring queueless operations and minimal latency of message traffic.

```cpp
#include <iostream>
#include <zmq.hpp>
#include <string>

int main() {
    zmq::context_t context(1);
    zmq::socket_t socket(context, ZMQ_ROUTER);
    socket.bind("tcp://*:5555");

    while (true) {
        zmq::message_t identity;
        zmq::message_t content;

        // Receive the identity frame
        socket.recv(&identity);

        // Receive the content frame
        socket.recv(&content);

        std::string reply_msg = "Response to Client: " + identity.to_string();
        std::cout << "Serving Response: " << reply_msg << std::endl;

        // Send reply with the same identity
        socket.send(identity, ZMQ_SNDMORE);
        socket.send(zmq::message_t(reply_msg.c_str(), reply_msg.size()));
    }
    return 0;
}
```

Here, our C++ router-server example reveals the receipt of dual message frames: one for identity and another for the request content itself. The ROUTER socket leverages this information to identify which client to respond to and formats a suitable reply before dispatch.

Flexibility in routing, encouraged by the Dealer-Router pattern, allows application architects to introduce sophisticated message routing policies. These might involve:

- Prioritization: Channeling messages from high-priority senders ahead of others.

- Filtering: Omitting messages from certain clients based on dynamic rules.

- Load Management: Allocating heavy-load messages conditionally across available worker resources.

The capacity to weave custom logic into the operation offers significant leverage when dealing with diverse application landscapes and imposing client-specific rules.

A significant advantage brought forth by this pattern is support for message pipelining. Here, clients can issue multiple requests without waiting for responses, enhancing throughput by minimizing idle time and ensuring maximum channel utilization. This non-sequential operation reduces apparent waiting times but demands adherence to message corollary and bookkeeping, guaranteeing responses are matched or logged in accordance to their originating order.

While sophisticated, the Dealer-Router pattern necessitates diligent error-handling mechanisms due to its asynchronous nature. Given that responses may arrive out of order or intervals between them might be nondeterministic, applications might leverage buffers or response timestamps for additional coherence.

The Dealer-Router pattern shines in scenarios dealing with complex workflows like task scheduling, where non-blocking execution is vital, or multi-phase workflows where processes must be contemporaneous but logically independent. Akin to request multiplexing, it's pivotal to effective thread-parallel operations, with scalability on high-load services being attainable without redundancy in channel allocations.

For message reliability, developers might choose to wrap logic with error-detection and recovery strategies such as retries, dead-letter queues, or persistent task logging. This allows applications to gracefully handle scenarios where component failures leave certain messages unattended or partially processed.

Moreover, developers might enforce security via ZeroMQ's CURVE technology, ensuring Dealer-Router communications remain encrypted and mutually authenticated. This is critical when disseminating sensitive data across networked environments which span administrative domains.

Complementing standard Distributed Mind models, the Dealer-Router configuration has become a mainstay in implementations ranging across financial reconciliations, cloud-compute application orchestration, and processing-unit workload balancing — testaments to its versatility in abstracts dealing with stateful versus stateless episodic messaging mechanisms.

Therefore, while implementing this pattern, it remains essential to tailor communication flows that reward clarity of design and logically isolate operational segments of larger data workflows. Through thorough crafting of messaging schemas, ZeroMQ's Dealer-Router pattern shapes dispersed computational paradigms into cohesive, responsive architectures aligned with organizational throughput, security, and process integration needs.

3.6 Advanced Pattern Combinations

In the intricate world of distributed systems, singular messaging patterns sometimes prove inadequate for meeting the complex and multifaceted requirements of modern applications. As a result, combining multiple messaging patterns provides a powerful framework for solving advanced communication challenges. Patterns like Request-Reply, Publish-Subscribe, Push-Pull, and Dealer-Router serve as building blocks that, when meticulously interwoven, foster systems capable of encompassing diverse communication needs, scalability targets, reliability requisites, and performance metrics.

Combining patterns allows for the creation of hybrid models that leverage the strengths of individual patterns while mitigating their weaknesses. Such pattern combinations foster robustness and flexibility, ensuring that distributed applications are well-equipped to handle a range of scenarios, from real-time streaming and analysis to complex transaction processing and data aggregation.

One illustrative case study of advanced pattern combinations involves the orchestration of microservices within an ecosystem requiring both synchronous and asynchronous communication. By integrating ZeroMQ messaging patterns, developers can achieve seamless service interactions, real-time data dissemination, and efficient workload distribution through a combination of Request-Reply, Publish-Subscribe, and Push-Pull patterns.

Hybrid Model: Request-Reply with Publish-Subscribe

A common pattern combination employs the Request-Reply pattern alongside the Publish-Subscribe pattern for real-time service updates intertwined with synchronous data retrieval. In this model, client applications invoke services using a Request-Reply interaction, effectively querying the state or executing operations. Concurrently, updates or service events are broadcast to subscribers using the Publish-Subscribe pattern.

```
import zmq
import threading

def service_provision():
    context = zmq.Context()
    rep_socket = context.socket(zmq.REP)
    rep_socket.bind("tcp://*:5555")

    pub_socket = context.socket(zmq.PUB)
    pub_socket.bind("tcp://*:5556")

    while True:
        # Handle request
        message = rep_socket.recv()
        print(f"Received request: {message}")
        # Responding back
        rep_socket.send(b"Response from service")

        # Broadcast update
        pub_socket.send_string("update: New data available")

def client():
    context = zmq.Context()
    req_socket = context.socket(zmq.REQ)
    req_socket.connect("tcp://localhost:5555")

    sub_socket = context.socket(zmq.SUB)
    sub_socket.connect("tcp://localhost:5556")
    sub_socket.setsockopt_string(zmq.SUBSCRIBE, "update")
```

3.6. ADVANCED PATTERN COMBINATIONS

```
# Sending request
req_socket.send(b"Service Request")
reply = req_socket.recv()
print(f"Received response: {reply}")

# Listening for updates
message = sub_socket.recv_string()
print(f"Received update: {message}")

# Starting the service provision and client in different threads
service_thread = threading.Thread(target=service_provision)
service_thread.start()

client_thread = threading.Thread(target=client)
client_thread.start()
```

In the above Python example, we see a hybrid pattern where a service process engages in both Request-Reply for direct synchronous interaction and Publish-Subscribe for disseminating updates. The service_provision() function represents the service logic that listens for incoming requests while broadcasting service updates to interested subscribers. The client's logic demonstrates receiving responses to synchronous queries while also listening for asynchronous updates.

Pattern Combination: Push-Pull with Publish-Subscribe

For scenarios that necessitate efficient task distribution and dynamic result dissemination, the Push-Pull pattern can be coupled with Publish-Subscribe. This integration is particularly effective in data processing pipelines, where tasks are distributed among workers and results or progress updates are broadcast to all relevant components.

```
#include <iostream>
#include <zmq.hpp>
#include <string>
#include <thread>

void task_distributor() {
    zmq::context_t context(1);
    zmq::socket_t push_socket(context, ZMQ_PUSH);
    push_socket.bind("tcp://*:5560");

    zmq::socket_t pub_socket(context, ZMQ_PUB);
    pub_socket.bind("tcp://*:5561");

    for (int i=0; i<100; ++i) {
        zmq::message_t message(20);
        snprintf((char*) message.data(), 20, "Task number %d", i);
        push_socket.send(message);

        zmq::message_t update(20);
```

```cpp
        snprintf((char*) update.data(), 20, "Published %d", i);
        pub_socket.send(update);

        std::this_thread::sleep_for(std::chrono::milliseconds(100));
    }
}

void data_processor(int id) {
    zmq::context_t context(1);
    zmq::socket_t pull_socket(context, ZMQ_PULL);
    pull_socket.connect("tcp://localhost:5560");

    while (true) {
        zmq::message_t message;
        pull_socket.recv(&message);
        std::string task(static_cast<char*>(message.data()), message.size());
        std::cout << "Worker " << id << " processing: " << task << std::endl;

        std::this_thread::sleep_for(std::chrono::milliseconds(500));
    }
}

void status_listener() {
    zmq::context_t context(1);
    zmq::socket_t sub_socket(context, ZMQ_SUB);
    sub_socket.connect("tcp://localhost:5561");
    sub_socket.setsockopt(ZMQ_SUBSCRIBE, "", 0);

    while (true) {
        zmq::message_t update;
        sub_socket.recv(&update);
        std::string status(static_cast<char*>(update.data()), update.size());
        std::cout << "Status: " << status << std::endl;
    }
}

int main() {
    std::thread distributor_thread(task_distributor);
    std::thread processor1_thread(data_processor, 1);
    std::thread processor2_thread(data_processor, 2);
    std::thread listener_thread(status_listener);

    distributor_thread.join();
    processor1_thread.join();
    processor2_thread.join();
    listener_thread.join();

    return 0;
}
```

In this C++ example, the task_distributor function sends tasks to workers using a PUSH socket and simultaneously broadcasts updates via a PUB socket. Individual workers receive tasks using a PULL socket, while a separate status listener subscribes to updates, illustrating a system capable of both dynamic scaling and real-time reporting across

3.6. ADVANCED PATTERN COMBINATIONS

distributed nodes.

Advanced pattern combinations empower the crafting of more resilient systems by:

- Providing Redundancy: Use redundant data streams to ensure availability and durability, even amidst failures at one or more nodes.

- Enabling Multilayer Architectures: Manage communication across layers—capture ingress events via Pub-Sub while tackling detailed processing through Dealer-Router or Push-Pull chains.

- Facilitating Cross-Service Syncing: Sync data states or events across disparate platforms through dedicated queues or update channels.

- Enhanced Security and Control: Establish fine-grained access controls, safeguarding sensitive data through secured interfaces, ideally using ZeroMQ's CURVE encryption for end-to-end security.

While these combinations add resilience, flexibility, and scalability, they may also introduce complexity. Handling asynchronous messages and state management requires careful orchestration. Each pattern must be meticulously integrated to prevent bottlenecks or asynchronous drifts that could affect message flow reliability and efficiency.

Advanced pattern configurations demand diligent documentation to taper cognitive overhead on the development and operations teams. Architectural diagrams and well-commented codebase formats often aid in reducing miscommunication among integrated components, strengthening coherence across the deployment landscape.

Moreover, performance tuning and resource optimization are imperative. Configuring socket options (like high-water marks and queue size) and conducting proper load testing ensure system stability under varied conditions, protecting against buffer overflows, service saturation, or deadlocks.

Overall, the synthesis of these pattern combinations, rooted in ZeroMQ's underlying architecture, facilitates a holistic communication ecosystem. It allows enterprises to deploy systems characterized by remarkable scalability, adaptability, and robustness, paving the way for high-efficiency operations capable of meeting the demands of today's ever-evolving technological landscape.

Chapter 4

Working with Sockets in ZeroMQ

ZeroMQ leverages a variety of socket types to implement its versatile messaging patterns, each playing a specific role within the framework. The socket lifecycle involves careful management—from creation and configuration to binding, connecting, and termination. This chapter covers the essential concepts related to binding and connecting sockets to establish reliable communication channels. It also emphasizes how ZeroMQ supports asynchronous I/O operations, facilitating non-blocking message exchanges. Additionally, understanding socket options and managing contexts are crucial for tailoring the library's behavior to specific application needs. Effective error handling and troubleshooting socket-related issues form an integral part of working efficiently with ZeroMQ.

4.1 ZeroMQ Socket Types

The architecture of ZeroMQ revolves around its socket types, each designed to accommodate specific communication patterns. These socket types pave the way for a high degree of flexibility in building distributed systems, where the correct socket type choice directly influences the efficiency and design of message-passing strategies.

Understanding the semantic description of ZeroMQ socket types illuminates the roles they play in implementing robust messaging frameworks.

- **REQ and REP Sockets**

The REQ (request) and REP (reply) socket types correspond to a synchronous request-reply pattern. This is one of the simplest communication models, offering straightforward semantics by implementing a fixed sequence where a request is always followed by a reply.

REQ sockets send an initial request and wait for a corresponding reply from a REP socket. This implies a strict locking of communication where operations are blocking. Each request sent must be matched by one reply, establishing a reliable way for implementing RPC-style communications.

```
// REQ socket example
void *context = zmq_ctx_new();
void *requester = zmq_socket(context, ZMQ_REQ);

zmq_connect(requester, "tcp://localhost:5555");

zmq_send(requester, "Hello", 5, 0);
char buffer[10];
zmq_recv(requester, buffer, 10, 0);
```

REP sockets, on the other hand, receive requests and are designed to return a response thereafter. Like REQ, they enforce strict alternating sends and receives, ensuring that every request is handled sequentially.

```
// REP socket example
void *context = zmq_ctx_new();
void *responder = zmq_socket(context, ZMQ_REP);

zmq_bind(responder, "tcp://*:5555");

char buffer[10];
zmq_recv(responder, buffer, 10, 0);
zmq_send(responder, "World", 5, 0);
```

- **PAIR Sockets**

4.1. ZEROMQ SOCKET TYPES

PAIR sockets are the most basic form of a ZeroMQ socket, offering a one-to-one communication model. The PAIR type is intended for connected peers where bidirectional communication is possible. However, it comes with limitations; it only supports a single peer, lacking resilience for complex messaging scenarios where more than two participants are involved.

```
// PAIR socket usage
void *context = zmq_ctx_new();
void *socket1 = zmq_socket(context, ZMQ_PAIR);
void *socket2 = zmq_socket(context, ZMQ_PAIR);

zmq_bind(socket1, "inproc://example");
zmq_connect(socket2, "inproc://example");

zmq_send(socket1, "Message", 7, 0);
char buffer[10];
zmq_recv(socket2, buffer, 10, 0);
```

The simplicity of PAIR sockets makes them unsuitable for complex routing needs. ZeroMQ advises against their use in production environments where more robust socket types offer necessary scalability and reliability.

- **PUB and SUB Sockets**

Leveraging the publish-subscribe pattern, PUB (publish) and SUB (subscribe) sockets form the backbone of many messaging scenarios that necessitate message broadcasting.

PUB sockets broadcast messages to any number of connected SUB sockets, which, in turn, can filter these messages based on specific needs. The filters help receive only messages that match particular criteria, enabling efficient handling of data.

```
// PUB socket example
void *context = zmq_ctx_new();
void *publisher = zmq_socket(context, ZMQ_PUB);

zmq_bind(publisher, "tcp://*:5556");

zmq_send(publisher, "Topic: Message contents", 25, 0);
```

The SUB socket's filtering mechanism employs a simple but powerful prefix matching system. Upon connecting to a PUB socket, a SUB socket subscribes to messages matching its filters.

```
// SUB socket example
void *context = zmq_ctx_new();
void *subscriber = zmq_socket(context, ZMQ_SUB);

zmq_connect(subscriber, "tcp://localhost:5556");
zmq_setsockopt(subscriber, ZMQ_SUBSCRIBE, "Topic", 5);

char buffer[256];
zmq_recv(subscriber, buffer, 256, 0);
```

- **PUSH and PULL Sockets**

The PUSH-PULL pattern offers a simple yet effective way to implement distributed data parallelism. PUSH sockets dispatch messages, which are then balanced between all connected PULL sockets, following a round-robin distribution policy.

```
// PUSH socket example
void *context = zmq_ctx_new();
void *sender = zmq_socket(context, ZMQ_PUSH);

zmq_bind(sender, "tcp://*:5557");

zmq_send(sender, "Task", 4, 0);
```

PULL sockets, in contrast, receive messages in a fair load-balanced fashion, allowing workers to be distributed across the network, each processing a unique task.

```
// PULL socket example
void *context = zmq_ctx_new();
void *receiver = zmq_socket(context, ZMQ_PULL);

zmq_connect(receiver, "tcp://localhost:5557");

char buffer[256];
zmq_recv(receiver, buffer, 256, 0);
```

- **DEALER and ROUTER Sockets**

For scenarios requiring more complex routing patterns, DEALER and ROUTER socket types serve as advanced versions of REQ and REP sockets, respectively. DEALER sockets provide an asynchronous connect-to-all model with efficient load balancing across multiple servers.

4.1. ZEROMQ SOCKET TYPES

```
// DEALER socket example
void *context = zmq_ctx_new();
void *dealer = zmq_socket(context, ZMQ_DEALER);

zmq_connect(dealer, "tcp://localhost:5558");

zmq_send(dealer, "Msg", 3, 0);
```

ROUTER sockets, which can be considered as a superset of REP, enable addressing of messages with more significant control over the message flow, thereby enabling the implementation of custom routing strategies.

```
// ROUTER socket example
void *context = zmq_ctx_new();
void *router = zmq_socket(context, ZMQ_ROUTER);

zmq_bind(router, "tcp://*:5558");

char buffer[256];
zmq_recv(router, buffer, 256, 0);
zmq_send(router, "Response", 8, 0);
```

- **XPUB and XSUB Sockets**

Extending the PUB-SUB model, XPUB and XSUB sockets allow for capturing of subscription messages, offering intricate access and management functionalities in advanced publish-subscribe scenarios.

```
// XPUB socket example
void *context = zmq_ctx_new();
void *xpub = zmq_socket(context, ZMQ_XPUB);

zmq_bind(xpub, "tcp://*:5559");

char buffer[256];
zmq_recv(xpub, buffer, 256, 0);
zmq_send(xpub, "Broadcast", 9, 0);
```

XSUB sockets behave like a regular SUB socket but with extended capabilities for intercepting messages related to subscriptions.

```
// XSUB socket example
void *context = zmq_ctx_new();
void *xsub = zmq_socket(context, ZMQ_XSUB);

zmq_connect(xsub, "tcp://localhost:5559");

zmq_send(xsub, "", 0, 0);
```

The variety of ZeroMQ socket types underscores its role as a versatile messaging library. Mastery of these socket types enables developers to implement complex and efficient message-passing architectures, leveraging patterns that best suit their application needs. Proficiency in selecting and utilizing these socket types is a cornerstone for effectively employing ZeroMQ in sophisticated messaging applications.

4.2 Socket Lifecycle: Creation to Termination

The lifecycle of a ZeroMQ socket spans several distinct phases, each critical to establishing effective communication in distributed systems. Understanding the socket lifecycle encompasses the processes from creation to termination, ensuring efficient resource management and robust communication channels.

Socket Creation

Sockets in ZeroMQ originate from a context, which acts as the parent environment managing socket connections. Creating a socket involves defining its type, aligning with the intended communication pattern. Each socket type caters to specific messaging paradigms, as previously elucidated.

The initial step requires creating a new context. This context acts as a container for the sockets acting within a particular scope, managing input and output operations as well as threading issues.

```
// Creating a ZeroMQ context
void *context = zmq_ctx_new();
```

Following the context creation, the desired socket type is instantiated by invoking the zmq_socket() function, specifying the context and the socket type.

```
// Socket creation
void *socket = zmq_socket(context, ZMQ_REQ);
```

Socket Configuration

The next phase involves configuring the socket options, an essential

4.2. SOCKET LIFECYCLE: CREATION TO TERMINATION

component providing control over behavior and performance characteristics. Common options include setting timeouts, message filtering, and behaviors such as whether the socket blocks operations.

Configuration typically employs the zmq_setsockopt() function, capable of adjusting various socket properties. An illustrative example is setting a socket timeout, crucial for handling delayed responses and preventing indefinite blocking.

```
// Setting a socket option
int timeout = 5000; // in milliseconds
zmq_setsockopt(socket, ZMQ_RCVTIMEO, &timeout, sizeof(timeout));
```

Binding and Connecting

With sockets prepared, the next logical step is establishing connections. This requires either binding or connecting sockets, depending on their role in communication.

Binding a Socket:

Binding involves assigning a socket to a network address, typically performed by server-side sockets waiting to accept connections.

```
// Binding a socket
zmq_bind(socket, "tcp://*:5555");
```

Connecting a Socket:

Conversely, client-side sockets connect to a bound server via the zmq_connect() function.

```
// Connecting a socket
zmq_connect(socket, "tcp://localhost:5555");
```

Data Transmission

Once connected, sockets commence data transmission, engaging in send-and-receive operations. The functions zmq_send() and zmq_recv() manage outgoing and incoming messages, respectively. These functions define the essential I/O operations governing message exchanges.

Sending a message involves specifying the message content and its length:

```
// Sending a message
```

```
zmq_send(socket, "Sample message", 14, 0);
```

Receiving a message necessitates managing the buffer for incoming data:

```
// Receiving a message
char buffer[256];
zmq_recv(socket, buffer, 256, 0);
```

In ZeroMQ, message delivery is reliable across all sockets, ensuring delivery only once, in contrast to transport-layer reliability mechanisms that may result in duplicates.

Socket Monitoring

ZeroMQ provides a facility for monitoring socket events, aiding in debugging and runtime diagnostics. By attaching a monitor to the socket, one can observe significant events like authentication errors, connection retries, and disconnections.

```
// Monitoring socket events
zmq_socket_monitor(socket, "inproc://monitor", ZMQ_EVENT_ALL);

char address[256];
void* monitor = zmq_socket(context, ZMQ_PAIR);
zmq_connect(monitor, "inproc://monitor");
zmq_recv(monitor, address, 256, 0);
```

Monitoring remains a crucial phase for gaining insights into socket lifecycles and diagnosing unexpected behaviors in communication patterns.

Socket Termination

Capping the socket lifecycle, termination ensures a graceful shutdown of connections and releases resources. Each socket should be closed with the zmq_close() function, safeguarding against potential resource leaks.

```
// Closing a socket
zmq_close(socket);
```

Post socket closing, the context must also be terminated with zmq_ctx_destroy(), ensuring any lingering resources are purged efficiently.

```
// Destroying the context
zmq_ctx_destroy(context);
```

Understanding these fundamental aspects of ZeroMQ socket lifecycles underscores their role in achieving optimal performance and reliability in distributed systems. Developers must integrate holistic lifecycle management into their architectures, aligning context, configuration, and termination tasks to harness ZeroMQ's full capabilities. A robust grasp of these phases enables the design of systems that are not only efficient but also scalable, providing a solid foundation for messaging frameworks.

4.3 Binding and Connecting Sockets

The establishment of robust communication channels in ZeroMQ relies heavily on the mechanisms of binding and connecting sockets. This interplay forms the backbone of messaging systems, where each phase introduces critical aspects of distributed network communication. A thorough understanding of binding and connecting empowers developers to design systems that scale efficiently and operate reliably over diverse network topologies.

Binding Sockets

Binding is the process of associating a socket with a specific network interface and port number, essentially designating it to accept incoming connections. This operation is primarily performed on server-side sockets intended to receive connections and messages.

The zmq_bind() function is pivotal for this process. It requires a valid network endpoint, specified as a transport protocol string defining the transport type, IP address, and port number.

```
// Binding a socket to a TCP address
void *context = zmq_ctx_new();
void *socket = zmq_socket(context, ZMQ_REP);
zmq_bind(socket, "tcp://*:5555");
```

In this example, the "*" placeholder signifies all available network interfaces on the host machine, embracing a versatile approach to listening for connections from any source. The choice of port is essential; it's crucial to ensure the chosen port is available and not conflicted by other services.

Beyond TCP, ZeroMQ facilitates binding over various transports, including:

- **IPC (Inter-Process Communication):**
  ```
  // Binding using IPC
  zmq_bind(socket, "ipc:///tmp/zmq-socket");
  ```

  IPC transport is particularly beneficial for local machine applications. It leverages named pipes, offering quality performance without network overhead, especially advantageous when applications demand high-throughput and low-latency communications internally.

- **In-process (inproc):**
  ```
  // Binding using in-process transport
  zmq_bind(socket, "inproc://example");
  ```

  In-process transport provides efficient communication between threads in the same process. This is exceptionally useful for applications implementing multithreaded architectures where thread-safe message passing is desired without external data serialization requirements.

Connecting Sockets

The complementary action of connecting links a client-side socket to a bound network endpoint. The zmq_connect() function facilitates this step, enabling socket communication across the network or within the same host.

```
// Connecting a client-side socket
void *requester = zmq_socket(context, ZMQ_REQ);
zmq_connect(requester, "tcp://localhost:5555");
```

In this example, the "localhost" address specifies that the connection is local. It can be substituted with an IP address for remote targets. The connection process inherently tries to establish communication, and, guided by the resilient nature of ZeroMQ, typically involves a reconnection policy in case of transient network failures.

Considerations in Binding and Connecting

1. **Order Independence:**

   ZeroMQ abstracts the traditional socket model where one must follow strict order executives of connecting post binding. It permits sockets to connect to endpoints irrespective of the binding order, reflecting ZeroMQ's agility and robustness in dynamic environments.

   ```
   // Example illustrating order independence
   zmq_connect(requester, "tcp://localhost:5555");
   zmq_bind(socket, "tcp://*:5555");
   ```

2. **Endpoint Address Flexibility:**

   Endpoints in ZeroMQ can be dynamic, supporting wildcard IP addresses. This flexibility is vital for services expected to run on machines without static IP addresses, frequently encountered in cloud-native applications.

3. **Transports and Security:**

   Different transports cater to different security needs. TCP-based transports may require encryption layers, such as TLS or a VPN, to ensure data privacy. ZeroMQ allows user-implemented security mechanisms given that it operates over raw sockets, providing the liberty to deploy custom security protocols.

4. **Load Balancing and Message Distribution:**

   Both binding and connecting operations intertwine with ZeroMQ's sophisticated internal messaging strategies, including load balancing. This permits scenarios such as connecting multiple clients to a single server, where messages are load-optimized via incoming socket configurations.

   ```
   // Load balancing setup
   zmq_socket(socket, ZMQ_ROUTER);
   zmq_bind(socket, "tcp://*:5555");

   zmq_socket(requester, ZMQ_DEALER);
   zmq_connect(requester, "tcp://localhost:5555");
   ```

   Here, the ROUTER-DEALER socket pair enhances flexibility and scalability, empowering the developer to implement tailored message routing rules within the connected architecture.

Connecting-In-Process with Threading

ZeroMQ supports a distinct tactic for thread-safe communications, using inproc transport coupled with multithreading techniques for high-performance settings. The following example demonstrates a producer-consumer pattern using threading coupled with in-process connections:

```
#include <pthread.h>

void *producer(void *context) {
    void *sender = zmq_socket(context, ZMQ_PUSH);
    zmq_bind(sender, "inproc://thread");

    for(int i = 0; i < 10; ++i) {
        zmq_send(sender, "Data", 4, 0);
    }
    zmq_close(sender);
    return nullptr;
}

void *consumer(void *context) {
    void *receiver = zmq_socket(context, ZMQ_PULL);
    zmq_connect(receiver, "inproc://thread");

    char buffer[5];
    for(int i = 0; i < 10; ++i) {
        zmq_recv(receiver, buffer, 5, 0);
    }
    zmq_close(receiver);
    return nullptr;
}

int main() {
    void *context = zmq_ctx_new();

    pthread_t producer_thread, consumer_thread;
    pthread_create(&producer_thread, nullptr, producer, context);
    pthread_create(&consumer_thread, nullptr, consumer, context);

    pthread_join(producer_thread, nullptr);
    pthread_join(consumer_thread, nullptr);

    zmq_ctx_destroy(context);
    return 0;
}
```

This demonstrates in-process communications, showcasing efficient intra-process message queues devoid of network IO, leveraging pthreads for threading efficiency.

Handling Failures in Connections

Errors and abrupt disconnections are inevitable in distributed networks. ZeroMQ's design anticipates these by incorporating robust reconnection strategies via internal socket management. ZeroMQ developers can manage the lifespan of connections, sometimes manually handling error states through built-in socket monitoring facilities as showcased previously.

In closing, careful consideration and understanding of binding and connecting sockets within ZeroMQ are pivotal for developers aiming to build highly performant, distributed systems. It involves not merely linking endpoints, but orchestrating a symphony of robust, fault-tolerant communications, from standalone prototypes to scalable production systems. Mastery of these principles sets the groundwork for any sophisticated implementation within the ZeroMQ ecosystem, serving efficiently as the backbone of distributed messaging solutions.

4.4 Asynchronous I/O with ZeroMQ

Asynchronous Input/Output (I/O) is a key concept in network programming, enabling efficient use of resources by overlapping communication with computation or other I/O tasks. ZeroMQ inherently supports asynchronous I/O, which is fundamental for constructing non-blocking messaging systems that remain responsive under heavy loads.

Core Principles of Asynchronous I/O

ZeroMQ's asynchronous methodology revolves around non-blocking operations, allowing the application to process other tasks rather than waiting for I/O completion. This paradigm is essential for high-performance applications, facilitating concurrency and improving throughput by effectively managing CPU and I/O bottlenecks.

- **Non-blocking Operations**: ZeroMQ sockets can operate in non-blocking mode, achieved by specifying flags such as ZMQ_DONTWAIT within the API functions. This avoids stalling program execution when a particular operation is not immediately possible.

- **Event-driven Architecture**: ZeroMQ encourages an event-driven approach, often implemented through polling mechanisms to monitor multiple sockets for various events.

- **Message Queues**: Each ZeroMQ socket possesses an internal queue, buffering outgoing and incoming messages, vital for decoupling producers and consumers of messages in the system architecture.

Implementing Asynchronous I/O

To implement asynchronous I/O, ZeroMQ provides several tools and features:

Non-blocking Messaging

ZeroMQ enables non-blocking send and receive operations by supplying the ZMQ_DONTWAIT flag in APIs, minimizing idle waiting time for sockets.

```
// Non-blocking message send
int flags = zmq_send(socket, "Data", 4, ZMQ_DONTWAIT);
if (flags == -1 && errno == EAGAIN) {
    // Handle scenario where message queue is full
}
```

Here, the send operation proceeds only if the socket's internal buffer has space. If full, it returns immediately, allowing the program to proceed without blockage.

```
// Non-blocking message receive
int received = zmq_recv(socket, buffer, 10, ZMQ_DONTWAIT);
if (received == -1 && errno == EAGAIN) {
    // Handle scenario where no messages are available
}
```

Polling for Socket Events

ZeroMQ's efficient multiplexing of socket events is driven by polling techniques. The zmq_poll() function enables developers to track multiple sockets concurrently, detecting readable/writeable states and acting accordingly.

```
// Polling multiple sockets
zmq_pollitem_t items[] = {
    { socket1, 0, ZMQ_POLLIN, 0 },
    { socket2, 0, ZMQ_POLLOUT, 0 }
};

int rc = zmq_poll(items, 2, timeout); // Timeout in milliseconds
if (rc == -1) {
    // Handle polling error
}
```

4.4. ASYNCHRONOUS I/O WITH ZEROMQ

```
if (items[0].revents & ZMQ_POLLIN) {
    // Handle readable state for socket1
}
if (items[1].revents & ZMQ_POLLOUT) {
    // Handle writeable state for socket2
}
```

Polling supports sophisticated, multi-event applications where the state of several handles is evaluated, facilitating reactive programming architectures in ZeroMQ.

Asynchronous Message Handling with Multithreading

The concurrent nature of ZeroMQ aligns well with multithreading, where separate threads manage different responsibilities:

- **Worker Threads**: Dedicated to handling processing tasks, offering a structured approach to balance load and perform parallel computations.

- **Background I/O Threads**: Responsible for communicating via ZeroMQ sockets, segregating I/O operations from the main application logic.

This separation improves responsiveness, prevents performance bottlenecks, and aligns with the asynchronous design philosophy.

```
#include <pthread.h>

void *worker_thread(void *socket) {
    while (true) {
        zmq_msg_t message;
        zmq_msg_init(&message);
        if(zmq_msg_recv(&message, socket, 0) == -1) break;

        // Process received message

        zmq_msg_close(&message);
    }
    return nullptr;
}

int main() {
    void *context = zmq_ctx_new();
    void *socket = zmq_socket(context, ZMQ_PULL);
    zmq_connect(socket, "tcp://localhost:5555");

    pthread_t thread_id;
```

```
    pthread_create(&thread_id, nullptr, worker_thread, socket);
    // Main thread can continue performing other tasks or managing the socket
    pthread_join(thread_id, nullptr);
    zmq_close(socket);
    zmq_ctx_destroy(context);
    return 0;
}
```

Advanced Techniques and Considerations

ZeroMQ's versatility extends to several advanced asynchronous techniques:

1. **Asynchronous Patterns**: Incorporate advanced patterns such as the DEALER-ROUTER or PUSH-PULL to balance workloads dynamically or manage tasks via distributed systems.

2. **High-water Mark**: Regulating socket message queue sizes prevents overloads, ensuring message flow remains controllable under pressure.
   ```
   // Setting high-water mark for a socket
   int highwatermark = 1000;
   zmq_setsockopt(socket, ZMQ_SNDHWM, &highwatermark, sizeof(
       highwatermark));
   ```

3. **ZeroMQ with Selectors**: Use platform-specific mechanisms for asynchronous I/O, permitting operations to take advantage of default OS-level optimizations for socket handling.

Challenges and Solutions

While asynchronous I/O with ZeroMQ offers significant advantages, it introduces complexities:

- **Message Ordering**: Non-blocking operations can disrupt natural message ordering; using robust sequence identifiers ensures correct processing sequence.

- **Error Handling**: Proper management of non-blocking errors, e.g., EAGAIN, is crucial to anticipate empty queues or full buffers, ensuring robust and recoverable code paths.

- **Concurrency Conflicts**: Managing shared data or resources across threads demands rigorous synchronization techniques, such as mutexes or conditional variables, to avert race conditions.

Opportunities for Optimizations

Consider the following optimizations:

- **Batch Processing**: Aggregate multiple operations or messages before execution, reducing context switch overhead and enhancing throughput.

- **Efficient Buffer Management**: Design applications with pre-allocated buffers to minimize memory allocation costs during runtime.

- **Prioritization of Events**: Implement mechanisms to prioritize certain events within a polling or threading architecture, ensuring critical tasks receive immediate attention.

Mastering asynchronous I/O within ZeroMQ compels developers to rethink traditional I/O paradigms, embracing a multifaceted approach that transcends simplistic synchronous operations. Techniques born from this paradigm enable the creation of responsive, high throughput applications capable of scaling seamlessly in dynamic distributed environments. Employing asynchronous I/O is not merely about achieving non-blocking operations but orchestrating an ensemble of interactions and handling complex event flows with elegance and precision.

4.5 Managing Socket Options and Contexts

In ZeroMQ, sockets and contexts are fundamental constructs that dictate the behavior and efficiency of messaging systems. Managing socket options and contexts effectively allows developers to tailor communication patterns, optimize performance, and ensure reliability.

This section delves into the intricate details of socket options and contexts in ZeroMQ, explaining their various aspects, functionalities, and applications.

Understanding Contexts in ZeroMQ

ZeroMQ contexts serve as a container for all sockets within a particular scope. They manage resources like I/O threads and ensure thread safety across operations. A context is essential for isolating messaging environments, particularly in applications requiring multiple independent messaging systems.

Creating a context is straightforward, accomplished with the zmq_ctx_new() function:

```
// Creating a new ZeroMQ context
void *context = zmq_ctx_new();
```

Each context can manage numerous sockets, yet contexts themselves are entirely isolated from one another, resulting in no cross-context interactions. This isolation offers a robust mechanism for managing distinct communication channels within a single application, from microservices to complex enterprise systems.

The lifecycle of a context is encapsulated by two essential operations: zmq_ctx_new() and zmq_ctx_destroy(). The latter ensures that all resources allocated during the context's existence are correctly released, promoting efficient cleanup operations.

```
// Destroying a ZeroMQ context
zmq_ctx_destroy(context);
```

Several pivotal context options dictate its behaviors, often set using zmq_ctx_set() and queried via zmq_ctx_get():

- **I/O Threads:** The number of I/O threads determines the concurrency level for internal message processing.
  ```
  // Setting the number of I/O threads
  zmq_ctx_set(context, ZMQ_IO_THREADS, 2);
  ```

- **Max Sockets:** Configures the maximum number of sockets that a context can handle simultaneously.
  ```
  // Setting maximum number of sockets
  ```

4.5. MANAGING SOCKET OPTIONS AND CONTEXTS

```
zmq_ctx_set(context, ZMQ_MAX_SOCKETS, 256);
```

Socket Options - Fundamentals and Techniques

ZeroMQ sockets benefit from a plethora of configuration options that augment their behavior, performance, and security. Understanding these options and how they interact empowers developers to tailor solutions to meet precise application specifications.

Options are negotiated and set using `zmq_setsockopt()`, while `zmq_getsockopt()` provides visibility into the current configuration.

Commonly Used Socket Options

- **Send and Receive Timeouts**: These options define how long send and receive operations can block before timing out.

```
// Setting a send timeout
int send_timeout = 3000; // 3000 milliseconds
zmq_setsockopt(socket, ZMQ_SNDTIMEO, &send_timeout, sizeof(
    send_timeout));
```

- **High-Water Mark**: Controls the queue size for outgoing/incoming messages, influencing flow control and resource allocations when limits are approached.

```
// Configuring send high-water mark
int send_hwm = 1000;
zmq_setsockopt(socket, ZMQ_SNDHWM, &send_hwm, sizeof(send_hwm));
```

- **Linger Period**: A crucial option defining how long a socket will attempt to send unsent messages before closing.

```
// Setting linger period before socket closure
int linger = 5000;
zmq_setsockopt(socket, ZMQ_LINGER, &linger, sizeof(linger));
```

- **Identity**: Sets the identity of a socket, which can be integral in scenarios involving ROUTER sockets where addressing is necessary.

```
// Assigning an identity to a socket
const char *identity = "Worker-1";
zmq_setsockopt(socket, ZMQ_IDENTITY, identity, strlen(identity));
```

Advanced Socket Options

- **Heartbeat Mechanisms**: Ensures continuous connectivity by sending/polling heartbeats, fortifying the robustness against network disruptions.

  ```
  // Configuring heartbeat interval
  int heartbeat_interval = 1000; // in milliseconds
  zmq_setsockopt(socket, ZMQ_HEARTBEAT_IVL, &heartbeat_interval, sizeof
      (heartbeat_interval));
  ```

- **Multicast Interfaces**: Used for PUB-SUB patterns over multicast networks, specifying interfaces for outgoing traffic is essential for optimal fairness and reachability.

  ```
  // Specifying multicast socket interface
  const char *mcast_interface = "eth0";
  zmq_setsockopt(socket, ZMQ_MULTICAST_IFACE, mcast_interface, strlen(
      mcast_interface));
  ```

- **Curve Encryption**: For secure messaging, CurveZMQ offers built-in encryption capabilities, enabling confidentiality and integrity in communications.

  ```
  // Configuring a socket for Curve encryption
  const char *server_key = "BASE64ENCODED_SERVER_KEY";
  zmq_setsockopt(socket, ZMQ_CURVE_SERVERKEY, server_key, strlen(
      server_key));
  ```

Performance Considerations and Optimizations

The flexibility of socket options and contexts in ZeroMQ demands careful consideration to harness their benefits fully. Performance can be fine-tuned via strategic option management, such as:

- **Balancing I/O Threads**: A careful calculation of I/O threads relative to the application's load can avert bottlenecks and enhance responsiveness.

- **Efficient Message Buffering**: Configuring suitable high-water marks ensures memory is efficiently allocated, avoiding overconsumption while maintaining throughput.

4.5. MANAGING SOCKET OPTIONS AND CONTEXTS

- **Optimal Linger Settings**: Estimating an optimal linger time prevents message loss during abrupt shutdowns, securing graceful terminations.

Context Isolation and Scalability

Separating logical contexts across components not only bolsters reliability by containing faults but also promotes modular scalability. Advanced applications leverage multiple contexts to compartmentalize functionalities, from scaling microservices to partitioning testing and production environments without interference.

Several exemplary strategies may include:

- **Multicontext Services**: Using distinct contexts per service reduces cross-service noise, especially in complex ecosystems like IoT where differentiated device communications converge.

- **Resource Management Through Context Level Tuning**: Isolating resource-intensive socket clusters into dedicated contexts can enhance performance predictability, minimizing adverse impacts on concurrent workloads.

- **Testing Environments**: Leveraging contexts in testing scenarios guarantees isolated test conditions, facilitating controlled evaluations without interrupting real-world applications.

Conclusion

The intricate domain of managing socket options and contexts in ZeroMQ unveils a panorama of possibilities for optimizing messaging frameworks. Grasping the wealth of configurable options advances the ability to design cohesive, high-performance messaging applications. From setting up basic configurations to delving into advanced features such as encryption and heartbeat mechanisms, developers are equipped with rigorous control over system behavior, leading to robust and versatile communication architectures across a myriad of deployment scenarios. Advances in this domain continue to influence and shape contemporary approaches to building efficient, responsive, and secure distributed systems.

4.6 Handling Socket Errors and Exceptions

Robust error handling is paramount in the design and implementation of distributed systems using ZeroMQ. Network anomalies, resource limitations, and protocol misalignments can all result in errors that must be meticulously managed. This section delves deeply into the strategies and mechanisms for handling socket-related errors and exceptions in ZeroMQ, ensuring the resilience and reliability of your applications.

Understanding Error Sources in ZeroMQ

ZeroMQ is engineered to abstract many traditional networking complexities, yet errors may still arise from multiple sources, including:

- **Network Unavailability**: Loss of connectivity can lead to failed send or receive operations, timeouts, or disconnections.

- **Resource Constraints**: Exceeding available file descriptors, memory, or socket count can precipitate errors.

- **Protocol Violations**: Misuse of socket types or incorrect protocol implementations could yield exceptions.

- **Configuration Issues**: Incorrect socket or context parameter settings might result in operational failures.

Errors are typically signaled by ZeroMQ functions returning a negative status value, with further diagnostics accessible through the global errno variable.

Common Socket Errors and their Management

1. **EAGAIN**: Signal of a non-blocking operation's inability to proceed.

When utilizing non-blocking sockets, operations that cannot be completed immediately are signaled by the EAGAIN error.

```
// Handling EAGAIN in non-blocking mode
int rc = zmq_recv(socket, buffer, sizeof(buffer), ZMQ_DONTWAIT);
if (rc == -1 && errno == EAGAIN) {
    // Try again later or proceed with alternative logic
}
```

4.6. HANDLING SOCKET ERRORS AND EXCEPTIONS

Approaches include reattempting the operation after a brief pause, transitioning to other tasks, or deploying time-sensitive logic in polling loops.

2. **ENOTSUP**: Indicates an unsupported operation, likely due to compatibility mismatches between socket types or protocol flags.

```
// Example of unsupported operation management
int rc = zmq_setsockopt(socket, ZMQ_NOT_AVAILABLE_OPT, &value, sizeof(value
    ));
if (rc == -1 && errno == ENOTSUP) {
    // Log and manage unsupported feature gracefully
}
```

Careful attention to API documentation ensures that only supported options and operations are attempted, though fallbacks may be necessary for cross-version compatibility.

3. **ETERM**: Context termination in progress, an error mostly seen during cleanup phases or shutdown sequences.

A closed or terminating context leads to an ETERM error on socket operations, signaling an attempt to leverage resources associated with a respected-but-no-longer-valid context.

```
// Context shutdown error handling
int rc = zmq_send(socket, message, size, 0);
if (rc == -1 && errno == ETERM) {
    // Safely abort pending operations and clean resources
}
```

Ensuring predictable shutdown orders by sequencing operations conservatively guards against premature context destruction.

4. **EFSM (Finite State Machine Error)**: Arising from incorrect socket operation sequences, particularly prevalent with stateful socket types like REQ-REP.

REQ sockets, when mismanaged (e.g., sending two requests in succession without an intervening reply), trigger EFSM.

```
// Handling state machine errors
int rc = zmq_send(socket, multiple_requests, size, 0);
if (rc == -1 && errno == EFSM) {
    // Correct sequence misalignment by enforcing correct flow
}
```

Establish stringent state checks and balance requests and replies accordingly to prevent sequence mismatches.

Exception Handling Frameworks: ZeroMQ and Language Bindings

While ZeroMQ in C utilizes standard error codes via errno, bindings in higher-level languages leverage native exception handling mechanisms conducive to more readable and maintainable code.

- **C++ Exception Handling with ZeroMQ**:

  ZeroMQ's C++ binding often maps errors to C++ exceptions. For example:

  ```
  try {
      zmq::context_t context(1);
      zmq::socket_t socket(context, ZMQ_REQ);
      socket.connect("tcp://localhost:5555");

      while (true) {
          // Send/Receive in try/catch to handle exceptions
          socket.send(zmq::buffer("Hello"));
          zmq::message_t reply;
          socket.recv(reply);
      }
  } catch (const zmq::error_t& e) {
      std::cerr << "Exception: " << e.what() << std::endl;
      // Error handling logic
  }
  ```

  Frames logical blocks where exceptions originate, catching and responding to them with application-specific logic.

- **Python ZeroMQ Error Handling Techniques**:

  Python traditionally uses exceptions for error propagation, with ZeroMQ's zmq module reflecting this paradigm via the zmq.ZMQError class.

  ```
  import zmq

  context = zmq.Context()
  socket = context.socket(zmq.REQ)
  socket.connect("tcp://localhost:5555")

  try:
      socket.send(b"Hello")
      message = socket.recv()
  except zmq.ZMQError as e:
      print(f"Error occurred: {e}")
      // Manage error based on type via e.errno
  ```

Facilitates differentiated exception handling strategies including logging, fallback operations, or corrective processes.

Resilience Strategies in ZeroMQ

Given the distributed system's dynamic nature, resilient patterns are crucial. Strategies encompassing network errors, node failures, and resource recovery solidify ZeroMQ's deployment under operational stressors.

1. **Automatic Reconnection Policies**: ZeroMQ supports automatic reconnection by default, emitting internal retries for transient network failures until success. Customized settings or manual control may enhance this further.

2. **Heartbeat Mechanisms**: Continuous stream health is preserved through periodic heartbeat checks, which can automatically identify and rectify failed connections.

3. **Backup and Fallback Systems**: Incorporate backup routes or sockets to transition operations seamlessly upon certain error thresholds, guaranteeing message delivery.

By understanding ZeroMQ's vast error landscape and executing defensive programming principles, developers can avert application downtimes, improve robustness, and maintain operational continuity. In high-performance, low-latency systems, mastering error and exception handling proves indispensable, crafting systems that thrive in asynchronous, distributed environments.

Chapter 5

Advanced Patterns and Use Cases

ZeroMQ enables the implementation of advanced messaging patterns by combining basic patterns to address complex communication requirements in distributed systems. These patterns are crucial for designing scalable architectures, such as those used in microservices and real-time data processing applications. Understanding their application can significantly enhance system performance and reliability, allowing for efficient load balancing and fault tolerance. Through practical examples and real-world scenarios, this chapter explores how ZeroMQ's versatility can be harnessed to solve intricate challenges in various industry contexts, ranging from high-performance computing to collaborative development environments.

5.1 Combining Patterns for Complex Workflows

Developing distributed systems involves addressing multiple communication challenges, and ZeroMQ provides a versatile suite of messaging patterns that can be combined to orchestrate complex workflows. This section delves into how these patterns can be integrated efficiently to create robust communication frameworks in distributed applications, focusing on both the technical implementation and the relevant considerations for real-world scenarios.

Central to combining messaging patterns is the concept of establishing a coherent flow of data and control across various system components. When designing such systems, it is crucial to examine the communication requirements, data coordination complexity, and fault tolerance needed to ensure optimal system performance.

Patterns Integration

ZeroMQ allows the integration of multiple messaging patterns by leveraging its socket abstractions. Some widely used patterns include *request-reply*, *publish-subscribe*, and *push-pull*. These basic patterns can be combined and augmented to form more sophisticated constructs, such as the *broker* or *device* pattern, to achieve complex workflows.

The request-reply pattern facilitates synchronous interactions between the client and server. It is particularly useful for command and control operations. Meanwhile, publish-subscribe is an asynchronous, one-to-many communication pattern that allows broadcasting of messages across a network of subscribers. The push-pull pattern provides a load-balanced, asynchronous mechanism for distributing tasks to workers, ensuring efficient parallel processing.

Consider the following exemplary scenario to effectively manage a complex workflow where a data processing system needs to integrate these patterns. The system collects data from sensors (publishers), processes them through several worker nodes, and sends aggregated results to a dashboard client via a request-reply mechanism. Such integrations can be implemented using the appropriate ZeroMQ socket types, as demonstrated below.

5.1. COMBINING PATTERNS FOR COMPLEX WORKFLOWS

```
import zmq

context = zmq.Context()

# Publisher socket for sensor data
publisher = context.socket(zmq.PUB)
publisher.bind("tcp://*:5555")

# Push socket for task dispatching
dispatcher = context.socket(zmq.PUSH)
dispatcher.bind("tcp://*:5556")

# Reply socket for client communication
replier = context.socket(zmq.REP)
replier.bind("tcp://*:5557")
```

Assembling Complex Workflows

In a practical system setup, assembling a network of interconnected patterns involves mapping out the data flow. A common design approach leverages the divide-and-conquer strategy and subsequently assembles subsystems into a real-time analytics engine. Here, ZeroMQ's smart queuing and multiplexing capabilities enhance performance and responsiveness.

To illustrate, consider a system that analyzes real-time traffic data. As traffic sensors publish data, a broker device forwards this input to worker nodes distributed geographically. Each node processes these messages asynchronously using the push-pull pattern to ensure scalability and fault tolerance. Processed results are then disseminated back to centralized nodes via a request-reply link for integration into the primary traffic monitoring systems.

```
# Broker node managing data flow between sensors and processing units.
publisher.connect("tcp://sensor_ip:5555")
dispatcher.bind("tcp://*:5560")

while True:
    # Receive from publisher and forward to worker nodes
    message = publisher.recv()
    dispatcher.send(message)

    # Aggregate response from workers and send reply
    if dispatcher.poll(1000):
        result = dispatcher.recv()
        replier.send(result)
```

Efficiency Considerations

Efficiency in a combined pattern architecture is largely dependent on how well the communication links are optimized. Ensuring minimal latency involves planning the socket communication topologies and configuring them for high throughput and low overhead. Considering optimal message size, socket options like ZMQ_CONFLATE, or tuning parameters such as HWM (High Water Mark) are crucial for avoiding bottlenecks in high-performance scenarios.

Moreover, implementing robust data delivery mechanisms is essential. Techniques like message filtering in publish-subscribe scenarios, and implementing request retries or timeouts in request-reply instances, contribute to enhancing communication reliability.

```
# Example tuning for a PUB socket - enabling message filtering
subscriber = context.socket(zmq.SUB)
subscriber.setsockopt_string(zmq.SUBSCRIBE, "relevant_data")
subscriber.connect("tcp://data_broker:5555")

# Setting a high water mark for the queue
dispatcher.setsockopt(zmq.SNDHWM, 1000)
```

Fault Tolerance and Reliability

Building fault tolerance into the workflow is essential for maintaining system integrity and availability. ZeroMQ's inherent handling capabilities can be expanded to include mechanisms like backup brokers, redundant paths, and heartbeat monitoring.

In instances where components must ensure durability and reliability of message delivery under varying network conditions, integrating an acknowledgment system is advisable. Consumers confirm receipt of messages, and producers can replay messages from a log if necessary, using ZeroMQ patterns like the dealer-router for flexibility managing these acknowledgments.

```
# Router socket handling acknowledgments (ACKs) for reliable delivery
router = context.socket(zmq.ROUTER)
router.bind("tcp://*:5559")

while True:
    # Routing requests and processing acknowledgement
    ident, message = router.recv_multipart()

    # Logic for message processing
    result = process_message(message)

    # Send ACK back to the requester
    router.send_multipart([ident, result])
```

Scalability and Dynamic Adaptation

Scalability in ZeroMQ-based systems allows dynamic adaptation of systems to handle varying loads efficiently. This can be accomplished by adjusting the number of worker node instances, effectively using the push-pull pattern to balance loads. Dynamically scalable architectures may require intelligent load distribution strategies or broker systems capable of adaptively allocating resources.

Furthermore, the ability to scale must be complemented with real-time monitoring and automatic scaling mechanisms, potentially integrating orchestration tools such as Kubernetes, which can leverage ZeroMQ's distributed capabilities effectively.

```
# Scaling logic for a dynamic pool of workers
worker_pool = []

for _ in range(initial_worker_count):
    worker = context.socket(zmq.PULL)
    worker.connect("tcp://dispatcher-address:5556")
    worker_pool.append(worker)

# Function to dynamically increase or reduce workers
def adjust_workers(desired_count):
    if len(worker_pool) < desired_count:
        add_workers(desired_count - len(worker_pool))
    elif len(worker_pool) > desired_count:
        remove_workers(len(worker_pool) - desired_count)
```

The multi-layered architecture afforded by combining ZeroMQ patterns significantly contributes to building distributed systems that are resilient, flexible, and scalable. By intelligently integrating and managing these messaging patterns, complex workflows can be executed seamlessly, meeting demanding communication requirements while ensuring system performance and reliability.

5.2 Scalable Architectures with ZeroMQ

Designing scalable architectures is a fundamental aspect of building systems that can accommodate increasing loads and evolving demands. ZeroMQ, renowned for its flexibility and efficiency in inter-process communication, provides a robust framework for developing scalable architectures. This section aims to elucidate key principles of scalable design using ZeroMQ, exploring load balancing, fault tolerance, and strategies for optimizing system performance.

Conceptual Underpinnings of Scalability

Scalability in software design refers to a system's capacity to handle growth, whether by increasing the throughput, supporting more users, or accommodating more data. Achieving scalability demands a blend of sound design principles, such as decoupling components, optimizing resource utilization, and employing asynchronous processing techniques.

ZeroMQ supports these principles by offering a set of messaging patterns that allow for efficient communication across distributed systems. Two key components driving scalability in ZeroMQ architectures are the *load balancer* and *fault-tolerant mechanisms*. These components work collaboratively to maintain optimal performance and reliability.

Load Balancing with ZeroMQ

Load balancing is critical in distributed systems to ensure the even distribution of workloads across available resources, preventing any single node from becoming a bottleneck. ZeroMQ's push-pull pattern inherently supports load balancing by distributing tasks among available worker nodes.

Consider a scenario where a ZeroMQ-driven service needs to process incoming data requests while ensuring maximum utilization of the compute nodes:

```
import zmq

context = zmq.Context()

# Push socket at the dispatcher
dispatcher = context.socket(zmq.PUSH)
dispatcher.bind("tcp://*:5558")

# Worker side pull socket
def worker_task():
    worker = context.socket(zmq.PULL)
    worker.connect("tcp://dispatcher-host:5558")
    while True:
        task = worker.recv_json()
        # Process the task
        process(task)

# Initiating multiple worker nodes
for _ in range(worker_count):
```

5.2. SCALABLE ARCHITECTURES WITH ZEROMQ

```
start_new_thread(worker_task, ())
```

In the above implementation, several worker threads connect to the dispatcher via a pull socket, receiving tasks dispatched by the push socket. This structure ensures that tasks are evenly distributed among the workers, enhancing load balancing.

Dynamic Load Balancing Strategies

Beyond static configurations, dynamic load balancing involves adjusting to real-time load conditions. ZeroMQ applications can incorporate such strategies by leveraging monitoring and feedback mechanisms to adapt resource allocation dynamically.

For example, incorporating a monitoring subsystem that gauges node load and adjusts task distribution or resource allocation can markedly enhance system scalability. The broker node can actively monitor worker performance and redistribute tasks to under-utilized nodes to maintain balance.

```
# Monitoring and adjusting workload dynamically
def monitor_and_adjust(dispatcher):
    while True:
        for worker_id in get_workers():
            load = check_load(worker_id)
            if load < threshold:
                dispatcher.adjust_weight(worker_id, increase=True)
            else:
                dispatcher.adjust_weight(worker_id, increase=False)
```

Fault Tolerance in Scalable Architectures

ZeroMQ's design facilitates fault-tolerant systems by abstracting transport details and providing straightforward recovery mechanisms. In distributed systems, fault tolerance involves designing applications that can continue operating in case of node failures or network partitions.

A common approach is to use the *dealer-router* pattern, providing bidirectional communication with the ability to handle request retries and worker acknowledgements. The router socket can route requests to healthy workers, maintaining system operations even if some components fail.

```
# Router-dealer socket configuration for fault tolerance
router = context.socket(zmq.ROUTER)
```

```
router.bind("tcp://*:5560")

dealer = context.socket(zmq.DEALER)
dealer.connect("tcp://worker-pool:5560")

while True:
    ident, message = router.recv_multipart()
    # If node fails, retry logic
    if not send_to_worker(dealer, ident, message):
        retry_logic(message)
```

These mechanisms assure that tasks are redundantly processed, and failed nodes can be seamlessly replaced or redistributed to preserve consistent throughput.

Latency and Throughput Optimization

Achieving low latency while sustaining high throughput is foundational to scalable system architectures. With ZeroMQ, optimizing these factors requires thoughtful configuration of socket options and architectural patterns.

Reducing latency involves minimizing message size, optimizing network paths, and using asynchronous messaging where applicable. ZeroMQ's lightweight design and advanced socket options, such as ZMQ_CONFLATE, help streamline message handling.

```
# Configuring to reduce latency through conflate
stream_socket = context.socket(zmq.SUB)
stream_socket.setsockopt(zmq.CONFLATE, 1) # Only the last message is queued
stream_socket.connect("tcp://source-stream:5559")
```

Architectural Patterns for Scalability

Implementing advanced architectural patterns is pivotal for harnessing the full potential of ZeroMQ in scalable systems. These patterns could involve multi-layered or hierarchical designs that delineate responsibilities and optimize data handling logically.

For instance, a *broker* architecture can segment tasks into discrete pipelines, each responsible for a specific function of the processing flow, helping to scale various subsystems independently.

```
# Broker architecture setup for independent scaling
frontend = context.socket(zmq.ROUTER)
frontend.bind("tcp://*:5570")

backend = context.socket(zmq.DEALER)
backend.bind("tcp://*:5571")
```

```
# Asynchronous broker loop
while True:
    items = dict(poller.poll())
    if frontend in items:
        message = frontend.recv_multipart()
        backend.send_multipart(message)
    if backend in items:
        message = backend.recv_multipart()
        frontend.send_multipart(message)
```

Horizontal Scalability and Resilience

ZeroMQ naturally supports horizontal scaling, which involves adding more nodes to a system to enhance capacity. This is achieved effortlessly by simply increasing the number of consumers or workers without modifying existing code.

Multiple redundant nodes ensure resiliency; if one node fails, others continue executing tasks, reinforcing the system's robustness.

```
# Adding a new worker node for horizontal scaling
worker_new = context.socket(zmq.PULL)
worker_new.connect("tcp://dispatcher-host:5558")
```

Deploying such ZeroMQ-based architectures ensures the systems are not only scalable but resilient to varying operational contexts. By understanding and implementing these design foundations effectively, developers can engineer systems capable of handling vast amounts of data and accommodating substantial user bases, providing efficient and reliable services in the face of dynamically changing needs.

5.3 Building Microservices with ZeroMQ

Microservices architecture is an increasingly popular software development approach, enabling scalable, flexible, and independent service design. ZeroMQ offers potent facilities for building microservices with efficient communication, promoting decoupled systems without centralized governance. This section explores how to leverage ZeroMQ to structure effective microservice architectures, focusing on communication patterns, system reliability, and optimizing inter-service interactions.

Key Concepts in Microservices Architecture

In microservices architecture, applications are broken into small, independent services, each running its own process and communicating through lightweight mechanisms like HTTP or messaging protocols. This architectural style supports continuous deployment, scalable development, and improves fault isolation.

ZeroMQ is a messaging library known for its simplicity and lightweight footprint, delivering message queuing, publish-subscribe, and peer-to-peer connectivity paradigms. Its inherent asynchronous non-blocking I/O patterns align closely with microservices principles, where services can interact without waiting on each other, enhancing throughput and fault tolerance.

Designing Microservices with Messaging Patterns

ZeroMQ's rich messaging patterns enable the development of microservices where each service can effectively communicate with others, potentially deployed across diverse environments. The choice of messaging pattern critically influences the architecture and system capabilities.

1. **Request-Reply Pattern**: This synchronous pattern can be used for querying services or retrieving data, where one service sends a request to another and waits for a reply.

    ```python
    import zmq

    context = zmq.Context()

    # Client service performing request
    client = context.socket(zmq.REQ)
    client.connect("tcp://serviceA:5566")

    client.send_json({"operation": "fetchData"})
    reply = client.recv_json()
    print("Received reply:", reply)
    ```

2. **Publish-Subscribe Pattern**: Employed for broadcasting information where services subscribe to shared event streams, suitable for logging, monitoring, or real-time updates.

    ```python
    # Publisher microservice broadcasting events
    publisher = context.socket(zmq.PUB)
    publisher.bind("tcp://*:5567")
    ```

5.3. BUILDING MICROSERVICES WITH ZEROMQ

```
# Broadcasting an event
publisher.send_string("event_name event_data")
```

3. **Push-Pull Pattern**: Facilitates task distribution among services without blocking. It's apt for workload distribution, enabling seamless scaling by simply adding more worker instances.

```
# Task dispatcher service (PUSH)
dispatcher = context.socket(zmq.PUSH)
dispatcher.bind("tcp://*:5568")

# Worker service (PULL)
def worker_task():
    worker = context.socket(zmq.PULL)
    worker.connect("tcp://dispatcher-host:5568")
    while True:
        task = worker.recv_json()
        process_task(task)

# Launch worker
for _ in range(number_of_workers):
    start_new_thread(worker_task, ())
```

Service Decoupling and Loose Coupling

ZeroMQ promotes service decoupling by allowing services to interact using transient messaging interfaces rather than tightly-bound API calls. This separation enhances system resilience, where individual services can be independently maintained and deployed without impacting the entire system.

Loose coupling is enhanced when using ZeroMQ by employing an intermediary, such as a broker, to mediate service communication. This acts as a service registry or event router, decoupling service endpoints from each other and enabling dynamic service discovery.

```
# Broker service - acts as a service registry
frontend = context.socket(zmq.ROUTER)
frontend.bind("tcp://*:5570")

backend = context.socket(zmq.DEALER)
backend.bind("tcp://*:5571")

# Routes messages between services
while True:
    events = poller.poll()
    message = frontend.recv_multipart()
    backend.send_multipart(message)
```

Designing for Resilience and Fault Tolerance

Microservice resilience and fault tolerance are critical for building robust systems. ZeroMQ facilitates strategies such as:

1. **Health Checks and Heartbeats**: Implementing heartbeat messages between microservices can ensure timely detection of failed services, allowing quick failover and recovery strategies.

   ```
   # Heartbeat mechanism for service health
   service = context.socket(zmq.REQ)
   service.connect("tcp://health-monitor:5559")
   service.send_string("heartbeat")
   ```

2. **Redundant Paths and Service Replication**: Implementing redundant service paths ensures alternative routes for communication, reducing the risk of service outages affecting operations.

   ```
   # Multi-path routing for redundancy
   router = context.socket(zmq.ROUTER)
   router.bind("tcp://*:5580")

   while True:
       ident, message = router.recv_multipart()
       try:
           handle_message(message, alternative_path=True)
       except RoutingError:
           route_fallback(message)
   ```

3. **Circuit Breaker Patterns**: Incorporating circuit breaker logic to isolate failing services, preventing total system failures by allowing specific responses during service disruptions.

   ```
   # Circuit breaker example
   try:
       response = call_external_service()
   except ServiceUnavailable:
       if not circuit_open:
           open_circuit()
       fallback_response()
   ```

Scalability and Elasticity

Microservices must scale seamlessly, responding dynamically to load variations. ZeroMQ's patterns allow horizontal scaling, where new service instances are spun up via orchestration platforms like Kubernetes, facilitating automatic scaling and load balancing.

Adding more instances of services that use the push-pull pattern effortlessly increases throughput without service coordination changes:

5.3. BUILDING MICROSERVICES WITH ZEROMQ

```
# Horizontal scaling by adding new workers
new_worker = context.socket(zmq.PULL)
new_worker.connect("tcp://dispatcher:5568")
```

Elasticity involves auto-scaling mechanisms that match service instance counts to current demand, minimizing resource wastage and optimizing cost efficiency.

Security Considerations

Security remains a paramount concern in microservice architectures. Implementing encryption, authentication, and authorization on ZeroMQ messages helps protect against unauthorized access and data breaches.

- **End-to-End Encryption**: ZeroMQ supports encryption using CurveZMQ, ensuring message contents remain confidential during transit.

    ```
    # Setting up CurveZMQ for encrypted communication
    socket = context.socket(zmq.REQ)
    socket.curve_publickey = zmq.curve_keypair()[0]
    socket.curve_secretkey = zmq.curve_keypair()[1]
    socket.curve_serverkey = server_public_key
    ```

- **Authentication**: Implementing authentication processes validates the identity of services attempting communication.

- **Authorization**: Controlling access based on service rights, ensuring only authorized services execute specific operations.

Designing microservices with ZeroMQ embraces agility, autonomy, and robustness. Implementing its flexible messaging patterns and integrating them with proper design principles results in systems that respond fluidly to change, scale seamlessly to meet demand, and remain resilient amid unexpected pressures. Systems built with ZeroMQ can thus embody the key attributes of microservices: scalability, flexibility, and resilience.

5.4 High-Performance Computing Applications

High-performance computing (HPC) plays a pivotal role in solving complex scientific, engineering, and commercial problems that require substantial computational resources. ZeroMQ contributes significantly to HPC by offering efficient, low-latency messaging frameworks that facilitate distributed compute environments. This section explores the application of ZeroMQ in HPC, detailing its relevance to parallel processing, resource management, and performance optimization.

Introduction to HPC Frameworks

HPC systems endeavor to achieve maximum computational efficiency by utilizing multiple processors or compute nodes working in parallel. Typical HPC frameworks comprise clusters, grids, or supercomputers involving dense networks with thousands of cores coordinated to perform intricate computations, often involving data-intensive tasks.

ZeroMQ's lightweight protocol provides significant advantages in these environments, where the flexible communication patterns and non-blocking I/O maximize resource utilization and accelerate computation interfacing.

ZeroMQ in Distributed Computation

ZeroMQ enables seamless distributed communication, crucial for HPC tasks relying on collective computation across multiple nodes.

- Task Distribution and Workload Balancing

    In distributed HPC systems, tasks are often split and distributed among computing nodes. Implementing the push-pull pattern is instrumental for balancing workloads dynamically, ensuring each compute node handles appropriate amounts of data processing without overloading any particular node.

```
import zmq

context = zmq.Context()

# Task manager for dispatching workloads
```

5.4. HIGH-PERFORMANCE COMPUTING APPLICATIONS

```
task_sender = context.socket(zmq.PUSH)
task_sender.bind("tcp://*:5551")

# Worker nodes pull tasks and execute
def compute_node():
    receiver = context.socket(zmq.PULL)
    receiver.connect("tcp://task-manager:5551")
    while True:
        task = receiver.recv_json()
        result = process_computation(task)
        results_sender.send_json(result)

# Results collector receiving computed data
results_sender = context.socket(zmq.PUSH)
results_sender.bind("tcp://*:5552")
```

This setup supports asynchronous task distribution, allowing the HPC system to handle large volumes of tasks concurrently while managing load variations effectively.

- Real-Time Data Processing

    Real-time processing in HPC applications requires efficient means to process continuous streams of data without lag. ZeroMQ's publish-subscribe pattern facilitates real-time data dissemination across different computation nodes, enabling parallel processing of incoming data streams and timely results dissemination.

```
# Publisher node broadcasting real-time data
data_source = context.socket(zmq.PUB)
data_source.bind("tcp://*:5560")

# Subscriber nodes receiving and processing the data
data_consumer = context.socket(zmq.SUB)
data_consumer.setsockopt_string(zmq.SUBSCRIBE, "")
data_consumer.connect("tcp://data-source:5560")

while True:
    data = data_consumer.recv_json()
    processed_data = process_real_time_data(data)
```

This pattern ensures scalability by allowing more subscriber nodes to be added without affecting the publisher's performance, enabling numerous computations in parallel.

Optimizing Communication in HPC

Optimization entails reducing message overhead, minimizing latency, and maximizing throughput. ZeroMQ provides succinct tools and techniques in achieving these objectives.

- Latency Reduction Techniques

    Minimizing latency impacts responsiveness in HPC operations. By configuring ZeroMQ's socket options, developers can effectively manage message buffering and routing, decreasing the time from request to response.

    Configuring socket options such as ZMQ_IMMEDIATE ensures messages are only sent if the remote peer is immediately ready to receive them, maintaining message integrity without unnecessary delays.

```
# Immediate socket configuration to reduce latency
socket = context.socket(zmq.REQ)
socket.setsockopt(zmq.IMMEDIATE, 1)
socket.connect("tcp://compute-node:5570")
```

- Batch Messaging for Enhanced Throughput

    In tasks that require bulk data movement, batching messages can significantly improve throughput by reducing the per-message overhead. Messages can be accumulated into larger packets and sent in a single network transfer.

```
# Batched message sending for high throughput
batch = []
while has_more_data:
    batch.append(collect_next_message())
    if len(batch) == batch_size:
        send_batch(batch)
        batch.clear()
```

Batch messaging is particularly effective in scenarios involving large data transfers, where bandwidth utilization becomes critical for performance.

Resource Management and Scheduling

Efficient scheduling and resource allocation are crucial in HPC setups to prevent resource conflict and maximize hardware utilization.

5.4. HIGH-PERFORMANCE COMPUTING APPLICATIONS

- Dynamic Resource Allocation

  HPC systems often deal with dynamic workloads, requiring resources to be allocated flexibly. ZeroMQ supports dynamic allocation through adaptive subscription mechanisms, where nodes can signal their availability or overload conditions dynamically, facilitating an intelligent resource allocation strategy.

```
# Adaptive node management based on resource availability
def resource_aware_node():
    node_socket = context.socket(zmq.SUB)
    node_socket.connect("tcp://resource-manager:5553")

    while True:
        status = get_current_status()
        node_socket.send_json({"status": status})
        response = node_socket.recv_json()
        adjust_resources(response)
```

Such adaptive mechanisms ensure that when demand spikes, additional resources can be seamlessly allocated without administrator intervention, enhancing the system's elasticity.

- Computational Scheduling Policies

  Integration with existing HPC scheduling frameworks, like Slurm or Torque, ensures tasks are submitted and managed efficiently. ZeroMQ can be used to relay real-time updates between schedulers and nodes, providing insights into job statuses and queued workloads.

```
# Communicating with a job scheduler
scheduler_interface = context.socket(zmq.REQ)
scheduler_interface.connect("tcp://scheduler:5554")

# Request job allocation
scheduler_interface.send_json({"task": "allocate", "resources": required_resources})
allocated_node_info = scheduler_interface.recv_json()
deploy_task_to_node(allocated_node_info)
```

Security and Data Integrity

In HPC environments, ensuring data integrity and communication security is paramount due to the sensitivity and magnitude of data being processed.

- Secure Messaging

CHAPTER 5. ADVANCED PATTERNS AND USE CASES

ZeroMQ supports CurveZMQ encryption, enabling secure communications between nodes. This encryption ensures messages are protected from unauthorized access or tampering, maintaining data confidentiality.

```
# Configuring Curve encryption for secure messages
secured_socket = context.socket(zmq.REQ)
secured_socket.curve_secretkey, secured_socket.curve_publickey = zmq.
    curve_keypair()
secured_socket.curve_serverkey = server_public_key
secured_socket.connect("tcp://secured-endpoint:5555")
```

- Data Integrity Validation

Implementing checksums or hash validations on data exchanged between nodes ensures integrity. Services verify the data upon receipt, ensuring computations are based on accurate inputs, essential in scientific and financial simulations where precision is critical.

```
# Validating data integrity using checksum
message, checksum_received = receive_with_checksum(socket)
if validate_checksum(message, checksum_received):
    process(message)
else:
    handle_checksum_error()
```

HPC in Real-World Applications

In practical scenarios, ZeroMQ's applicability extends to bioinformatics, fluid dynamics simulations, astrophysics, and climate modeling. Its ability to support large-scale computations, real-time data analysis, and high-throughput situations becomes evident when tackling computationally intensive problems.

For example, climate modeling involves simulating large datasets over adjacent grid points, often broadcasting updates on model evolution or potential changes to maintain a cohesive simulation:

```
# Complex climate model distribution coordination
climate_node = context.socket(zmq.SUB)
climate_node.connect("tcp://model-distribution:5566")
climate_node.setsockopt_string(zmq.SUBSCRIBE, "update-channel")

while True:
    model_update = climate_node.recv_json()
    integrate_model_update(model_update)
```

ZeroMQ empowers HPC applications by capitalizing on efficient data distribution, adaptable resource management, and secure communication channels, making it an invaluable tool for advancing computational science and industry precision.

5.5 Real-time Data Processing Use Cases

Real-time data processing has become imperative across industries, enabling immediate analysis and decision-making based on live data streams. This capability materially impacts domains such as finance, healthcare, telecommunications, and IoT ecosystems. ZeroMQ provides an effective framework for such applications due to its inherent support for fast, decentralized, and asynchronous messaging patterns. This section presents a detailed exploration of ZeroMQ's role in real-time data processing, highlighting use cases, core challenges, and best practices for implementation.

Overview of Real-time Data Processing

Real-time data processing involves ingesting, processing, and analyzing data as it arrives to produce timely insights or actions. The effectiveness of real-time processing systems anchors on low-latency communication, high throughput, and scalability. Systems must adeptly handle data bursts while maintaining high availability and resilience.

ZeroMQ servers these requirements with its lightweight protocol ensuring minimal overhead, non-blocking I/O for seamless message propagation, and diverse communication patterns allowing developers to tailor specific tasks efficiently.

Use Case 1: Financial Market Data Analysis

In financial markets, real-time data processing is critical for analyzing trading data to generate buy/sell signals, risk assessments, and compliance reports. An integral part of this is ingesting market data continuously, analyzing it using complex algorithms, and dispatching the results with minimal delay.

- **Data Ingestion and Pre-processing**

  Financial data streams can be high-frequency, necessitating ef-

CHAPTER 5. ADVANCED PATTERNS AND USE CASES

ficient message handling under bandwidth constraints. The publish-subscribe pattern is expertly suited for disseminating market data to multiple analysts simultaneously.

```
import zmq

context = zmq.Context()

# Data distributor for market feed
market_feed = context.socket(zmq.PUB)
market_feed.bind("tcp://*:5575")

# Broadcast market data
market_feed.send_json({"ticker": "AAPL", "price": 150.75})
```

Subscribers to the market feed receive real-time updates, allowing them to deploy rapid analysis algorithms.

- **Quantitative Analysis and Trading Signals**

Analysis engines subscribe to the feed, executing trading strategies based on computational models, and using push-pull for distributed computation among numerous computation nodes enhances scalability.

```
# Subscribing to market data feed
market_listener = context.socket(zmq.SUB)
market_listener.setsockopt_string(zmq.SUBSCRIBE, "AAPL")
market_listener.connect("tcp://data-source:5575")

# Trigger analysis on received data
while True:
    market_data = market_listener.recv_json()
    analyze_and_trade(market_data)
```

The analyzed results are sent back to trading systems via request-reply for further actions, ensuring rapid execution.

Use Case 2: Telemedicine and Patient Monitoring

The healthcare sector increasingly looks towards real-time monitoring to enhance patient care, monitor critical health metrics, and respond swiftly to emergencies. ZeroMQ assists in reliably transporting sensor data from medical devices to healthcare providers for real-time monitoring and alerts.

- **Continuous Health Monitoring**

5.5. REAL-TIME DATA PROCESSING USE CASES

In a telehealth environment, patient devices continuously stream vital signs (e.g., heart rate, glucose levels) using ZeroMQ's reliable messaging patterns to the centralized healthcare system.

```
# Device broadcasting patient vitals
patient_device = context.socket(zmq.PUB)
patient_device.connect("tcp://health-monitor:5580")

while True:
    heartbeat = read_sensor_data()
    patient_device.send_json({"patient_id": "1234", "heart_rate": heartbeat})
```

Providers receive the data, effectively monitoring patient statuses in real time, potentially triggering alerts in critical situations.

- **Alert Systems and Emergency Responses**

  ZeroMQ enables alert systems to broadcast critical event notifications to multiple care providers, ensuring that emergency teams are promptly informed and activated.

```
# Alert broadcasting system
alerts_broadcaster = context.socket(zmq.PUB)
alerts_broadcaster.connect("tcp://care-team:5585")

def check_and_alert(vital_data):
    if vital_data["heart_rate"] < THRESHOLD:
        alerts_broadcaster.send_string("Alert: Emergency for patient 1234")
```

This setup guarantees that critical patient conditions are not left unattended, significantly enhancing response efficacy.

Use Case 3: IoT Network Management

In IoT, real-time processing manages vast numbers of devices producing high-velocity data streams. From smart city applications to autonomous vehicles, ZeroMQ assists in both data collection and decision-making processes across distributed nodes.

- **Sensor Network Data Aggregation**

  Real-time control systems collect and process data from numerous IoT devices efficiently using routing and multiplexing patterns to aggregate data logically across networks.

```
# Data collection from IoT devices
iot_collector = context.socket(zmq.PULL)
```

CHAPTER 5. ADVANCED PATTERNS AND USE CASES

```
iot_collector.bind("tcp://*:5590")

# Receiving data from sensors
while True:
    sensor_data = iot_collector.recv_json()
    aggregate_and_analyze(sensor_data)
```

Aggregating data streams ensures coherent input to analytics components, crucial for orchestrating IoT ecosystem activities.

- **Automated Actuation and Feedback Loops**

    Decision-making algorithms utilize real-time data for automated actuation, such as adjusting traffic lights in smart cities or managing utility loads in smart grids.

```
# Control decision system influencing an automated response
decision_system = context.socket(zmq.PUSH)
decision_system.connect("tcp://actuator-system:5595")

def control_decision_logic(sensor_data):
    actuation_decision = compute_control_analytics(sensor_data)
    decision_system.send_json({"action": actuation_decision})
```

    These real-time feedback mechanisms create seamless automation loops and immediate actions, enabling smarter IoT infrastructures.

Performance Considerations and Optimization

Ensuring the real-time efficacy of processing systems necessitates performance optimization strategies aligned with ZeroMQ capabilities.

- **Reducing Message Latency**

    Performance hinges on reducing communication latencies. ZeroMQ supports socket-level configurations, such as using ZMQ_DELAY_ATTACH_ON_CONNECT to prevent message overloads during node discovery.

```
# Optimizing socket for low latency
opt_socket = context.socket(zmq.PUB)
opt_socket.setsockopt(zmq.DELAY_ATTACH_ON_CONNECT, 1)
opt_socket.bind("tcp://*:5600")
```

- **Scaling with Multicore Utilization**

Utilizing ZeroMQ's compatibility with multi-threading scales read and write operations concurrency, optimizing multicore CPU setups for handling high data rates.

```
# Concurrency for multi-core processing
def worker_function():
    context = zmq.Context()
    local_socket = context.socket(zmq.SUB)
    local_socket.connect("tcp://main-node:5605")

start_new_thread(worker_function, ())
```

Security and Data Integrity

In real-time data processing, securing the data pipeline and ensuring the integrity of streamed information is as important as in traditional data systems.

- **Secure End-to-End Transmission**

    ZeroMQ supports encrypting data streams with CurveZMQ, vital for preventing eavesdropping and tampering, especially over public networks.

    ```
    # Secure message settings for sensitive data
    secure_client = context.socket(zmq.PUB)
    secure_client.curve_secretkey, secure_client.curve_publickey = zmq.curve_keypair()
    secure_client.curve_serverkey = service_server_key
    secure_client.bind("tcp://*:5610")
    ```

- **Data Validation Mechanisms**

    Incorporating validation routines to ensure message correctness and authenticity helps maintain continuity and relevance of processing outputs.

    ```
    # Validation routine of incoming messages
    def validate_message_format(data_packet):
        if 'sensor_id' in data_packet and 'value' in data_packet:
            return True
        return False
    ```

Combining ZeroMQ with innovative processing strategies empowers systems to access real-time data utilities efficiently, delivering quick responses, intelligent insights, and rock-solid reliability across diverse application domains. Through these pursuits, ZeroMQ aids industries in leveraging real-time data for operational and strategic benefit.

5.6 Case Studies of ZeroMQ in Industry

ZeroMQ has established itself as a cornerstone in industries where fast, reliable, and efficient messaging is paramount. From financial services to telecommunications and beyond, ZeroMQ supports the backbone of systems requiring high throughput and low latency. This section entails a detailed exploration of real-world case studies where ZeroMQ has been instrumental in addressing unique industry challenges, showcasing its versatility and impact.

Case Study 1: Financial Trading Systems

In financial markets, rapid trade execution, real-time data analytics, and risk assessment are crucial for sustaining competitive advantage. ZeroMQ's efficient messaging capabilities are leveraged to streamline operations in high-frequency trading (HFT) systems and analytical platforms.

- **HFT and Real-time Analytics**

    High-frequency trading necessitates processing extensive market data feeds and executing transactions within microseconds. A prominent brokerage firm implemented ZeroMQ to optimize its market data distribution network and execution layer.

    ```
    import zmq

    context = zmq.Context()

    # Broker node to handle market feeds
    price_broker = context.socket(zmq.XSUB)
    price_broker.bind("tcp://*:5655")

    # Distributing and aggregating market data
    market_subscriber = context.socket(zmq.SUB)
    market_subscriber.setsockopt_string(zmq.SUBSCRIBE, "")
    market_subscriber.connect("tcp://broker:5655")

    while True:
        market_data = market_subscriber.recv_json()
        analyze_and_respond(market_data)
    ```

ZeroMQ's asynchronous messaging and non-blocking I/O ensure messages are processed quickly, maintaining the speed demanded by HFT operations.

- **Risk Management Systems**

  For risk management, a global investment firm uses ZeroMQ to monitor exposure across multiple trading desks. Data from various endpoints is collected, processed, and analyzed in real-time to provide centralized risk dashboards.

  ```
  # Gathering risk exposure data
  risk_monitor = context.socket(zmq.SUB)
  risk_monitor.setsockopt_string(zmq.SUBSCRIBE, "")
  risk_monitor.connect("tcp://risk-data-source:5660")

  # Managing aggregated risk data
  while True:
      risk_data = risk_monitor.recv_json()
      update_risk_dashboard(risk_data)
  ```

  The flexibility of ZeroMQ patterns allows for dynamic reconfiguration of systems, facilitating real-time adaptation to fluctuations in trading volumes or market conditions.

Case Study 2: Telecommunications and IoT Networks

In telecommunications, the escalating demand for bandwidth has driven operators to overhaul their network architectures to support real-time communication and device interconnectivity. ZeroMQ aids in alleviating these operational complexities.

- **IoT Device Networking**

  A telecommunications provider used ZeroMQ to facilitate communication between millions of IoT devices, providing a distributed network that ensures low-latency data transport across city-wide networks.

  ```
  # Environmental sensors data streaming
  sensor_streamer = context.socket(zmq.PUB)
  sensor_streamer.bind("tcp://*:5675")

  # Streaming sensor data across the network
  while True:
      sensor_data = gather_sensor_readings()
      sensor_streamer.send_json(sensor_data)
  ```

CHAPTER 5. ADVANCED PATTERNS AND USE CASES

This enabled the seamless integration of numerous devices, ensuring scalability and robustness that can accommodate continuous device addition.

- **Network Performance Monitoring**

    Network operators employed ZeroMQ to implement real-time network performance monitoring solutions, providing carriers with comprehensive insights into line health, throughput, and latency variations on a granular level.

    ```
    # Monitoring node for network health analytics
    performance_monitor = context.socket(zmq.SUB)
    performance_monitor.connect("tcp://network-analyzer:5680")

    # Evaluating live data for performance insights
    while True:
        performance_data = performance_monitor.recv_json()
        process_performance_metrics(performance_data)
    ```

    By achieving superior network visibility, operators can optimize resource allocation, improve service quality, and reduce downtime effectively.

Case Study 3: Cloud Services and Data Centers

In the era of cloud computing, data centers provide backbone services supporting consumer applications at an unprecedented scale. ZeroMQ has been integrated into several IT infrastructure systems to improve communication protocols.

- **Distributed Machine Learning Pipelines**

    A tech enterprise employs ZeroMQ in its distributed machine learning pipelines, enhancing the scalability and efficiency of model training processes across geographically dispersed data centers.

    ```
    # Model update dissemination node
    model_node = context.socket(zmq.PUB)
    model_node.bind("tcp://*:5690")

    # Propagating model updates to regional nodes
    while True:
        model_update = generate_model_update()
        model_node.send_json(model_update)
    ```

5.6. CASE STUDIES OF ZEROMQ IN INDUSTRY

Data-driven decisions hinge on effectively collecting, distributing, and analyzing vast datasets, a challenge met by ZeroMQ's versatility across varied computing environments.

- **Service Orchestration and Management**

  Prestigious cloud providers utilized ZeroMQ to enable service orchestration engines, which manage vital cloud services dynamically based on demand, ensuring both resource optimization and service reliability.

  ```
  # Task orchestration management node
  orchestrator = context.socket(zmq.DEALER)
  orchestrator.bind("tcp://*:5700")

  # Managing service requests and executions
  while True:
      request = orchestrator.recv_json()
      allocate_resources_for_service(request)
  ```

  This orchestration framework allows for continuous deployment resilience, bolstering the ability to efficiently serve growing numbers of concurrent users.

Case Study 4: Multimedia Streaming Services

The multimedia industry is undergoing a metamorphosis with increasing demand for high-definition content and seamless streaming experiences. ZeroMQ facilitates efficient data transport ensuring uninterrupted content delivery.

- **Stream Distribution Networks**

  A leading media services company integrated ZeroMQ to enhance their streaming distribution network architecture, optimizing content delivery across diverse endpoints while maintaining high availability.

  ```
  # Video stream distribution node
  video_distributor = context.socket(zmq.PUB)
  video_distributor.bind("tcp://*:5710")

  # Distributing video feeds to subscribers
  while True:
      video_data = read_video_feed()
      video_distributor.send(video_data)
  ```

Leveraging ZeroMQ's low message overhead, the company achieves uninterrupted streaming quality, crucial for maintaining subscriber satisfaction.

- **Live Content Broadcasting**

  A broadcasting platform utilized ZeroMQ to synchronize live sports content dissemination globally, ensuring viewers experience seamless broadcast regardless of location or platform confined by regional communication constraints.

  ```
  # Broadcasting live event updates
  broadcast_node = context.socket(zmq.PUB)
  broadcast_node.bind("tcp://*:5720")

  # Sending live event information
  while True:
      event_update = create_broadcast_update()
      broadcast_node.send_json(event_update)
  ```

By employing ZeroMQ's robust messaging models, they can handle peak loads efficiently, such as during significant sporting events, ensuring consistent real-time viewing quality.

Performance Optimization and Lessons Learned

Across these industries, practical experience delineates several key lessons when implementing ZeroMQ in live environments:

- **Optimizing Latency and Throughput**

  Tuning sockets for specific operational needs, such as lowering high-water marks or enabling ZMQ_CONFLATE, ensures consistent low-latency and high-throughput operations.

  ```
  # Optimizing socket configuration for latency
  optimized_socket = context.socket(zmq.DEALER)
  optimized_socket.setsockopt(zmq.RCVHWM, 10)
  optimized_socket.setsockopt(zmq.SNDHWM, 10)
  optimized_socket.bind("tcp://*:5730")
  ```

- **Ensuring Resilience and Redundancy**

  Architecting redundant communication paths where broker systems can failover to alternate routes improves system resilience and ensures operational continuity.

- **Scaling Architectures Dynamically**
  ZeroMQ's inherent capability to scale horizontally across nodes allows systems to adjust gracefully to load variations, catering to peak traffic without requiring intricate redesigns.

As these cases illustrate, ZeroMQ offers versatile solutions adaptable to varied industrial needs, delivering performance and resilience necessary to support complex, critical operations across technological landscapes. From optimizing computational efficiencies to enhancing service delivery, ZeroMQ has proven its invaluable role in the strategic advancement of numerous industries.

Chapter 6

Integrating ZeroMQ with Various Programming Languages

ZeroMQ offers extensive support for multiple programming languages, providing bindings that facilitate its integration into diverse software ecosystems. This cross-language compatibility enables developers to implement ZeroMQ's messaging capabilities in languages such as Python, C/C++, Java, and JavaScript, among others. Each language presents unique integration techniques and performance considerations, necessitating tailored approaches to leverage ZeroMQ's full potential. This chapter provides detailed guidance on integrating ZeroMQ with these languages, supported by examples and best practices. Additionally, strategies are explored for achieving seamless cross-language communication, enhancing interoperability and scalability across heterogeneous systems.

6.1 ZeroMQ Language Bindings Overview

ZeroMQ serves as a highly versatile messaging library with robust support for multiple programming languages, offering a well-orchestrated framework for developers to implement messaging systems across varied platforms. The core of its cross-language capabilities resides in its language bindings, which allow ZeroMQ to be integrated into both compiled languages such as C/C++ and interpreted languages like Python, JavaScript, and more. This section delves into the comprehensive landscape of ZeroMQ language bindings, illuminating their installation procedures and utility within application contexts.

The ZeroMQ library itself is implemented in C++, which ensures optimal performance and flexibility. However, to facilitate its use across different development ecosystems, ZeroMQ provides language bindings - essentially, a set of functions and frameworks - that enable the native features of ZeroMQ to be accessed from within different programming environments. Below, we explore some of the most popular ZeroMQ language bindings, consider the installation nuances of each, and explore how they integrate with respective language paradigms, emphasizing the importance of leveraging these bindings to harness ZeroMQ's full capabilities.

Python Bindings (PyZMQ)

Python, renowned for its readability and ease of use, is a popular choice among developers working on rapid prototyping and data-driven applications. ZeroMQ's Python binding, PyZMQ, is a straightforward bridge between Python applications and ZeroMQ's message-passing capabilities.

Installation of PyZMQ is typically conducted through the Python Package Index (PyPI) using pip, a standard package installer for Python:

```
pip install pyzmq
```

The PyZMQ module provides interfaces to most of ZeroMQ's functionality, allowing for the creation of sockets, connection patterns (like PUB-SUB, REQ-REP), and message framing all using Python's syntax. Consider the basic implementation of a ZeroMQ PUB-SUB pattern in

6.1. ZEROMQ LANGUAGE BINDINGS OVERVIEW

Python:

```
import zmq

context = zmq.Context()
socket = context.socket(zmq.PUB)
socket.bind("tcp://*:5555")

while True:
    # Publishing messages
    socket.send_string("Hello ZeroMQ")
```

PyZMQ aligns with Python's garbage collection, and its asynchronous features harmonize well with Python's asyncio framework, optimizing performance for concurrent execution.

C/C++ Bindings

In systems programming, C and C++ maintain their dominance due to their high performance and close-to-hardware manipulation capabilities. ZeroMQ's native interface is in C, with an elegant API extending to C++ applications. This offers an imperative control over threading, memory management, and execution context.

Incorporating ZeroMQ with C or C++ involves the use of header files and linking against the ZeroMQ library. Developers typically begin by including the library header:

```
#include <zmq.hpp>
#include <iostream>

int main() {
    zmq::context_t context;
    zmq::socket_t socket(context, zmq::socket_type::push);
    socket.bind("tcp://*:5555");
    socket.send(zmq::buffer("Hello ZeroMQ"), zmq::send_flags::none);
    return 0;
}
```

The primary advantage of using ZeroMQ in C/C++ is its low overhead and direct OS-level interaction, making it an optimal choice for high-throughput, low-latency applications. Furthermore, detailed control over the connection lifecycle via explicit context and socket management is afforded to the developer.

Java Bindings (JeroMQ)

The Java language, known for its portability across operating systems and robust ecosystem, can utilize ZeroMQ through JeroMQ, a pure

Java implementation of the ZeroMQ protocol. Unlike other language bindings that wrap the native C++ implementation, JeroMQ is standalone, eliminating the need for native code.

To integrate JeroMQ into a Java project, developers can include it as a dependency in build management tools like Maven or Gradle:

```
<dependency>
    <groupId>org.zeromq</groupId>
    <artifactId>jeromq</artifactId>
    <version>0.5.2</version>
</dependency>
```

A sample Java implementation of a ZeroMQ REQ-REP pattern is straightforward:

```java
import org.zeromq.ZContext;
import org.zeromq.ZMQ;

public class ZeroMQExample {
    public static void main(String[] args) {
        try (ZContext context = new ZContext()) {
            ZMQ.Socket socket = context.createSocket(ZMQ.REP);
            socket.bind("tcp://*:5555");

            while (!Thread.currentThread().isInterrupted()) {
                byte[] reply = socket.recv(0);
                System.out.println("Received: " + new String(reply, ZMQ.CHARSET));
                socket.send("Reply from Server", 0);
            }
        }
    }
}
```

JeroMQ's abstraction over socket management and its integrated support for Java's concurrency libraries like ExecutorService facilitate robust, non-blocking messaging applications.

JavaScript Bindings (Node.js)

JavaScript's rise has been monumental, particularly in server-side development through Node.js. ZeroMQ's binding for Node.js, often accessed through the 'zeromq' package, provides extensive capabilities for building non-blocking, event-driven applications.

Installation uses the Node Package Manager (npm):

```
npm install zeromq
```

Implementing a simple PUSH-PULL pattern in Node.js with ZeroMQ

6.1. ZEROMQ LANGUAGE BINDINGS OVERVIEW

is illustrated as follows:

```
const zmq = require('zeromq')

async function run() {
    const sock = new zmq.Push

    await sock.bind("tcp://127.0.0.1:3000")
    console.log("Producer bound to port 3000")

    while (true) {
        console.log("Sending a message...")
        await sock.send("Hello from ZeroMQ")
    }
}
run()
```

ZeroMQ's event loop integration with Node.js enhances the scalability of network applications written in JavaScript by using asynchronous I/O patterns.

Cross-language Interoperability

ZeroMQ's cross-language bindings extend its utility beyond standalone implementations in a single language to facilitating seamless messaging across applications written in different languages. This capability is harnessed through ZeroMQ's protocol-independent message framing and advanced routing, allowing messages to be seamlessly exchanged without regard to language-specific differences.

For instance, a C++ backend can serve high-performance analytics services, while a Python-based web application can serve as the frontend interface, communicated seamlessly through ZeroMQ sockets. The ability to mix and match languages enables developers to maximize the strengths of multiple programming languages within a single distributed system solution.

Despite the tremendous advantages, developers should be aware of the synchronization pitfalls and error-handling differences inherent to the languages being integrated. Careful consideration of atomic message delivery and error propagation mechanisms will ensure the integrity of cross-language communication.

ZeroMQ's language bindings provide the versatility needed for today's software needs, ensuring that developers can choose the best languages and frameworks for their specific application requirements, while maintaining consistent messaging protocols across platforms. This section has outlined the strategic importance and functional depth of ZeroMQ's language bindings, accompanied by illustrative examples to guide integration. The following sections build on this foundation, exploring specific use cases within each language context.

6.2 Using ZeroMQ with Python

ZeroMQ offers a powerful yet simple toolkit for building distributed software systems. When paired with Python, a language known for its simplicity and broad applicability, ZeroMQ becomes even more potent. This section explores the integration of ZeroMQ with Python, examining detailed aspects of using ZeroMQ's message-passing capabilities within Python applications through PyZMQ, which is the official Python binding for ZeroMQ.

PyZMQ, valued for its seamless cross-platform compatibility, allows Python programs to leverage ZeroMQ's flexible messaging patterns such as PUB-SUB, REQ-REP, and PUSH-PULL. Its syntactic harmony with Python's async features like asyncio, along with support for both synchronous and asynchronous I/O models, makes it a robust choice for developers seeking scalability and performance.

Installation of PyZMQ

Installation of PyZMQ is streamlined through Python's package management system, PyPI. The recommended method is using the pip command, ensuring the latest version compatible with the existing Python environment is installed. Here is how PyZMQ can be installed:

```
pip install pyzmq
```

This command installs PyZMQ along with any dependencies. It is crucial to ensure that Python and pip are updated to avoid compatibility issues. On some systems, especially those with isolated python environments, using virtual environments can help manage dependencies cleanly.

Basic Concepts and Message Patterns

ZeroMQ departs from traditional client-server communication by en-

6.2. USING ZEROMQ WITH PYTHON

abling sockets to employ different communication patterns. With PyZMQ, these patterns can be efficiently utilized in Python applications. Here is a brief overview of essential ZeroMQ message patterns and how they map to various application scenarios:

- **REQ-REP (Request-Reply):** A synchronous pattern where each request sent from a client receives a reply from the server. This pattern is useful for RPC (Remote Procedure Call) scenarios.

- **PUB-SUB (Publish-Subscribe):** An asynchronous pattern in which messages are published to multiple subscribers. This is useful for broadcast and multicast communication.

- **PUSH-PULL:** A pipeline model where messages are pushed from producers to consumers. It is beneficial for tasks distribution and work queue management.

Implementing the REQ-REP Pattern

The REQ-REP pattern is elegant for echo servers or RPC scenarios, where each call to a server has a well-defined response. Below is a basic Python implementation of a client-server application using the REQ-REP pattern:

```
# Server code
import zmq

context = zmq.Context()
socket = context.socket(zmq.REP)
socket.bind("tcp://*:5555")

while True:
    message = socket.recv_string()
    print(f"Received request: {message}")
    socket.send_string("World")
```

```
# Client code
import zmq

context = zmq.Context()
socket = context.socket(zmq.REQ)
socket.connect("tcp://localhost:5555")

for request in range(10):
    print(f"Sending request {request}")
    socket.send_string("Hello")
    reply = socket.recv_string()
    print(f"Received reply {request}: {reply}")
```

In this example, the server binds to a TCP port and waits for incoming requests. The client connects to the server's address and sends out requests. For each request sent, the server responds with a message, exemplifying a classic request-reply cycle.

Utilizing the PUB-SUB Pattern

In public-subscribe systems, a publisher sends out messages which are received by all subscribers listening on the channel. This is particularly useful for real-time updates and logging. Below is an example of using the PUB-SUB pattern in PyZMQ:

```
# Publisher code
import zmq
import time

context = zmq.Context()
socket = context.socket(zmq.PUB)
socket.bind("tcp://*:5556")

while True:
    topic = "weather"
    message = "Temperature: 20°C"
    socket.send_string(f"{topic} {message}")
    time.sleep(1)
```

```
# Subscriber code
import zmq

context = zmq.Context()
socket = context.socket(zmq.SUB)
socket.connect("tcp://localhost:5556")

topicfilter = "weather"
socket.setsockopt_string(zmq.SUBSCRIBE, topicfilter)

while True:
    message = socket.recv_string()
    print(f"Received message: {message}")
```

Here, the publisher sends out weather updates every second, and the subscriber filters messages by subscribing to the 'weather' topic. This is a classic example of the pub-sub model that ensures each of the connected subscribers receives every published message.

Advanced Usage and Features

PyZMQ provides comprehensive support for advanced features like message filtering, high-water mark settings, and context pool optimization. For scenarios involving large volumes of data or high concur-

6.2. USING ZEROMQ WITH PYTHON

rency, these features can be adjusted to fine-tune performance.

ZeroMQ allows the configuration of a socket's high-water mark (HWM), which is the maximum number of outstanding messages a socket can hold in memory before server-side backpressure is applied. For instance, setting a specific HWM:

```
socket.set_hwm(1000)
```

This operation is crucial for preventing memory overload situations in publish-subscribe patterns during burst message publication.

ZeroMQ's context class, which manages socket connections, can be leveraged to optimize performance. Contexts are thread-safe but not thread-specific, meaning you can create and cache a context across threads to manage sockets:

```
context = zmq.Context()
# Context can manage multiple sockets
```

Asynchronous I/O with PyZMQ

Additionally, PyZMQ's integration with Python's asyncio module facilitates non-blocking execution of I/O operations, which is especially effective when developing applications that handle numerous concurrent operations. Here is how to implement a simple async REP server:

```
import zmq
import zmq.asyncio
import asyncio

ctx = zmq.asyncio.Context()

async def server():
    socket = ctx.socket(zmq.REP)
    socket.bind("tcp://*:5555")

    while True:
        message = await socket.recv_string()
        print(f"Received request: {message}")
        await asyncio.sleep(1) # Simulate some asynchronous processing
        await socket.send_string("World")

asyncio.run(server())
```

By exploiting asyncio capabilities, PyZMQ extends its usage to scalable applications that can handle vast numbers of asynchronous network operations concurrently.

Error Handling and Debugging

Error handling in PyZMQ takes advantage of Python's exception handling. Network-related exceptions, such as timeouts or unreachable connections, are raised as zmq-specific exceptions, allowing them to be caught and handled gracefully.

```
try:
    socket.send_string("Message", flags=zmq.NOBLOCK)
except zmq.Again as e:
    print("Resource temporarily unavailable, skipping this message")
```

This non-blocking approach avoids hindrances during message sends over full queues, enabling the application to continue functioning smoothly while ensuring proper error logging.

Cross-language Communication

One of the remarkable features of ZeroMQ when paired with PyZMQ is its ability to interact seamlessly with services written in different languages. Using standardized protocols, a Python application can interact with a C++ microservice or a Java graphical user interface component, thereby fostering interoperability within distributed systems.

For example, using the same message framing, a Python client can communicate with ZeroMQ sockets implemented in any of the supported languages by employing consistent socket connections and message structures.

The flexibility and versatility of ZeroMQ, complemented by Python's dynamism, provide a robust platform for developers tackling the challenges of modern software design. By leveraging PyZMQ's functionalities, developers gain access to a sophisticated yet straightforward mechanism for creating performant, scalable distributed applications suited to meet the demands of contemporary computing environments. PyZMQ empowers developers to explore innovative solutions with a focus on ease-of-use, robust messaging patterns, and cross-platform communication.

6.3 ZeroMQ in C/C++ Applications

ZeroMQ provides a highly efficient and flexible platform for messaging in C/C++ applications. Characterized by its high-performance core written in C++, ZeroMQ integrates seamlessly into C and C++ projects, providing the capabilities needed to build sophisticated network applications. Its low-latency communication and minimal overhead make it a prized tool in the arsenal of developers focusing on both real-time systems and high-throughput data processing tasks.

The integration of ZeroMQ within C/C++ applications leverages the full power of the language's system capabilities, offering precise control over threading, memory management, and error handling. This section explores the intricacies of using ZeroMQ in C/C++ applications, detailing installation, implementation of messaging patterns, and best practices for optimizing performance.

Installation and Integration

The ZeroMQ C++ library, often referred to as libzmq, is open-source and can be obtained from its GitHub repository or installed through a package manager. The library provides a well-documented API accessible via header files, alongside a shared or static library for linking. Installation using a package manager such as apt (on Ubuntu/Debian-based systems) can be done with:

```
sudo apt-get install libzmq3-dev
```

For CentOS or Red Hat systems, the command is typically:

```
sudo yum install zeromq-devel
```

In C++ projects, linking against ZeroMQ is essential, which can be handled by appending -lzmq to the compilation command:

```
g++ zmq_example.cpp -o zmq_example -lzmq
```

Developers working with build automation tools like CMake can include ZeroMQ by finding the package and linking it:

```
find_package(ZeroMQ REQUIRED)
target_link_libraries(my_application PRIVATE ZeroMQ::libzmq)
```

Basic Messaging Patterns in C++

ZeroMQ's power is derived from multiple messaging patterns that it implements. In C++, these patterns are realized using the zmq.hpp binding.

- **Request-Reply Model:** Offers a straightforward synchronized messaging pattern where a request is sent and a corresponding reply is awaited. Here is an elementary illustration of a REQ-REP server-client:

```cpp
// Server.cpp
#include <zmq.hpp>
#include <string>
#include <iostream>

int main() {
    zmq::context_t context{1};
    zmq::socket_t socket{context, zmq::socket_type::rep};
    socket.bind("tcp://*:5555");

    for (;;) {
        zmq::message_t request;
        socket.recv(request, zmq::recv_flags::none);
        std::cout << "Received " << request.to_string() << std::endl;

        zmq::message_t reply{5};
        memcpy(reply.data(), "World", 5);
        socket.send(reply, zmq::send_flags::none);
    }
    return 0;
}
```

```cpp
// Client.cpp
#include <zmq.hpp>
#include <string>
#include <iostream>

int main() {
    zmq::context_t context{1};
    zmq::socket_t socket{context, zmq::socket_type::req};
    socket.connect("tcp://localhost:5555");

    for (int request_nbr = 0; request_nbr < 10; request_nbr++) {
        zmq::message_t request{5};
        memcpy(request.data(), "Hello", 5);
        socket.send(request, zmq::send_flags::none);

        zmq::message_t reply;
        socket.recv(reply, zmq::recv_flags::none);
        std::cout << "Received " << reply.to_string() << std::endl;
    }
    return 0;
}
```

These programs demonstrate synchronous communication; the client sends a message and waits for the reply from the server.

- **Publisher-Subscriber Model:** In the PUB-SUB model, a publisher sends messages to all subscribers interested in a topic. This is ideal for scenarios requiring message dissemination to multiple listeners:

```cpp
// Publisher.cpp
#include <zmq.hpp>
#include <iostream>
#include <chrono>
#include <thread>

int main() {
    zmq::context_t context{1};
    zmq::socket_t socket{context, zmq::socket_type::pub};
    socket.bind("tcp://*:5556");

    while (true) {
        zmq::message_t message{12};
        memcpy(message.data(), "Update Time", 12);
        socket.send(message, zmq::send_flags::none);

        std::this_thread::sleep_for(std::chrono::seconds(1));
    }
    return 0;
}
```

```cpp
// Subscriber.cpp
#include <zmq.hpp>
#include <iostream>

int main() {
    zmq::context_t context{1};
    zmq::socket_t socket{context, zmq::socket_type::sub};

    socket.connect("tcp://localhost:5556");
    socket.setsockopt(ZMQ_SUBSCRIBE, "", 0); // Subscribe to all topics

    for (;;) {
        zmq::message_t message;
        socket.recv(message, zmq::recv_flags::none);
        std::cout << "Received Message: " << message.to_string() << std::::
            endl;
    }
    return 0;
}
```

This exemplifies message broadcasting where any number of subscribers can listen for updates published to their topics of interest, effectively supporting real-time broadcast systems.

- **Push-Pull Model:** The PUSH-PULL setup facilitates a pipeline where tasks can be distributed to multiple workers by a ventilator for processing, enabling heavy load balancing across different worker units.

```cpp
// Push.cpp
#include <zmq.hpp>
#include <iostream>
#include <thread>

int main() {
    zmq::context_t context{1};
    zmq::socket_t socket{context, zmq::socket_type::push};
    socket.bind("tcp://*:5557");

    for (int i = 0; i < 100; i++) {
        zmq::message_t task(10);
        snprintf((char*) task.data(), 10, "Task %03d", i);
        socket.send(task, zmq::send_flags::none);
        std::cout << "Sent Task: " << (char*)task.data() << std::endl;
        std::this_thread::sleep_for(std::chrono::milliseconds(100));
    }
    return 0;
}
```

```cpp
// Pull.cpp
#include <zmq.hpp>
#include <iostream>

int main() {
    zmq::context_t context{1};
    zmq::socket_t socket{context, zmq::socket_type::pull};

    socket.connect("tcp://localhost:5557");

    while (true) {
        zmq::message_t task;
        socket.recv(task, zmq::recv_flags::none);
        std::cout << "Processing " << task.to_string() << std::endl;
    }
    return 0;
}
```

This model emphasizes scalability as more workers can be added to handle increasing load, thus ensuring balanced workloads across processors.

Advanced ZeroMQ Features in C++

ZeroMQ offers customization by configuring socket options such as timeouts, linger period settings, and more. For example, setting a linger period helps define the socket's behavior on closure while mes-

6.3. ZEROMQ IN C/C++ APPLICATIONS

sages are still potentially in transit:

```
socket.setsockopt(ZMQ_LINGER, 0);
```

The ZeroMQ poller functionality aids in managing multiple sockets more efficiently by allowing non-blocking IO:

```
zmq::pollitem_t items[] = {
    { static_cast<void*>(socket), 0, ZMQ_POLLIN, 0 }
};
while (true) {
    zmq::poll(items, 1, std::chrono::milliseconds(10));
    if (items[0].revents & ZMQ_POLLIN) {
        zmq::message_t message;
        socket.recv(message, zmq::recv_flags::none);
        std::cout << "Polled message: " << message.to_string() << std::endl;
    }
}
```

This offers a powerful means to execute tasks only when data is available, contributing significantly to CPU utilization efficiency.

Error Handling

ZeroMQ in C++ uses exceptions to handle errors, enabling developers to encompass error-prone code within try-catch blocks. Proper use of exception handling mitigates unexpected disruptions in service operations.

```
try {
    socket.send(request, zmq::send_flags::none);
} catch (const zmq::error_t& e) {
    std::cerr << "Error: " << e.what() << std::endl;
}
```

This approach ensures that any issue in the message transport process is logged and handled effectively, allowing the application to maintain stability.

Performance Considerations

The performance of ZeroMQ applications can significantly vary based on the operational environment and configuration. Pointers for maximizing performance in C/C++ applications include:

- **Batch Processing:** Sending in batches can considerably enhance throughput.

- **Minimize Context Switching:** Optimize the number of threads to mitigate the cost associated with context switches.

- **Network Configuration:** Evaluate and tune the underlying network stack for latency and throughput considerations.

ZeroMQ's performance can be crucially boosted by adjusting buffer sizes, employing direct physical connections where possible, and utilizing efficient memory management practices to reduce latency and increase throughput.

By leveraging C/C++ for ZeroMQ applications, developers can create highly efficient, responsive, and scalable solutions tailored to demanding computational requirements. ZeroMQ's comprehensive C++ API empowers developers to craft applications adaptable to numerous networking paradigms, all while ensuring that systems remain responsive, robust, and maintainable.

6.4 Integrating ZeroMQ with Java

Java, with its platform independence and extensive library ecosystem, is a robust choice for building cross-platform applications. When paired with ZeroMQ, which complements Java's versatility with powerful messaging capabilities, the duo forms a potent backbone for distributed systems. ZeroMQ's integration in Java is primarily facilitated through JeroMQ, a pure Java implementation of ZeroMQ that eliminates the requirement for native bindings, thus simplifying deployment across different systems. This section explores the integration process, fundamental messaging patterns, and advanced features of ZeroMQ within the Java environment.

Getting Started with JeroMQ

To begin with JeroMQ, it is necessary to incorporate the library into your Java project. This can be managed effectively using build tools like Maven or Gradle, ensuring that all dependencies are handled appropriately.

For Maven, add the following dependency to your pom.xml:

```
<dependency>
```

6.4. INTEGRATING ZEROMQ WITH JAVA

```
    <groupId>org.zeromq</groupId>
    <artifactId>jeromq</artifactId>
    <version>0.5.2</version>
</dependency>
```

For Gradle, include the following in your build.gradle file:

```
implementation 'org.zeromq:jeromq:0.5.2'
```

This setup ensures that JeroMQ is readily available in your Java project environment, seamlessly integrating ZeroMQ's capabilities without the need for external C libraries or additional configuration.

Core Messaging Patterns

ZeroMQ provides several messaging patterns that cater to different communication paradigms in network applications. Java developers can leverage these patterns directly through JeroMQ, facilitating a range of communication architectures.

- **Request-Reply Pattern:** A simple synchronous communication model, ideal for client-server setups. This pattern allows for clear request handling with a one-to-one message ratio.

- **Publish-Subscribe (PUB-SUB):** Facilitates message distribution to multiple subscribers. Used extensively in scenarios requiring real-time data dissemination, such as market data feeds.

- **Push-Pull Pattern:** Used for distributing workloads among processors. This model supports task distribution, with workers pulling in new tasks as they are ready to process them.

Implementing the Request-Reply Pattern

The Request-Reply pattern is often used in scenarios necessitating synchronous exchanges, such as traditional client-server models. Below is a basic implementation using JeroMQ:

```
// ReqRepServer.java
import org.zeromq.ZMQ;

public class ReqRepServer {
    public static void main(String[] args) {
        ZMQ.Context context = ZMQ.context(1);
        ZMQ.Socket socket = context.socket(ZMQ.REP);
        socket.bind("tcp://*:5555");
```

```
        while (!Thread.currentThread().isInterrupted()) {
            byte[] request = socket.recv(0);
            System.out.println("Received request: " + new String(request, ZMQ.
                CHARSET));
            socket.send("World".getBytes(ZMQ.CHARSET), 0);
        }
        socket.close();
        context.term();
    }
}
```

```
// ReqRepClient.java
import org.zeromq.ZMQ;

public class ReqRepClient {
    public static void main(String[] args) {
        ZMQ.Context context = ZMQ.context(1);
        ZMQ.Socket socket = context.socket(ZMQ.REQ);
        socket.connect("tcp://localhost:5555");

        for (int request = 0; request < 10; request++) {
            String requestString = "Hello";
            System.out.println("Sending request " + request + ": " + requestString);
            socket.send(requestString.getBytes(ZMQ.CHARSET), 0);
            byte[] reply = socket.recv(0);
            System.out.println("Received reply " + request + ": " + new String(reply,
                ZMQ.CHARSET));
        }
        socket.close();
        context.term();
    }
}
```

Here, the server listens on a specified TCP port and processes requests sequentially, while the client iterates over multiple requests, showcasing the blocking nature of the REQ-REP pattern.

Exploring Publish-Subscribe

The PUB-SUB pattern in JeroMQ supports scenarios where multiple receivers need access to the same data stream, such as notifications or log updates.

```
// Publisher.java
import org.zeromq.ZMQ;

public class Publisher {
    public static void main(String[] args) {
        ZMQ.Context context = ZMQ.context(1);
        ZMQ.Socket socket = context.socket(ZMQ.PUB);
        socket.bind("tcp://*:5556");

        while (!Thread.currentThread().isInterrupted()) {
```

6.4. INTEGRATING ZEROMQ WITH JAVA

```java
        String topic = "news";
        String message = "Latest update!";
        socket.send((topic + " " + message).getBytes(ZMQ.CHARSET), 0);
        try {
            Thread.sleep(1000);
        } catch (InterruptedException e) {
            Thread.currentThread().interrupt();
        }
    }
    socket.close();
    context.term();
    }
}
```

```java
// Subscriber.java
import org.zeromq.ZMQ;

public class Subscriber {
    public static void main(String[] args) {
        ZMQ.Context context = ZMQ.context(1);
        ZMQ.Socket socket = context.socket(ZMQ.SUB);
        socket.connect("tcp://localhost:5556");

        String filter = "news";
        socket.subscribe(filter.getBytes(ZMQ.CHARSET));

        while (!Thread.currentThread().isInterrupted()) {
            String message = socket.recvStr(0);
            System.out.println("Received message: " + message);
        }
        socket.close();
        context.term();
    }
}
```

In this setup, the publisher prepares a one-way broadcast of messages, and any number of subscribers can dynamically join to receive message streams that match their subscription criteria.

Push and Pull Work Distribution

The Push-Pull pattern is ideal for scenarios where tasks are dynamically pulled by workers from a task source. This supports workload distribution among multiple worker processes.

```java
// Push.java
import org.zeromq.ZMQ;

public class Push {
    public static void main(String[] args) {
        ZMQ.Context context = ZMQ.context(1);
        ZMQ.Socket socket = context.socket(ZMQ.PUSH);
        socket.bind("tcp://*:5557");
```

```
        for (int i = 0; i < 100; i++) {
            String task = "Task " + i;
            socket.send(task.getBytes(ZMQ.CHARSET), 0);
            System.out.println("Sent: " + task);
            try {
                Thread.sleep(100);
            } catch (InterruptedException e) {
                Thread.currentThread().interrupt();
            }
        }
        socket.close();
        context.term();
    }
}
```

```
// Pull.java
import org.zeromq.ZMQ;

public class Pull {
    public static void main(String[] args) {
        ZMQ.Context context = ZMQ.context(1);
        ZMQ.Socket socket = context.socket(ZMQ.PULL);
        socket.connect("tcp://localhost:5557");

        while (!Thread.currentThread().isInterrupted()) {
            String task = socket.recvStr(0);
            System.out.println("Received Task: " + task);
        }
        socket.close();
        context.term();
    }
}
```

Inherently scalable, this pattern is optimal for architectures requiring dynamic task scheduling and load balancing.

Advanced Features and Configuration

JeroMQ allows for extensive configuration of socket behavior and network settings, essential for performance tuning and adapting to different application needs.

- **Socket Options:** Customize socket operations, including send and receive timeouts, queue lengths, and linger periods. For example, setting a LINGER period:

  ```
  socket.setLinger(0); // Immediately discard pending messages when closing
  ```

- **Poller Integration:** Use ZeroMQ's polling mechanisms to manage multiple sockets effectively, allowing IO operations concurrently without blocking the application:

6.4. INTEGRATING ZEROMQ WITH JAVA

```
ZMQ.Poller poller = context.poller(1);
poller.register(socket, ZMQ.Poller.POLLIN);
while (!Thread.currentThread().isInterrupted()) {
    poller.poll();
    if (poller.pollin(0)) {
        System.out.println("Message received: " + socket.recvStr(0));
    }
}
```

Polling provides a robust way to manage socket events and improves overall responsiveness.

Error Handling and Reliability

ZeroMQ's error handling is streamlined through Java's exception model. Ensuring reliable message delivery and handling network-related issues are crucial in distributed systems.

```
try {
    socket.send("Reliable message".getBytes(ZMQ.CHARSET), ZMQ.DONTWAIT);
} catch (ZMQException e) {
    System.err.println("ZeroMQ Error: " + e.getMessage());
}
```

Designing reliable systems with ZeroMQ involves considering various network conditions and incorporating reconnection strategies to handle temporary connectivity losses.

Cross-Platform Interoperability

ZeroMQ's language-agnostic message framing ensures interoperability across different programming environments. By adhering to consistent socket patterns, Java applications can seamlessly communicate with other systems built in languages such as Python, C++, or Node.js.

To maximize the advantages of ZeroMQ in Java, leveraging JeroMQ's features and best practices fosters the development of efficient, scalable, and dependable networked applications. Whether for microservice architectures, high-frequency trading systems, or robust data pipelines, ZeroMQ's flexibility and performance capabilities integrate seamlessly with Java's expansive ecosystem to meet the complex demands of modern software engineering tasks.

6.5 ZeroMQ with JavaScript and Node.js

JavaScript's versatility and the event-driven architecture of Node.js have made them a popular choice for both client-side and server-side application development. When paired with ZeroMQ, this combination brings high-performance messaging capabilities to JavaScript environments, facilitating the development of scalable network applications. ZeroMQ's integration with JavaScript and Node.js is facilitated through well-maintained libraries that encapsulate ZeroMQ's messaging patterns in an easy-to-use API. This section provides an in-depth exploration of using ZeroMQ in JavaScript and Node.js, including setup, core messaging patterns, advanced features, and best practices.

Setting Up ZeroMQ in Node.js

To get started with ZeroMQ in Node.js, the `zeromq` package provides Node.js bindings for ZeroMQ. This package can be installed via npm, the Node Package Manager, making it straightforward to incorporate into your Node.js projects:

```
npm install zeromq
```

This installation not only adds ZeroMQ support to your project but also ensures any underlying C library dependencies specific to your platform are managed appropriately. Once installed, ZeroMQ can be required and used within your Node.js scripts.

Core Messaging Patterns in Node.js

The versatility of ZeroMQ's messaging patterns can be effectively leveraged within Node.js applications. Key patterns include:

- **Request-Reply (REQ-REP):** Suitable for synchronous operations where a request is sent, followed by a single reply.

- **Publish-Subscribe (PUB-SUB):** Ideal for broadcasting messages to multiple subscribers, supporting real-time data dissemination.

- **Push-Pull:** Utilized for task distribution among workers, offering a load-balancing mechanism for queued tasks.

Let's examine these patterns in the context of Node.js applications.

6.5. ZEROMQ WITH JAVASCRIPT AND NODE.JS

Implementing the Request-Reply Pattern

The Request-Reply pattern is widely used in client-server communications, where each request awaits a corresponding response.

```
// reqrep_server.js
const zmq = require('zeromq');
let sock = new zmq.Reply;

sock.bind("tcp://*:5555")
  .then(() => {
    console.log("Server bound to port 5555");
    sock.on('message', (msg) => {
      console.log('Received request:', msg.toString());
      sock.send('World');
    });
  });
```

```
// reqrep_client.js
const zmq = require('zeromq');
let sock = new zmq.Request;

sock.connect("tcp://localhost:5555");
console.log("Client connected to port 5555");

for (let i = 0; i < 10; i++) {
  sock.send('Hello');
  sock.receive().then(reply => {
    console.log('Received reply:', reply.toString());
  });
}
```

In this example, the server listens for incoming requests and responds to each with a predetermined message. The client iterates over multiple requests, reflecting the synchronous interaction characteristic of the REQ-REP pattern.

Exploring the Publish-Subscribe Pattern

The PUB-SUB pattern enables the dissemination of messages to multiple receivers, commonly used in scenarios requiring real-time data distribution.

```
// publisher.js
const zmq = require('zeromq');
let sock = new zmq.Publisher;

sock.bind('tcp://*:5556')
  .then(() => {
    console.log('Publisher bound to port 5556');
    setInterval(() => {
      console.log('Sending message...');
      sock.send('news latest update!');
```

159

```
    }, 1000);
});
```

```
// subscriber.js
const zmq = require('zeromq');
let sock = new zmq.Subscriber;

sock.connect('tcp://localhost:5556');
sock.subscribe('news');
console.log('Subscriber connected and subscribed to news');

sock.on('message', (topic, message) => {
  console.log('Received message:', topic.toString(), message.toString());
});
```

Publishing is achieved through a simple broadcast to interested subscribers, where clients must first subscribe to a topic before receiving messages. This reduces data transmission overhead and ensures messages are delivered only to the relevant listeners.

Employing the Push-Pull Pattern

The Push-Pull model suits scenarios needing workload distribution among processing nodes, enhancing throughput by balancing tasks across available workers.

```
// push.js
const zmq = require('zeromq');
let sock = new zmq.Push;

sock.bind('tcp://*:5557')
  .then(() => {
    console.log('Push socket bound to port 5557');
    for (let i = 0; i < 100; i++) {
      let msg = `Task ${i}`;
      console.log('Sending:', msg);
      sock.send(msg);
    }
  });
```

```
// pull.js
const zmq = require('zeromq');
let sock = new zmq.Pull;

sock.connect('tcp://localhost:5557');
console.log('Pull socket connected to port 5557');

sock.on('message', (msg) => {
  console.log('Received task:', msg.toString());
});
```

This model effectively balances tasks across multiple consumers, with

6.5. ZEROMQ WITH JAVASCRIPT AND NODE.JS

each worker pulling tasks as resources become available, allowing for scalable and efficient processing environments.

Handling Asynchronous Operations

Node.js's asynchronous nature is beneficial for non-blocking operations in ZeroMQ, allowing for handling multiple sockets concurrently without stalling application execution. Since ZeroMQ operations are asynchronous, integrating with JavaScript's event loop ensures responsive application behavior:

```
async function handleRequests() {
  while (true) {
    const [msg] = await sock.receive();
    console.log('Handling request:', msg.toString());
    await sock.send('Response');
  }
}

handleRequests();
```

This structure leverages 'async/await' to manage non-blocking IO, ensuring continuity even when network operations are pending.

Advanced Features and Error Handling

ZeroMQ supports extensive configuration to fine-tune network performance and reliability, a critical aspect in production settings where robustness and error mitigation are paramount. Options such as message buffering, retry mechanisms, high-water marks, and failover strategies are integral to ensure scalable systems:

- **High-Water Mark (HWM):** Controls the queue size before blocking:
  ```
  sock.sendHighWaterMark = 1000; // Set high water mark for sending queue
  ```

- **Error Handling:** Ensure robust application logic by catching errors during socket operations:
  ```
  sock.on('error', (err) => {
    console.error('ZeroMQ Error:', err);
  });
  ```

Implementing these features mitigates risks related to network instability or excessive message rates, contributing to a seamless user experience.

Security Considerations

When deploying ZeroMQ in environments that require secure communication channels, incorporating zmq's encryption mechanisms, such as CurveZMQ, can safeguard message data:

- **CurveZMQ Encryption:**
  ```
  sock.curve_server = true; // Configure socket as CurveZMQ server
  sock.curve_publickey = publicKey; // Set public key
  sock.curve_secretkey = secretKey; // Set secret key
  ```

Utilizing CurveZMQ offers encryption and authentication, protecting data integrity and authenticity in distributed applications.

Cross-language Message Interoperability

ZeroMQ's protocol-independence ensures interoperability between JavaScript and other language services, fostering a polyglot environment where services are developed in the language best suited for their functionality. By adhering to consistent messaging interfaces, a JavaScript client can interact with services written in Python, C++, Java, and more, seamlessly facilitating complex system architectures.

In summary, ZeroMQ's integration within JavaScript and Node.js environments significantly amplifies development capabilities, allowing developers to craft high-performing, scalable network applications. Through practical implementations of ZeroMQ's core messaging patterns and advanced configurations, developers can harness the full potential of Node.js in distributed system landscapes, enabling robust solutions that meet the stringent demands of modern interconnected systems.

6.6 Cross-language Messaging with ZeroMQ

The landscape of modern software development demands solutions that facilitate interoperability across diverse programming languages.

6.6. CROSS-LANGUAGE MESSAGING WITH ZEROMQ

ZeroMQ's architecture inherently supports this need by enabling seamless cross-language messaging within distributed systems. Through its language bindings, ZeroMQ empowers developers to integrate disparate systems — each written in the most suitable language for its purpose — into a cohesive, intercommunicating whole. This section unveils the methodologies, patterns, and best practices for implementing cross-language messaging using ZeroMQ, illustrating its utility in enhancing system interoperability and scalability.

Understanding Cross-language Communication

Cross-language communication refers to the ability of systems implemented in different programming languages to exchange data. ZeroMQ achieves this by providing language-agnostic message formats and a flexible communication protocol that remain consistent regardless of the underlying language. At the core of this capability is the ZeroMQ message model, based on simple message envelopes that facilitate transport over network sockets.

The ZeroMQ messaging ecosystem incorporates language bindings for Python, C++, Java, JavaScript, and more, allowing applications in these languages to utilize ZeroMQ's message-passing semantics. ZeroMQ's abstracted socket paradigms, such as REQ/REP, PUB/SUB, and PUSH/PULL, are shared across these bindings, ensuring a uniform messaging experience.

Common Scenarios and Patterns

Cross-language messaging is particularly beneficial in several scenarios:

- **Microservices Architectures:** Within these systems, each service is often developed using the language best suited to its specific functionality, such as high-performance services in C++ and rapid development services in Python.

- **Hybrid Application Frameworks:** Applications that integrate legacy systems with new services can leverage ZeroMQ to provide a unified communication protocol across varied codebases.

- **Data Processing Pipelines:** Systems involving sequential processing stages may use different languages for each stage, optimizing tasks such as data ingestion, analysis, and storage.

The following sections delve into detailed implementations and considerations for achieving effective cross-language messaging using ZeroMQ.

Implementing Cross-language Communication

Integrating ZeroMQ for cross-language communication typically involves establishing message formats and endpoints while using consistent ZeroMQ socket patterns. Below, we explore a sample implementation involving Python and C++.

Python Server with REQ/REP Pattern

The Python server responds to incoming requests using the ZeroMQ REQ/REP pattern:

```python
# server.py
import zmq

context = zmq.Context()
socket = context.socket(zmq.REP)
socket.bind("tcp://*:5555")

while True:
    message = socket.recv_string()
    print(f"Received request: {message}")
    # Do some work
    socket.send_string("Response from Python server")
```

This server listens on a TCP socket, receiving messages and responding accordingly.

C++ Client with REQ/REP Pattern

A C++ client communicating with the Python server using the same REQ/REP pattern demonstrates cross-language connectivity:

```cpp
// client.cpp
#include <zmq.hpp>
#include <string>
#include <iostream>

int main() {
    zmq::context_t context{1};
    zmq::socket_t socket{context, zmq::socket_type::req};
    socket.connect("tcp://localhost:5555");

    for (int request_nbr = 0; request_nbr < 10; request_nbr++) {
```

6.6. CROSS-LANGUAGE MESSAGING WITH ZEROMQ

```
    zmq::message_t request{"Hello from C++ client", 21};
    socket.send(request, zmq::send_flags::none);

    zmq::message_t reply;
    socket.recv(reply, zmq::recv_flags::none);
    std::cout << "Received: " << reply.to_string() << std::endl;
  }
  return 0;
}
```

This C++ client initiates requests to the Python server, awaiting responses, showcasing a complete message exchange.

Simplicity through Message Formats

To facilitate interoperability, the message payload should be simple, such as strings or JSON objects, which can be easily parsed in multiple languages. When using complex data structures, it is advisable to serialize data using standard serialization libraries, such as Protocol Buffers or JSON.

Consider the scenario where Python and C++ systems exchange JSON-encoded data:

```
import json

data = {"key": "value"}
json_message = json.dumps(data)
socket.send_string(json_message)
```

And in C++, parsing the JSON string could be done using a JSON library such as nlohmann/json:

```
#include <nlohmann/json.hpp>

auto json_data = nlohmann::json::parse(reply.to_string());
std::cout << "Parsed Key: " << json_data["key"] << std::endl;
```

This approach ensures clarity in communication by using a human-readable, universally supported data format.

Utilizing PUB/SUB for Broadcast Communication

Some systems require distributing messages to multiple languages using a publish-subscribe pattern. Consider a C++ publisher communicating with Python subscribers:

```
// publisher.cpp
#include <zmq.hpp>
#include <string>
```

```cpp
#include <iostream>
#include <chrono>
#include <thread>

int main() {
    zmq::context_t context{1};
    zmq::socket_t socket{context, zmq::socket_type::pub};
    socket.bind("tcp://*:5556");

    while (true) {
        zmq::message_t message{"Update from C++", 15};
        socket.send(message, zmq::send_flags::none);
        std::this_thread::sleep_for(std::chrono::seconds(1));
    }
    return 0;
}
```

```python
# subscriber.py
import zmq

context = zmq.Context()
socket = context.socket(zmq.SUB)
socket.connect("tcp://localhost:5556")
socket.setsockopt_string(zmq.SUBSCRIBE, "")

while True:
    message = socket.recv_string()
    print(f"Received update: {message}")
```

The C++ publisher broadcasts periodic updates consumed by any connected Python subscribers, reinforcing the strength of ZeroMQ's PUB-/SUB model in multi-language contexts.

Ensuring Reliability and Scalability

Reliability in cross-language communication includes considerations for message delivery, error handling, and reconnect strategies. ZeroMQ's built-in features, such as high-water marks, message buffering, and retry policies, contribute significantly to robust messaging between services.

In implementations with high-volume messaging or varying network conditions, fine-tuning these configurations can enhance performance:

1. **Set High-Water Mark:** Controls the maximum number of queued messages before blocking further sends.

   ```
   socket.setsockopt(zmq.SNDHWM, 1000)
   ```

2. **Timeout Management:** Configure timeouts to manage periods of inactivity during message sends/receives.

```
socket.setsockopt(zmq.RCVTIMEO, 5000) # 5 seconds timeout
```

3. **Message Consistency:** Employ message delimiters or protocols to avoid incomplete message misinterpretation across systems.

Security Considerations and Encryption

Cross-language applications often operate across public networks; ensuring data security using ZeroMQ's CurveZMQ encryption is advisable. This library provides asymmetric encryption capabilities, securing messages exchanged between server and client, regardless of the language:

1. **Generating Key Pairs:** Create CurveZMQ keys for client and server.

2. **Configuring Security:**

```
sock.curve_server = true;
sock.curve_publickey = publicKey;
sock.curve_secretkey = secretKey;
```

Incorporating these security measures ensures that cross-language message integrity is maintained, safeguarding against unauthorized access or data tampering.

Concluding Thoughts on Cross-language Integration

Cross-language messaging offers developers flexibility to optimize individual services while maintaining coherent system communication. ZeroMQ's emphasis on simplicity, coupled with its robust support across languages, positions it as an ideal tool for enabling interoperability among diverse systems. The importance of building clear and extensible message protocols, coupled with strategic error handling, cannot be overstated in ensuring systems scale and respond effectively to user demands. As applications grow increasingly complex and distributed, ZeroMQ's cross-language capabilities will remain central to developing interconnected, efficient, and resilient modern software architectures.

Chapter 7

Security and Error Handling in ZeroMQ

Ensuring secure communication and effective error handling are pivotal aspects of ZeroMQ's application in distributed systems. ZeroMQ implements a robust security model, incorporating encryption and authentication mechanisms such as CurveZMQ to protect data integrity and confidentiality. Understanding these security features is critical for safeguarding applications against potential threats. Additionally, ZeroMQ provides comprehensive error handling techniques, enabling developers to efficiently detect, manage, and recover from various communication issues. Techniques for handling timeouts, message failures, and debugging are essential for maintaining resilient and reliable systems. This chapter delves into these security features and error management strategies, offering practical insights for developers.

7.1 Understanding ZeroMQ's Security Model

ZeroMQ, often abbreviated as ØMQ, is a high-performance, asynchronous messaging library aimed at scalable distributed or concurrent applications. It differs from traditional message-oriented middleware by not having a central message broker, which necessitates a robust security model to protect communications effectively across distributed nodes. In this section, we explore ZeroMQ's security model, emphasizing its goals and constraints in safeguarding the communications that it facilitates.

ZeroMQ does not have a built-in security model but provides a framework upon which security features can be implemented. The primary goals of ZeroMQ's security model are to ensure confidentiality, integrity, and authenticity of the data being communicated between nodes. This involves implementing strategies that protect against unauthorized data access and modification, as well as verifying the identities of communication participants.

- **Confidentiality**: This involves protecting the content of messages from being understood by anyone other than the intended recipient. ZeroMQ offers encryption capabilities to ensure that even if a message is intercepted, it cannot be deciphered by unauthorized parties.

- **Integrity**: Ensuring that messages are not tampered with during transmission is paramount. ZeroMQ uses cryptographic mechanisms to verify that the content received is unchanged from what the sender transmitted.

- **Authenticity**: Authenticity is about ensuring that messages are genuinely from the claimed sender. ZeroMQ implements identity verification methods that prevent impersonation attacks, where malicious actors pretend to be legitimate participants in the communication.

These objectives are crucial in creating a secure communication environment, particularly in distributed applications where data can traverse multiple untrusted networks.

7.1. UNDERSTANDING ZEROMQ'S SECURITY MODEL

While addressing these security objectives, ZeroMQ operates under specific constraints that influence its security model:

- **Performance Overhead**: The introduction of security mechanisms inevitably adds computational overhead. ZeroMQ aims to minimize this overhead to maintain high throughput and low latency.

- **Scalability**: ZeroMQ is designed to handle numerous simultaneous connections and vast volumes of data. Any security implementation must support this scalability without degradation in performance.

- **Ease of Use**: Developers need straightforward tools for integrating security within their applications. ZeroMQ seeks to provide user-friendly interfaces for implementing its security features.

ZeroMQ's security model, therefore, balances these constraints by leveraging cryptographic libraries such as CurveZMQ for encryption and authentication while aligning with ZeroMQ's core principles of simplicity and performance.

CurveZMQ is a cryptographic library that extends ZeroMQ's capabilities with a focus on securing communications. It implements the Curve25519 elliptic curve cryptography, which provides robust security with efficient computations. This section explores how CurveZMQ is leveraged within the ZeroMQ security framework:

- **Key Exchange**: CurveZMQ uses a key exchange mechanism to establish encrypted communication channels. Both the client and server generate public-private key pairs and exchange their public keys. This process allows them to compute a shared secret that can be used to encrypt messages.

Illustrating the key exchange scenario in ZeroMQ, consider the following pseudocode for initializing a safe communication channel:

```
import zmq
from nacl import public

# Generate a Curve25519 key pair for the server
server_private_key = public.PrivateKey.generate()
```

CHAPTER 7. SECURITY AND ERROR HANDLING IN ZEROMQ

```
server_public_key = server_private_key.public_key

context = zmq.Context()
socket = context.socket(zmq.REP)

# Set server's key pair
socket.curve_secretkey = server_private_key._private_key
socket.curve_publickey = server_public_key._public_key

# Bind the socket to an address
socket.bind("tcp://*:5560")
```

This example demonstrates the generation and application of a pair of keys for a server within ZeroMQ, utilizing CurveZMQ to secure communication.

- **Encryption**: Once the keys are exchanged, CurveZMQ uses them to encrypt messages. The use of symmetric encryption, derived from the Diffie-Hellman exchange, ensures that the shared secret key is employed to encrypt and decrypt the messages.

- **Message Authentication**: Each message sent over a CurveZMQ connection is accompanied by an authentication tag. The recipient verifies this tag to ensure that the message has not been tampered with, achieving both integrity and authenticity.

In addition to the basic encryption and key exchange, ZeroMQ's model incorporates advanced mechanisms to enhance security further:

- **ZAP (ZeroMQ Auth Protocol)**: ZAP provides the framework for authentication. When a new connection request is received, the ZAP handler checks the client's credentials against the server's policy. ZAP allows for a pluggable architecture, enabling developers to define custom authentication policies as needed.

Here is an illustration of how ZAP might be configured for a simple username-password authentication:

```
def zap_handler(zap_socket):
    while True:
        msg = zap_socket.recv_multipart()
        version, sequence, domain, address, identity, mechanism, *credentials = msg

        if mechanism == b"PLAIN" and valid_credentials(credentials):
            zap_socket.send_multipart([
```

7.1. UNDERSTANDING ZEROMQ'S SECURITY MODEL

```
                version, sequence, b"200", b"OK", domain, identity, b""])
        else:
            zap_socket.send_multipart([
                version, sequence, b"400", b"Invalid", domain, identity, b""])
```

In this example, a ZAP handler is set to validate incoming connections based on predefined criteria. The response codes denote the acceptance (200) or rejection (400) of the request based on validity checks.

- **Null Authentication**: For use cases where authentication is unnecessary, or where communication occurs over a trusted network, ZeroMQ allows for null authentication. This configuration reduces overhead but should be used cautiously, as it offers no protection against impersonation.

ZeroMQ supports various communication topologies, such as publish-subscribe (PUB-SUB), request-reply (REQ-REP), and push-pull (PUSH-PULL). Each topology presents unique security challenges and solutions:

- **Publish-Subscribe**: In a PUB-SUB model, subscribers typically do not authenticate themselves to publishers, potentially allowing unauthorized entities to receive messages. To mitigate this, publishers can encrypt messages broadcast, ensuring that only subscribers with the correct keys can decrypt and access the content.

- **Request-Reply**: The REQ-REP topology typically involves direct connections where both parties often authenticate each other, providing a secure form of communication once keys are correctly exchanged.

- **Push-Pull**: PUSH-PULL models can implement encryption and authentication similarly, ensuring that only authorized workers (pull sockets) can receive and process messages from push sockets.

```
# Example: Encrypted Request-Reply Pattern

server = context.socket(zmq.REP)
server.bind("tcp://*:5555")
```

```
client = context.socket(zmq.REQ)
client.connect("tcp://localhost:5555")

# Encrypting message on client-side
client.send(encrypt("Hello, Server"))

# Decrypting message on server-side
message = decrypt(server.recv())
```

Here, we demonstrate encrypting and decrypting messages in a REQ-REP pattern to ensure data confidentiality.

ZeroMQ's versatility in integrating security mechanisms requires careful considerations and adherence to best practices:

- **Key Management**: Secure storage and rotation of cryptographic keys is essential. ZeroMQ applications need mechanisms for protecting keys in memory and on disk, possibly using hardware security modules if available.

- **Regular Audits**: Conducting security audits of ZeroMQ implementation can uncover vulnerabilities and help in strengthening defenses. Regular updates to libraries, especially those involving cryptographic functions like CurveZMQ, are indispensable to maintain a strong security posture.

- **Secure Defaults**: Utilizing secure defaults in configurations minimizes the risk of human error leading to security gaps. ZeroMQ applications need to ensure that encryption and authentication are enabled by default.

- **Network Security**: Once the application layer security is established through ZeroMQ, additional measures such as firewall rules, secure configurations of network devices, and intrusion detection systems can further bolster the network security.

Understanding the nuanced considerations of ZeroMQ's security model empowers developers to implement robust, reliable applications capable of enduring complex security landscapes inherent in distributed systems. Combining ZeroMQ's native security frameworks like CurveZMQ and ZAP with broader security strategies ensures application resilience and data integrity across networked environments.

7.2 Encryption and Authentication in ZeroMQ

In distributed systems, encryption and authentication are paramount to ensuring secure communication between endpoints. ZeroMQ, a flexible and lightweight messaging library, provides robust mechanisms to achieve these goals. This section delves into the encryption and authentication techniques available within ZeroMQ, shedding light on the libraries and protocols utilized to protect messages and authenticate communication participants.

Encryption in ZeroMQ

ZeroMQ incorporates encryption to ensure message confidentiality, protecting them from unauthorized access or interception. While ZeroMQ itself does not natively include encryption facilities, it can be woven together with other cryptographic libraries such as CurveZMQ to implement secure communication protocols.

Asymmetric Encryption with CurveZMQ

CurveZMQ, an extension of the ZeroMQ suite, employs Curve25519 elliptic curve cryptography for public-key encryption. Public-key encryption allows two parties to establish a shared secret over an untrusted network without having previously exchanged a secret.

- **Public and Private Keys**: In asymmetric encryption, each party possesses a public and private key pair. The public key is shared with others, while the private key is kept secret. The public key encrypts messages that only the corresponding private key can decrypt.

- **Encryption Process**: When a client wants to communicate securely with a server, it encrypts the message using the server's public key. The server decrypts it using its private key, ensuring that only the intended recipient can read the message.

Illustrating the asymmetric encryption process within ZeroMQ using CurveZMQ, consider the following example:

```
import zmq
```

```
import zmq.auth

# Generate public/private key pair
client_public, client_secret = zmq.auth.create_curve_keypair()
server_public, server_secret = zmq.auth.create_curve_keypair()

# Client connects to server, encrypting messages with server's public key
context = zmq.Context()
client = context.socket(zmq.REQ)
client.curve_secretkey = client_secret
client.curve_publickey = client_public
client.curve_serverkey = server_public

client.connect("tcp://localhost:5555")

# Sending encrypted message
client.send(b"Secure Message")
```

In this code, a client sends an encrypted message to a server using asymmetric keys, ensuring only the server can decrypt and read the content.

Symmetric Encryption and Session Keys

While asymmetric encryption ensures secure key exchange, it is computationally expensive for large data transfers. ZeroMQ addresses this by using symmetric encryption once a session has started, leveraging session keys derived from the initial asymmetric key exchange. This approach combines the security of asymmetric encryption with the efficiency of symmetric encryption for continuous communication.

- **Session Keys**: After the initial key exchange, both parties compute a shared session key used for encrypting and decrypting message payloads.

- **Efficient Message Handling**: Symmetric encryption algorithms like AES (Advanced Encryption Standard) handle large payloads efficiently, reducing the processing overhead on communication nodes.

Here is an illustration of deriving and using session keys in ZeroMQ:

```
from cryptography.hazmat.primitives.ciphers import Cipher, algorithms, modes
import os

# Example key exchange process output
shared_key = os.urandom(32)  # Derived shared key from CurveZMQ exchange
```

7.2. ENCRYPTION AND AUTHENTICATION IN ZEROMQ

```
# Initialization vector for AES
iv = os.urandom(16)

# Encrypt a message
def encrypt_message(message, key, iv):
    cipher = Cipher(algorithms.AES(key), modes.CFB(iv))
    encryptor = cipher.encryptor()
    return encryptor.update(message)

# Decrypt a message
def decrypt_message(ciphertext, key, iv):
    cipher = Cipher(algorithms.AES(key), modes.CFB(iv))
    decryptor = cipher.decryptor()
    return decryptor.update(ciphertext)

# Encrypt and decrypt example
ciphertext = encrypt_message(b"Hello, Secure World!", shared_key, iv)
plaintext = decrypt_message(ciphertext, shared_key, iv)
```

In this example, AES is used to encrypt and decrypt messages using a session key established through the initial asymmetric exchange.

Authentication Mechanisms

Beyond encryption, ensuring participant authenticity is essential to thwart impersonation and replay attacks. ZeroMQ provides mechanisms to authenticate communication endpoints through protocols like the ZeroMQ Authentication Protocol (ZAP).

ZeroMQ Authentication Protocol (ZAP)

ZAP acts as a gatekeeper in the authentication process, supporting various authentication mechanisms. It operates as an intermediary between ZeroMQ sockets and user-defined logic to determine if a connection is authorized.

- **PLAIN Mechanism**: ZAP supports simple username-password pairs for authentication.

- **CURVE Mechanism**: More robust, leveraging CurveZMQ's elliptic curve encryption to authenticate clients using digital signatures.

An example of a simple ZAP authentication handler is shown below, focusing on authentication using the CURVE mechanism:

```
def zap_server(auth):
    while True:
```

```
msg = auth.recv_multipart()
identity, request_id, domain, address, identity, mechanism, *credentials = msg

# Verify mechanism
if mechanism == b"CURVE":
    client_key, metadata = credentials
    # Assume we have a function to verify client_key
    if verify_client_key(client_key):
        auth.send_multipart([identity, request_id, b"200", b"OK"])
    else:
        auth.send_multipart([identity, request_id, b"400", b"Unauthorized"])
else:
    auth.send_multipart([identity, request_id, b"400", b"Unknown"])
```

Here, the handler checks for a CURVE mechanism and verifies client credentials, granting access based on the validation results.

Pluggable Authentication Models

ZeroMQ's flexibility enables developers to implement custom authentication models more suited to specific needs. For instance, leveraging third-party authentication servers or incorporating multi-factor authentication mechanisms are feasible with ZAP's infrastructure.

- **Custom Policies**: Define bespoke policies for unique requirements, such as token-based authentication or TLS certificates.

- **Integration with External Systems**: Seamlessly integrate with centralized access management systems, leveraging directory services such as LDAP or identity platforms like OAuth.

Secure Transport Across ZeroMQ Patterns

ZeroMQ supports various messaging patterns, such as PUB-SUB or REQ-REP. Each pattern implies distinct security considerations, demanding suitable encryption and authentication strategies.

- **Publish-Subscribe (PUB-SUB)**: Encryption ensures that even in an openly accessible publishing stream, unauthorized subscribers cannot discern the message content.

- **Request-Reply (REQ-REP)**: Authentication becomes particularly vital, ensuring request-respond pairs genuinely originate from and are directed to legitimate entities within the network.

Below is an example of setting up encryption in a REQ-REP pattern, using CurveZMQ:

```
# Server setup
server = context.socket(zmq.REP)
server.bind("tcp://*:5555")
server.curve_secretkey = server_secret
server.curve_publickey = server_public

# Client setup
client = context.socket(zmq.REQ)
client.curve_serverkey = server_public
client.connect("tcp://localhost:5555")

# Secure communication
client.send(b"Request")
message = server.recv()
server.send(b"Reply")
```

In this secure REQ-REP setup, both client and server are configured with CurveZMQ to assure securely exchanged messages.

Security Best Practices

Implementing encryption and authentication effectively requires adherence to certain best practices:

- **Key Strength and Management**: Regularly rotate cryptographic keys and ensure their secure storage. Avoid hard-coding keys in application code and consider using secure storage solutions or services.

- **Secure Protocols**: Opt for secure and up-to-date cryptographic protocols, such as those provided by CurveZMQ, to prevent exploitation of deprecated encryption standards.

- **Network Segmentation**: Use network architectures that isolate sensitive communications to further mitigate risks, employing techniques such as VLANs or dedicated VPNs.

- **Code Reviews and Testing**: Regularly review the security aspects of code, and employ penetration testing to identify potential vulnerabilities before deployment.

Encryption and authentication within ZeroMQ form the bedrock of secure distributed systems. Leveraging tools like CurveZMQ alongside ZeroMQ's inherent configurability provides comprehensive security tailored to bespoke communication needs, reinforcing ZeroMQ's prowess in enabling robust, resilient architectures across diverse scenarios. Through diligent adherence to secure coding practices, including stringent key management and astute authentication strategies, ZeroMQ applications stand fortified against emerging threats and security challenges.

7.3 Implementing CurveZMQ for Secure Communications

CurveZMQ is an extension of the ZeroMQ messaging library leveraged for secure communications. It implements Curve25519 elliptic curve technology which forms the backbone of its encryption and authentication mechanisms. This section systematically explores the intricacies of implementing CurveZMQ, delving into its cryptographic principles, deployment strategies, and practical application scenarios essential for safeguarding ZeroMQ communications.

Understanding Curve25519 and Its Importance:

Curve25519 is a high-speed, high-security elliptic curve offering 128 bits of security with 256-bit keys. Known for its efficiency and security, it is particularly suitable for devices with limited computational resources. The core operations in Curve25519 are scalar multiplication on the elliptic curve, providing robust key exchange capabilities without exposing private keys.

Cryptographic Principles Behind CurveZMQ:

CurveZMQ utilizes several cryptographic principles to create secure channels:

- **Elliptic Curve Cryptography (ECC)**: ECC provides the mathematical algorithms allowing small key sizes to offer strong security, with operations based on the algebraic structures of elliptic curves over finite fields.

- **Diffie-Hellman Key Exchange**: CurveZMQ leverages this method to securely exchange cryptographic keys over a public

7.3. IMPLEMENTING CURVEZMQ FOR SECURE COMMUNICATIONS

channel, allowing two parties to generate a shared secret independently.

- **Symmetric Encryption**: Once the shared key is established via ECC, symmetric encryption based on AES or ChaCha20 encrypts message payloads. Symmetric encryption is computationally less expensive than its asymmetric counterpart, suitable for larger data processing.

Configuration and Deployment of CurveZMQ:

Implementing CurveZMQ involves key pair generation, configuration of ZeroMQ sockets, and encryption of messages. Below is a detailed walkthrough of these steps:

Key Pair Generation:

Key generation is the first step toward employing CurveZMQ. Both communication endpoints must generate public-private key pairs. The private key remains confidential, whereas the public key is shared with counterparts.

```
import zmq.auth

# Generate key pairs
client_public, client_secret = zmq.auth.create_curve_keypair()
server_public, server_secret = zmq.auth.create_curve_keypair()

# Save keys securely
with open("client.key", "w") as client_key_file:
    client_key_file.write(client_public)
    client_key_file.write(client_secret)

with open("server.key", "w") as server_key_file:
    server_key_file.write(server_public)
    server_key_file.write(server_secret)
```

The code above generates CurveZMQ key pairs and persists them securely for client and server use.

Socket Configuration with CurveZMQ:

After key generation, the next phase is configuring ZeroMQ sockets to utilize CurveZMQ for secure communications. This entails setting the curve-related properties on the sockets to include private keys, public keys, and peer server keys.

```
# Setup Context
```

```
context = zmq.Context()

# Server socket setup
server = context.socket(zmq.REP)
server.curve_secretkey = server_secret
server.curve_publickey = server_public
server.curve_server = True  # Set the server mode
server.bind("tcp://*:5555")

# Client socket setup
client = context.socket(zmq.REQ)
client.curve_secretkey = client_secret
client.curve_publickey = client_public
client.curve_serverkey = server_public
client.connect("tcp://localhost:5555")
```

The above example focuses on preparing the REP (server) and REQ (client) sockets for a secure communication session using CurveZMQ.

Message Encryption and Decryption Process:

Once the sockets are configured, messages sent between the client and server undergo encryption/decryption using the shared session key deduced from the key exchange process.

```
# Client sends encrypted message
client.send(b"Hello Secure World!")

# Server receives and decrypts message
message = server.recv()
print("Decrypted Message:", message.decode())

# Server replies
server.send(b"Encrypted Hello!")
```

Key Points:

- Upon setting up CurveZMQ, all send/receive operations automatically utilize encryption based on the established session keys for secure communication.

- Applications can now exchange data securely without requiring additional cryptographic operations within the message flow logic.

Analyzing the Security of CurveZMQ:

The security efficacy of CurveZMQ hinges on several core factors:

- **Key Management**: Securely generating, storing, and distributing keys is critical. Hardware Security Modules (HSM) or dedicated services like HashiCorp Vault can manage keys heuristically.

- **Minimal Exposure**: Immediate clearing of private keys from memory post-usage diminishes exposure risks, aligning with principles of least privilege and minimal exposure.

- **Resistance to Side-Channel Attacks**: Curve25519's design resists several attack vectors, including side-channel and timing attacks, owing to its fixed-time operations.

Integration with ZeroMQ Patterns:

CurveZMQ can be implemented across various ZeroMQ messaging patterns:

- **Request-Reply (REQ-REP)**: Ideal for scenarios requiring acknowledgment of secure message delivery. Messages are secured, verified, and confirmed through explicit requests and replies.

- **Publish-Subscribe (PUB-SUB)**: While encryption ensures secure broadcast, endpoint authentication allows verification of legitimate subscribers. To implement CurveZMQ's secure PUB-SUB, keys are shared and verified only amongst trusted entities.

- **Push-Pull (PUSH-PULL)**: Suitable for distributed processing systems requiring secure task distribution across worker nodes. Utilizing CurveZMQ, the task sender (push) encrypts messages, and worker nodes (pull) authenticate the source and decrypt tasks for processing.

Each pattern requires tailored configurations to optimize both security and performance parameters ensuring mission-critical systems function seamlessly in diverse environments.

Real-World Applications of CurveZMQ:

CurveZMQ's practical applications span various domains, from secure financial transactions to protected data transfer in IoT:

- **Internet of Things (IoT)**: IoT devices benefit greatly from CurveZMQ's efficient encryption. This lightweight protocol facilitates secure device-to-device communication, vital for sensitive applications such as smart home devices and connected vehicles.

- **Financial Services**: In financial markets, ensuring privacy and integrity of transactions is paramount. Secure communication facilitated by CurveZMQ defends against market manipulation and protects monetary exchanges from breaches.

- **Healthcare Systems**: Protected patient data exchange mandates encryption and authentication. Implementing CurveZMQ ensures secure transfer of patient records across healthcare institutions or devices.

- **Distributed Computing and Blockchain**: Secure consensus and data-sharing mechanisms within blockchain networks can deploy CurveZMQ to encrypt distributed ledgers and transactions, reinforcing trust in decentralized operations.

Best Practices for Implementing CurveZMQ:

Ensuring a robust deployment of CurveZMQ involves adhering to the following best practices:

- **Comprehensive Key Management**: Regularly update change keys ensuring outdated keys are not inadvertently reused, and securely delete obsolete keys.

- **Security Audits**: Undertake regular security audits and penetration tests to verify the resilience of deployed CurveZMQ setups. Identify and rectify vulnerabilities proactively.

- **Adopt Least Privilege Principle**: Limit access to messaging services and keys to only those entities that absolutely require it. Employ access controls rigorously within infrastructure to enforce least privilege principles.

- **Complementary Security Measures**: Despite CurveZMQ's strength, complement cryptographic measures with broader network security strategies including firewalls, intrusion detection systems (IDS), and secure organizational policies.

Implementing CurveZMQ within ZeroMQ is a strategic choice for any application demanding high-performance secure communications. ZeroMQ's attribute to integrate CurveZMQ seamlessly within its architectural design underpins its efficacy to ensure confidentiality, integrity, and availability. By leveraging the powerful cryptographic features of CurveZMQ, applications enjoy significant enhancements in their security postures while adhering to ZeroMQ's paradigms of scalability and simplicity. Carefully implementing, maintaining, and managing cryptographic elements form essential components of agility and resilience in dealing with evolving security landscapes.

7.4 Error Detection and Management Techniques

In distributed communication systems powered by ZeroMQ, managing errors effectively is as crucial as securing communications. Given the intricate networks and potential points of failure inherent in distributed architectures, ZeroMQ provides a myriad of techniques for error detection and management, aimed at ensuring system robustness and reliability. This section discusses these techniques, elucidating various error scenarios and their corresponding strategies for effective management.

Understanding Error Detection in ZeroMQ

Error detection in ZeroMQ involves employing mechanisms to identify faults during message transmission or reception, ensuring prompt resolution to minimize system impact. Key challenges include network latencies, unavailable endpoints, packet loss, and protocol mismatches. Proactively detecting these issues is instrumental in maintaining system health, requiring:

- **Message Acknowledgment**: Critical for ensuring that messages are delivered successfully. Implementing acknowledgments provides feedback loops to confirm receipt, enabling retries or alternative flows when necessary.

- **Heartbeats and Monitoring**: ZeroMQ supports heartbeat messages which serve as periodic signal checks between nodes to ascertain their availability. When a node misses several consecutive heartbeats, it is marked as potentially unavailable, prompting further actions such as reconnection attempts or failover strategies.

- **Logging and Alerts**: Centralized logging systems capture error events across ZeroMQ setups, offering a consolidated view enabling prompt response and analysis. Real-time alert systems trigger notifications for developers or administrators when anomalies are observed.

```
import zmq
import time

# Heartbeat mechanism example
context = zmq.Context()
socket = context.socket(zmq.REQ)

# Configuring heartbeats
socket.setsockopt(zmq.LINGER, 0)
socket.setsockopt(zmq.HEARTBEAT_IVL, 1000) # Send heartbeat every 1000 ms
socket.setsockopt(zmq.HEARTBEAT_TIMEOUT, 3000) # Timeout in 3000 ms
socket.setsockopt(zmq.HEARTBEAT_TTL, 6000) # Max time-to-live for heartbeat

# Connect socket
socket.connect("tcp://localhost:5555")

while True:
    try:
        socket.send(b"Ping")
        message = socket.recv()
        print(f"Received: {message.decode()}")
    except zmq.ZMQError as e:
        print(f"Heartbeat failed: {e}")
    time.sleep(1)
```

This Python snippet demonstrates setting up a ZeroMQ REQ socket with heartbeat options, enabling it to detect disconnections proactively through missed heartbeats.

Common ZeroMQ Error Scenarios

ZeroMQ, despite its robust design, can encounter several error scenarios prevailing in distributed systems:

- **Connection Timeouts**: Occurs when a message socket fails to connect to a remote peer within an expected timeframe.

7.4. ERROR DETECTION AND MANAGEMENT TECHNIQUES

- **Message Drops**: A message drop happens due to buffer overflows or insufficient memory resources when a message fails to queue in the receiver's socket.

- **Protocol Violations**: When two communicating sockets don't adhere to the same protocol definition, resulting in corrupt or undesirable communication flow.

- **Resource Exhaustion**: Exceeding maximum allowable sockets, CPU, or memory limits can lead to refusal of further connections, causing service degradation.

Implementing Fault Tolerance with ZeroMQ

To address such errors effectively, implementing fault-tolerant designs in ZeroMQ applications is necessary. Consider these techniques:

- **Retries and Backoff Strategies**: Design the client to automatically retry sending messages upon failure, utilizing backoff strategies to stagger retries over time, preventing flood conditions.

```
import random

def send_with_retries(socket, message, max_attempts=5, initial_interval=1):
    attempts = 0
    while attempts < max_attempts:
        try:
            socket.send(message)
            response = socket.recv() # Wait for response
            return response
        except zmq.ZMQError:
            attempts += 1
            interval = initial_interval * (2 ** attempts) # Exponential backoff
            interval += random.uniform(0, 0.5) # Small random increment
            time.sleep(interval) # Wait before retrying
    raise Exception("Max retries exceeded")
```

This algorithm implements message retries on a ZeroMQ socket using exponential backoff, introducing a stochastic element to distribute load in high contention scenarios.

- **Load Balancing Across Endpoints**: Distribute messages evenly across multiple workers or endpoints, ensuring continued availability when individual nodes fail. ZeroMQ's PUSH-PULL pattern is adept for such balancing.

```
# Simple Load Balancer for ZeroMQ Push-Pull
context = zmq.Context()
load_balancer = context.socket(zmq.ROUTER)
load_balancer.bind("tcp://*:5555")

worker = context.socket(zmq.DEALER)
worker.bind("ipc://worker")

# Forwarding messages between PUSH and PULL sockets
zmq.proxy(load_balancer, worker)
```

By introducing a ROUTER-DEALER proxy between PUSH-PULL sockets, the load balancer dynamically redistributes messages, enhancing fault tolerance through endpoint redundancy.

- **Failover Mechanisms**: Configure replicas or alternate servers, automatically redirecting clients when primary services become unavailable.

- **Transactional Messaging**: Transactional approaches entail messaging sleeves that pair requests with replies, enabling atomic operations (either fully completed or altogether aborted), providing greater consistency against disconnections.

Advanced Message Recovery Techniques

For more advanced recovery and management scenarios, consider these methods:

- **Message Queue Persistence**: Storing unprocessed or failed messages on disk or within databases to be retrieved and sent for subsequent opportunities, preserving state and progress beyond application shutdowns.

```
import sqlite3

# Save message to persistent queue
def save_message(queue_db, message):
    with sqlite3.connect(queue_db) as conn:
        cursor = conn.cursor()
        cursor.execute("INSERT INTO message_queue (message) VALUES (?)", (
            message,))
```

7.4. ERROR DETECTION AND MANAGEMENT TECHNIQUES

```
        conn.commit()
# Retrieve unprocessed message
def retrieve_messages(queue_db):
    with sqlite3.connect(queue_db) as conn:
        cursor = conn.cursor()
        cursor.execute("SELECT id, message FROM message_queue WHERE
            processed = 0")
        messages = cursor.fetchall()
    return messages
```

This snippet outlines how ZeroMQ messages are persistently stored in an SQLite database, ensuring recovery after unexpected shutdowns.

- **Sequence Numbers and Ordering Guarantees**: Sequence numbers may accompany messages, allowing recipients to identify and handle sequence anomalies, reordering them as necessary. Software retries extend restorability guarantees by allowing packets to rebuild seamless communication flows.

- **Checkpoints and State Recovery**: Introduce checkpointing mechanisms capturing the state at intervals, from which systems can resume operations following disruptions or crashes. These consistent snapshots ensure that in-progress transactions have minimal overlap or data loss post-recoveries.

Configuring Error Monitors and Alerts

To transform error insights into proactive system responses, ZeroMQ deployments should integrate monitoring frameworks:

- **System Health Dashboards**: Implement interactive dashboards presenting real-time ZeroMQ health metrics, including nodal uptimes, message trends, or anomaly detections.

- **Automated Alerts**: Employ alerting services like Grafana or Prometheus, with integrations enabling developers to configure thresholds that, when breached, automatically escalate issues through channels like SMS, email, or other messaging services.

```
import prometheus_client
# Basic ZeroMQ Metrics Server
```

```
REQUESTS_METRIC = prometheus_client.Counter('zmq_requests_total', 'Total
    Requests')
ERRORS_METRIC = prometheus_client.Counter('zmq_errors_total', 'Total Errors')

def process_message(socket):
    REQUESTS_METRIC.inc()
    try:
        # message processing logic
        pass
    except Exception as e:
        ERRORS_METRIC.inc()
        raise e

# Start the metrics server on a separate process or thread
prometheus_client.start_http_server(8000)
```

In this example, a Prometheus client tracks ZeroMQ requests and errors, facilitating the collection of metrics and enabling monitoring.

The adoption of these practices tightly integrates error management into ZeroMQ's lifecycle, elevating overall system dependability. Effective error management transforms potential disruptions into manageable events, reinforcing ZeroMQ's dedication to resilient and scalable communication infrastructures. Digging deeper, confidence in ZeroMQ's ability to handle errors allows developers to focus efforts on building innovative solutions that harness and amplify ZeroMQ's vast capabilities.

7.5 Handling Timeouts and Message Failures

In distributed and concurrent messaging systems like ZeroMQ, handling timeouts and message failures is crucial for maintaining communication resilience and application reliability. As complex network environments often experience varying levels of latency, packet loss, or node failures, ZeroMQ provides mechanisms to mitigate these issues effectively. This section delves into methods for managing timeouts and recovering from message failures, ensuring robustness and continuity in messaging operations.

Understanding Timeouts in ZeroMQ

Timeouts in ZeroMQ occur when a message sender does not receive an

7.5. HANDLING TIMEOUTS AND MESSAGE FAILURES

expected acknowledgment or response within a predefined time interval. They can be attributed to several unmet conditions, such as network latencies, server unavailabilities, or misconfigurations of socket parameters.

- **Connection Timeouts**: Occur during the initial handshake or connection setup phase, often due to network instability or server-side issues.

- **Send and Receive Timeouts**: Impacted by sending a message without successful acknowledgment or expecting a message that fails to arrive.

To cope with these scenarios, applications must implement robust mechanisms to detect and react to timeout events, preserving the communication channel's integrity.

Configuring Timeout Parameters in ZeroMQ

ZeroMQ provides flexible configuration options to set timeouts, catering to different operational needs and latency characteristics:

1. **Linger Option**: Determines how long a socket remains open after a close call to send outstanding messages. Setting this option appropriately helps ensure message delivery under high latency.

2. **Receive Timeout**: Controls the maximum duration a socket waits before raising an exception if no messages arrive. This can prevent the application from indefinitely blocking when awaiting messages.

3. **Send Timeout**: Defines the time a socket spends trying to send messages before timing out, mitigating risks associated with unreachable network paths or overflowing buffers.

```
import zmq

context = zmq.Context()

# Set up a ZeroMQ socket with timeout configurations
socket = context.socket(zmq.REQ)
socket.setsockopt(zmq.LINGER, 0) # Immediately drop pending messages on close
socket.setsockopt(zmq.RCVTIMEO, 5000) # Set receive timeout to 5000 ms
```

```
socket.setsockopt(zmq.SNDTIMEO, 2000)  # Set send timeout to 2000 ms
socket.connect("tcp://server-address:5555")
```

The above configuration highlights setting the linger, receive, and send timeouts on a ZeroMQ REQ socket, helping manage latency-induced delays by effectively timing out operations that exceed acceptable thresholds.

Managing Message Failures

Message failures arise when transmissions do not initially succeed, necessitating retries or alternate handling methods. They may stem from network disconnections, resource limitations, or unforgivable protocol deviations. ZeroMQ addresses these failures using various resilient strategies:

1. **Retries with Backoff Algorithms**: Utilizing automatic retry attempts upon failure introduction, spacing retries with exponential or incremental backoff algorithms to prevent overwhelming the network with repeated requests without resolution.

```
import time
import random

def retry_with_backoff(socket, message, max_retries=5):
    attempt = 0
    while attempt < max_retries:
        try:
            socket.send(message)
            response = socket.recv()  # Await successful reception
            return response
        except zmq.Again:
            attempt += 1
            backoff_time = 2 ** attempt + random.random()  # Calculating
                exponential backoff with jitter
            time.sleep(backoff_time)
    raise RuntimeError("Exceeded max retries without response.")
```

This approach handles message failures employing a retry mechanism with exponential backoff, efficiently controlling the load on communication paths while mitigating the effect of transient failures.

2. **Alternate Route Messaging**: In strategically distributed environments, adopt routing options directing messages through alternative paths when primary routes are incapacitated, ensuring

transmissions reach intended destinations using backup communication links.

3. **Fallback Mechanisms**: Implement fallback routines facilitating seamless message transfer across auxiliary services, caching mechanisms, or storage solutions, dynamically redirecting messages penned for failing systems elsewhere for eventual destination reach.

4. **Acknowledgment and Confirmation Protocols**: For critical communications, employ explicit acknowledgment protocols that verify message delivery, requiring recipients to confirm successful receipt before proceeding further, reducing chances of undetected failures.

Design Patterns for Resilience Against Timeouts and Failures

Leveraging design patterns that enhance fault tolerance when dealing with timeouts and failures can significantly bolster application stability:

- **Circuit Breaker Pattern**: Integrate circuit breaker mechanisms for monitoring failure rates between communication endpoints, temporarily halting attempts to connect when failures surpass a certain threshold, thereby preventing waste of resources and aggravated network strain.

- **Health Check Mechanisms**: Persistently assess the availability status of nodes through automated health checks, keeping real-time assessments reflective of system conditions. This informs decisions about rerouting or throttling under high failure incidences.

```
# Sample Circuit Breaker implementation
class CircuitBreaker:
    def __init__(self, failure_threshold=3, reset_timeout=10):
        self.failure_threshold = failure_threshold
        self.reset_timeout = reset_timeout
        self.failure_count = 0
        self.last_failed_time = 0
        self.state = "CLOSED"
```

```
def call(self, func, *args, **kwargs):
    if self.state == "OPEN":
        if time.time() - self.last_failed_time > self.reset_timeout:
            self.state = "HALF-OPEN"
        else:
            raise Exception("Circuit Breaker is Open")

    try:
        result = func(*args, **kwargs)
        self.state = "CLOSED"
        self.failure_count = 0
        return result
    except Exception:
        self.failure_count += 1
        self.last_failed_time = time.time()
        if self.failure_count >= self.failure_threshold:
            self.state = "OPEN"
        raise
```

In this example, a circuit breaker is established to automatically inhibit further attempts to perform actions that repeatedly result in failure, thus distinguishing persistent chaos from surfacing issues.

Ensuring High Availability Through ZeroMQ Features

ZeroMQ innately promotes high availability by situationally taking advantage of its various socket types and topologies, ensuring continuity amidst dynamic error conditions:

- **Built-in Multipath Routing**: Leverage ZeroMQ's inherent multi-path routing by structuring networks that naturally benefit from alternative serving processes or linkages, promoting traffic dispersion when primary paths experience timeouts.

- **Connection Resilience**: Utilize ZeroMQ's optimistic reconnection properties, allowing sockets to automatically attempt reconnections when disrupted by known endpoint changes or temporary network interruptions.

- **Heartbeat Mechanisms**: Regular heartbeats can sustain session activity by maintaining liveliness between continuous communications, prompting remedial measures proactively upon infrequent acknowledgments.

The constancy of these built-in features provides significant error mitigation without burdening development processes, yielding a naturally robust operational backdrop for continued service availability.

7.5. HANDLING TIMEOUTS AND MESSAGE FAILURES

Monitoring and Alerting for Proactive Management

To enforce proactive protection against timeouts and message failures, employ sophisticated monitoring systems capturing metrics indicative of system health:

- **Telemetry Systems**: Deploy telemetry to collect and graph ZeroMQ socket statuses, error frequencies, and bandwidth efflux, cross-referencing thresholds for anomaly detection.

- **Real-Time Alerts**: Trigger notifications upon threshold infringements, achieving lead time for corrective measures through integrations within centralized monitoring frameworks, such as Prometheus or ELK Stack.

- **Predictive Analytics**: Implement predictive algorithms that provide insights into future failure patterns based on historical occurrences, improving plan responses and maintaining system integrity.

```
from prometheus_client import start_http_server, Counter, Gauge

# Prometheus metrics for monitoring ZeroMQ interactions
failure_count = Counter('zero_mq_failures', 'Number of message failures')
timeout_gauge = Gauge('zero_mq_timeout_duration', 'Average timeout duration')

def monitor_timeout(socket, start_time):
    # Simulate monitoring of message exchange
    try:
        socket.recv() # await message
        timeout_gauge.set(time.time() - start_time)
    except zmq.Again:
        failure_count.inc()
```

This snippet provides an example where Prometheus metrics track failures and timeout durations, enabling intelligent monitoring and metric-based management.

Dealing effectively with timeouts and message failures involves establishing resilient protocols, architectural strategies, and adaptive responses within ZeroMQ systems. Through meticulous configurations, acknowledging real-world scenarios, and adopting fail-safe mechanisms, application operations remain consistent even under worsening network conditions. Consequently, uniformly applying these methods bolsters confidence, operation continuity, and reinforces ZeroMQ's role as a versatile and steadfast constituent of distributed communications.

7.6 Debugging and Logging in ZeroMQ

In the development of distributed systems, debugging and logging are essential processes that ensure system transparency and robustness. ZeroMQ presents distinct challenges and opportunities for efficient debugging and logging, given its highly decentralized architecture and asynchronous message passing nature. This section expounds on strategies, tools, and methodologies for effective debugging and logging within ZeroMQ environments, offering insights into identifying and resolving issues that arise throughout the application lifecycle.

Importance of Debugging and Logging in ZeroMQ

The asynchronous nature and flexible messaging patterns of ZeroMQ, while providing numerous benefits, can complicate the identification of issues during development and runtime. Logging provides a historical trace of events, crucial for retrospection, while debugging enables point-in-time inspection and correction.

- Diagnosing Communication Failures: Identifying instances of dropped messages, broken connections, or mismatched protocols can prevent disruptions in message flow.

- Performance Monitoring: Logging allows for tracking throughput, latency, and resource utilization, which are key to maintaining optimal performance levels across distributed nodes.

- End-to-End Tracking: ZeroMQ spans across diverse topologies where tracking message lifecycles can reveal bottlenecks or unexpected divergences in flow.

Core Debugging Techniques in ZeroMQ

Debugging ZeroMQ applications requires a blend of standard debugging practices and ZeroMQ-specific strategies:

7.6. DEBUGGING AND LOGGING IN ZEROMQ

1. Socket Inspection: Utilize socket inspection to ascertain state and configuration specifics of each ZeroMQ socket, assessing options such as identity, linger settings, and buffer statuses to unearth configuration-based issues.

2. Protocol Verification: Confirm the compatibility of connected sockets by ensuring adherence to defined messaging patterns (e.g., REQ-REP, PUB-SUB) to eliminate protocol-based failures.

3. Message Tracing: Incorporate message tracing to scrutinize the paths and states of messages as they traverse the system, identifying bottlenecks or inaccuracies in routing logic.

4. Environment Emulation: Reproduce the environment locally with similar network conditions, concurrency levels, and workload variabilities to simulate and diagnose complex issues in controlled settings.

Using Built-In ZeroMQ Diagnostics

ZeroMQ provides several in-built diagnostics features that aid in debugging:

- zmq_msg_t API: Expose message diagnostics using the zmq_msg_t API to inspect size, attributes, and content of messages that fail to transmit correctly.

- zmq_monitor: Establish monitoring sockets to realize comprehensive socket state notifications, capturing events such as connection acceptance, disconnection, and message drops.

```
import zmq
import zmq.asyncio

# Setting up a monitor socket
zmq_socket = context.socket(zmq.REQ)
zmq_socket.connect("tcp://localhost:5555")
zmq_socket.monitor('tcp://monitor-address:5566', zmq.EVENT_ALL)

# Monitor event logging
event = zmq_socket.recv_monitor_message()
print(f"Event: {event['event']}, Address: {event['address']}, Value: {event['value']}")
```

This example demonstrates how ZeroMQ's built-in monitoring captures and prints connection-related events, providing insight into the socket status and operational irregularities.

Employing Comprehensive Logging Strategies

To harness the full potential of logging within ZeroMQ applications, developers should deploy robust logging frameworks:

1. Structured Logging: Use structured logging formats like JSON to enable easily parsable and searchable logs, facilitating automated analysis and troubleshooting efforts.

2. Centralized Logging Systems: Aggregate logs across distributed nodes into centralized systems using tools like ELK Stack (Elasticsearch, Logstash, Kibana) or Fluentd, promoting cohesive analysis from scattered log data.

3. Log Levels and Filtering: Implement graded logging practices, leveraging varying log levels (debug, info, warning, error, critical) to filter messages appropriate for real-time monitoring or historical review, mitigating log noise issues.

4. Contextual Enrichment: Integrate contextual information such as timestamps, socket identifiers, and execution paths alongside logs to provide holistic insights into each logged event.

```
import logging
import json

# Set up logging configuration
logging.basicConfig(level=logging.DEBUG, format='%(asctime)s %(levelname)s %(
    message)s')
logger = logging.getLogger(__name__)

def log_message(event_type, event_details):
    log_entry = json.dumps({
        'event_type': event_type,
        'details': event_details,
        'timestamp': time.time()
    })
    logger.info(log_entry)
```

The application of structured logging using JSON improves retrieval and analysis capabilities by including event-specific data paired with detailed descriptive logging statements.

7.6. DEBUGGING AND LOGGING IN ZEROMQ

Real-Time Analysis and Monitoring

Integrating real-time analysis into your ZeroMQ setups provides immediate insights into the application's health and issue patterns:

- Metrics and Dashboards: Utilize monitoring tools like Grafana paired with Prometheus to visualize metrics associated with ZeroMQ's operation graphically, helping identify anomalies or performance discrepancies against established baselines.

- Alerting Mechanisms: Configure alerts to proactively address pervasive issues, dispatching warnings or escalation messages when monitored conditions exceed certain operational thresholds. Integration with services like PagerDuty or OpsGenie can automate on-call responses.

```
from prometheus_client import start_http_server, Counter

# Define Prometheus metrics
message_count = Counter('zmq_message_count', 'Number of processed messages')
error_count = Counter('zmq_error_count', 'Number of errors encountered')

def process_message(socket):
    try:
        message = socket.recv()
        message_count.inc() # Track message processing
        # Process the message
    except Exception as e:
        error_count.inc() # Increment error counter
        logger.error(f"Error processing message. {e}")

# Start the Prometheus metrics server
start_http_server(8000)
```

In this example, Prometheus tracks ZeroMQ message and error counts, enhancing observability through metric collection reflected in real-time dashboards and alerts.

Advanced Debugging Tools and Techniques

Beyond built-in capabilities, developers may employ symmetrical debugging techniques dedicated to ZeroMQ:

- Integration with Debuggers: Utilize GDB or LLDB for C/C++ applications and Python's PDB tailored towards step-by-step execution review, inspecting value states throughout ZeroMQ method calls.

- Network Analyzers: Tools like Wireshark facilitate deep packet inspection of traffic between ZeroMQ nodes, offering network-layer visibility that complements socket-level logging.

- Third-party Testing and Simulation Frameworks: Employ specialized test frameworks, such as ZeroMQ's czmq C bindings or MockZMQ, tailored for crafting unit tests and simulating realistic messaging scenarios, enabling validation of application logic under varied circumstances.

Using these advanced tools, developers can delve into detailed examination of issues, tracing logic execution and network traffic comprehensively to pinpoint root causes.

Debugging and Logging Best Practices

To maximize efficiency, consistency, and relevancy within debugging and logging approaches, adhere to these best practices:

- Revision Control: Maintain revision histories within logs, marking significant changes in logic or infrastructure and correlating them with system health metrics, offering post-update retrospectives.

- Secure Logging: Exclude sensitive information from logs (e.g., credentials, personal identifiers), adhering to security policies and regulations while safeguarding compliance indictments.

- Log Rotation and Expiry: Implement automated log rotation and retention policies to manage log sizes. Regularly purge logs exceeding utility lifespans, maintaining a balance of historical coverage and storage feasibility.

- Chain of Responsibility: Establish a clear chain of responsibility for log access, ensuring only authenticated and authorized personnel interact with log data to reinforce security parameterization.

Debugging and logging are foundational to maintaining ZeroMQ applications' overall reliability and performance. Careful integration of structured methods supported by comprehensive tooling ensures developers can efficiently address and resolve issues, driving forward the

7.6. DEBUGGING AND LOGGING IN ZEROMQ

creation of robust and responsive distributed systems. Through cohesive practices and an awareness of available diagnostics, developers can fortify ZeroMQ implementations against evolving operational complexities, embedding resilience deep within communication infrastructures.

Chapter 8

Performance Tuning and Best Practices

Optimizing the performance of ZeroMQ applications is essential to meet the demands of high-throughput and low-latency environments. This involves fine-tuning ZeroMQ's configuration settings, such as buffer sizes and socket options, to enhance messaging efficiency. Network considerations also play a crucial role in achieving optimal performance, with strategies required for managing concurrency and load distribution. This chapter explores various performance tuning techniques and shares best practices to ensure robust, scalable ZeroMQ deployments. Additionally, it emphasizes the importance of monitoring and profiling ZeroMQ applications to identify and address potential bottlenecks, thus maintaining system stability and performance.

8.1 Optimizing ZeroMQ Configuration

ZeroMQ is a high-performance asynchronous messaging library used for building scalable, distributed applications. To leverage its full potential, configuring ZeroMQ appropriately is crucial. This section

CHAPTER 8. PERFORMANCE TUNING AND BEST PRACTICES

delves into fine-tuning ZeroMQ configurations, focusing on buffer sizes, socket options, and other critical parameters that influence performance.

ZeroMQ offers various socket types, such as REQ, REP, PUB, SUB, PUSH, PULL, each serving different communication patterns. Understanding these socket types' configuration intricacies is key to optimizing application performance. The optimization process involves examining socket options, assessing buffer sizes, and tuning parameters to suit specific application requirements.

Buffer Sizes: Buffer sizes are a pivotal parameter impacting ZeroMQ performance. They determine how many messages can be queued in memory, affecting throughput and latency. ZeroMQ provides send and receive buffer options, ZMQ_SNDBUF and ZMQ_RCVBUF. By default, the buffer sizes are adjusted by the underlying operating system, but can be manually set to optimize performance based on application demands.

```
#include <zmq.h>

int main() {
    void *context = zmq_ctx_new();
    void *socket = zmq_socket(context, ZMQ_PUSH);

    // Setting the send buffer size to 4MB
    int sndbuf = 4096 * 1024;
    zmq_setsockopt(socket, ZMQ_SNDBUF, &sndbuf, sizeof(sndbuf));

    // Setting the receive buffer size to 4MB
    int rcvbuf = 4096 * 1024;
    zmq_setsockopt(socket, ZMQ_RCVBUF, &rcvbuf, sizeof(rcvbuf));

    zmq_close(socket);
    zmq_ctx_destroy(context);
    return 0;
}
```

The choice of buffer size should be influenced by the expected volume of messages and the available system memory. A larger buffer can improve throughput in high-load scenarios but might increase latency if messages are delayed in the queue. Conversely, a smaller buffer might enhance latency but could lead to message loss under sudden load spikes. Profiling and load testing offer insights into the optimal buffer size.

Socket Options: Apart from buffer sizes, several socket options play

8.1. OPTIMIZING ZEROMQ CONFIGURATION

a critical role in ZeroMQ's performance optimization.

- ZMQ_LINGER: This option specifies how long a socket should block on a send or close operation. ZMQ_LINGER allows pending messages to be sent before the socket is closed. Setting it to zero discards unsent messages, useful for ensuring non-blocking scenarios.

```
int linger = 0; // Set linger to 0 for non-blocking close
zmq_setsockopt(socket, ZMQ_LINGER, &linger, sizeof(linger));
```

- ZMQ_SNDHWM and ZMQ_RCVHWM: The send and receive high-water mark options control the maximum number of outstanding messages ZeroMQ can queue. Configuring high-water marks is essential in preventing message pile-up, thereby maintaining a steady message flow. It allows for back-pressure to be effectively communicated within the system.

```
int sndhwm = 1000; // Max 1000 messages
zmq_setsockopt(socket, ZMQ_SNDHWM, &sndhwm, sizeof(sndhwm));

int rcvhwm = 1000; // Max 1000 messages
zmq_setsockopt(socket, ZMQ_RCVHWM, &rcvhwm, sizeof(rcvhwm));
```

Setting high-water mark values appropriately avoids message loss in high-throughput scenarios while enabling the application to remain responsive.

Tuning Network Parameters: Network parameters also influence ZeroMQ's performance. Network latency and bandwidth are primary factors. Given ZeroMQ's dependency on the underlying network infrastructure, adjusting network-level settings can improve messaging efficiency.

- TCP_KEEPALIVE: This parameter controls whether TCP keep-alive messages are sent to maintain connections. Enabling keep-alives is beneficial for long-lived connections, ensuring that temporary network interruptions do not lead to connection drops.

```
int keepalive = 1; // Enable TCP keep-alive
zmq_setsockopt(socket, ZMQ_TCP_KEEPALIVE, &keepalive, sizeof(keepalive
    ));
```

Fine-tuning TCP window sizes, timeouts, and congestion control settings at the operating system level further optimizes ZeroMQ performance, especially in environments with varying network qualities.

Context and Thread Management: ZeroMQ context management and thread utilization also necessitate careful configuration. A ZeroMQ context encapsulates all operations for a given threading domain. Typically, multiple threads should share a single context, but it also handles thread affinity, affecting inter-thread communication efficiency.

- `zmq_ctx_set`: Allows modifications to context-level attributes, such as the maximum number of I/O threads.

```
void *context = zmq_ctx_new();
// Set the I/O threads to 2
zmq_ctx_set(context, ZMQ_IO_THREADS, 2);
```

Setting the number of I/O threads should correspond with the number of cores available on the host machine and align with anticipated messaging workloads.

Additional Considerations: Beyond these technical parameters, the architectural design of the messaging patterns also dictates ZeroMQ optimization. Choosing appropriate topologies, like brokered versus peer-to-peer models, and carefully designing message serialization contribute to the messaging system's efficiency. It's crucial to evaluate application-specific requirements to harness ZeroMQ's full capabilities while maintaining system responsiveness.

Overall, optimal ZeroMQ configuration is about balancing competing demands—throughput versus latency, resource utilization versus responsiveness—to achieve a harmonious setup that adequately supports the application's operational profile. Profiling, load testing, and iterative adjustments allow for insights into system behavior, iteratively arriving at the most performant configuration.

8.2 Efficient Message Handling

Handling messages efficiently is a cornerstone of any high-performance application utilizing ZeroMQ, a platform-agnostic messaging library. Efficient message handling entails not just correct delivery but also optimizing for throughput and minimizing latency. Insufficient message handling can lead to bottlenecks, ultimately degrading application performance. This section explores various techniques and principles crucial for achieving efficient message handling in ZeroMQ-driven applications.

ZeroMQ provides several messaging patterns, including request-reply, publish-subscribe, and pipeline, each suited for different use cases. Choosing the right pattern is the first step towards efficient message handling. Subsequently, understanding how to implement these patterns effectively in conjunction with ZeroMQ's advanced socket mechanisms ensures enhanced message throughput and reduced latency.

Polling and Asynchronous Message Processing: ZeroMQ supports non-blocking message reception through polling mechanisms. Polling allows an application to manage multiple sockets without resorting to multi-threading or complicated event-loop permutations. This is an efficient way to handle incoming messages, enabling the application to perform other tasks while waiting for inputs.

ZeroMQ implements a unified interface for polling using the zmq_poll function, which integrates natively with its socket abstraction. This method permits the simultaneous monitoring of multiple sockets, optimizing resource usage and improving the application's responsiveness.

```
#include <zmq.h>
#include <stdio.h>
#include <string.h>

int main() {
    void *context = zmq_ctx_new();
    void *receiver = zmq_socket(context, ZMQ_PULL);
    zmq_bind(receiver, "tcp://*:5557");

    zmq_pollitem_t items[] = { { receiver, 0, ZMQ_POLLIN, 0 } };

    while (1) {
        zmq_poll(items, 1, -1); // Wait indefinitely for input
        if (items[0].revents & ZMQ_POLLIN) {
            char buffer[256];
            zmq_recv(receiver, buffer, 255, 0);
```

```
        printf("Received message: %s\n", buffer);
    }
}
zmq_close(receiver);
zmq_ctx_destroy(context);
return 0;
}
```

Asynchronous processing of messages alongside polling further amplifies the efficiency of message handling. This model allows applications to continue processing or handling other tasks while waiting for message events, thus standardizing the non-blocking communication model ZeroMQ aims to achieve.

Minimizing Message Latency: While ZeroMQ abstracts many complexities inherent in network communication, reducing message latency remains a pertinent challenge. Latency can be minimized by appropriately configuring ZeroMQ sockets and application logic to reduce wait times and the overhead of message serialization/deserialization.

- **Batching Messages:** Sending messages in batches instead of individually can amortize the overhead of function calls and increase throughput efficiently. ZeroMQ provides mechanisms for sending multiple messages atomically using multiple-frame messages, effectively reducing the latency that accompanies frequent network transmissions.

- **Message Prioritization:** ZeroMQ's flexible message-passing architecture affords the implementation of message prioritization schemes to handle time-critical messages. By monitoring socket events and adjusting message handling logic accordingly, higher priority messages can be dispatched expeditiously, preserving low-latency for critical operations.

- **Corrective Routing Patterns:** In scenarios involving complex routing logic, like those employing zero-cost routing overlays, optimizing the network topology directly influences latency metrics. Minimizing hops and ensuring messages take efficient end-to-end paths are critical steps in latency management.

Concurrent Handling and Load Balancing: Load balancing

8.2. EFFICIENT MESSAGE HANDLING

across multiple sockets and threads using ZeroMQ patterns like REQ-REP or PUSH-PULL enables the application to scale horizontally and handle increasing loads more effectively.

- PUSH-PULL pattern: This pattern is valuable in distributing workloads among available processing units, fitting well with task distribution scenarios typical in parallel processing contexts.

```
void *context = zmq_ctx_new();
void *push = zmq_socket(context, ZMQ_PUSH);
zmq_bind(push, "tcp://*:5558");

// Worker thread creation and task delegation
for (int i = 0; i < NUM_WORKERS; ++i) {
    char* task_data = generate_task_data(i);
    zmq_send(push, task_data, strlen(task_data), 0);
}
```

The PUSH-PULL pattern not only streamlines message distribution but also facilitates natural load leveling—where workers can process tasks independently, thus scaling with application demands.

Fault Tolerance and Redundancy Mechanisms: To maintain robust message handling in the face of network and system faults, ZeroMQ supports various fault tolerance techniques. These include but are not limited to implementing redundancy through mirrored queues, ensuring messages are reliably delivered or persisted in the presence of failures.

Deploying architectures like broker-based solutions, where message routing and storage can be centrally managed, allows for the creation of fault-tolerant systems. Such systems often integrate seamlessly with ZeroMQ's library capabilities, offering duplicative routing paths and message persistence to safeguard against message loss due to node failures.

Message Serialization Formats: Utilizing efficient serialization formats is essential for ZeroMQ applications exchanging complex data structures. ZeroMQ does not confine the user to a specific format, thereby enabling the flexibility to adopt efficient serialization techniques like Google's Protocol Buffers or Apache Thrift.

Selecting an efficient serialization mechanism optimizes the encoding/decoding process, reducing serialization overheads, minimizing message sizes, and consequently reducing transmission latency.

Monitoring and Profiling Message Operations: Profiling and monitoring ZeroMQ's operations via its built-in surveillance facilities is invaluable. Tools such as ZMQ_CURVE enable the secure monitoring of ZeroMQ messages, detecting potential inefficiencies or bottlenecks in the message pipeline.

```
zmq_curve_keypair(public_key, secret_key);
zmq_setsockopt(socket, ZMQ_CURVE_SERVER, &curve_server_status, sizeof(
    curve_server_status));
```

By providing visibility into message transit operations, application developers can diagnose inefficiencies—preemptively adapting message processing logic to address identified concerns.

A nuanced, meticulous understanding of ZeroMQ's capabilities, combined with strategic implementation choices catered to specific application requirements, leads to proficient message handling. Efficient message handling in ZeroMQ involves continuous evaluation and adaptation of deployment environments—including process architecture, message patterns, and network conditions—to continuously improve application performance across diverse operational constraints.

8.3 Network Considerations for High Performance

Achieving high performance in distributed systems utilizing ZeroMQ involves careful consideration of network factors. Network considerations are pivotal in optimizing message throughput and minimizing latency, directly impacting the responsiveness and efficiency of ZeroMQ applications. This section explores the network-related elements essential for maximizing ZeroMQ performance, addressing aspects such as network topology, latency reduction techniques, bandwidth management, and load distribution strategies.

Understanding Network Topologies: Network design significantly influences system performance. ZeroMQ supports various topologies, and selecting the appropriate one according to the application's requirements enhances performance. Common topologies include:

8.3. NETWORK CONSIDERATIONS FOR HIGH PERFORMANCE

- **Point-to-Point:** Suitable for direct communication between two nodes, minimizing unnecessary routing and reducing latency.

- **Publish-Subscribe:** Effective for broadcasting messages to multiple subscribers but requires careful configuration to manage message overhead and ensure all subscribers receive updates efficiently.

- **Pipeline (PUSH-PULL):** Facilitates task distribution across various nodes, balancing load by distributing messages evenly among workers.

Consideration of network topology should also involve evaluating factors like the number of intermediary nodes, expected message rates, and processing capabilities of each node in the network.

Latency Minimization Strategies: Latency can significantly impact the overall performance of ZeroMQ applications. Minimizing latency requires a multi-faceted approach, incorporating both software and hardware optimizations.

1. **Direct Connections:** Establishing direct TCP connections between communicating nodes avoids the overheads associated with multiple hops, thereby reducing latency. Direct connections are crucial in latency-sensitive applications such as real-time trading systems or live monitoring solutions.

2. **Optimizing Data Serialization:** Choosing efficient serialization formats reduces the amount of data transmitted over the network. Efficient serialization not only speeds up data transmission but also reduces deserialization time on the receiving end. Formats like Protocol Buffers and Avro achieve significant performance improvements compared to heavier XML or JSON structures.

3. **Message Batching:** Batching messages together over the network reduces the impact of network latencies inherent in connection setups and acknowledgments. ZeroMQ can be configured to send multiple distinct messages in rapid succession as a

batch, thus enhancing throughput and reducing total time spent in transmission.

```
void batch_send_messages(void *socket, char *messages[], int count) {
    for (int i = 0; i < count; i++) {
        zmq_send(socket, messages[i], strlen(messages[i]), ZMQ_SNDMORE);
        if (i == count - 1) {
            zmq_send(socket, "", 0, 0); // End of batch
        }
    }
}
```

4. **Network Protocol Tuning:** Adapting network protocol settings, such as TCP_NODELAY, can help. Disabling Nagle's algorithm allows small packets to be sent immediately rather than waiting to accumulate enough data, which is beneficial in low-latency required environments.

```
int tcp_nodelay = 1;
zmq_setsockopt(socket, ZMQ_TCP_NODELAY, &tcp_nodelay, sizeof(
    tcp_nodelay));
```

5. **Quality of Service (QoS):** Implementing network-level Quality of Service policies ensures high-priority traffic is given precedence. This can be vital in environments requiring guaranteed low-latency, such as financial sectors or emergency response solutions.

Bandwidth Management: Managing bandwidth efficiently is crucial for avoiding network congestion, which can degrade performance. Effective strategies include:

- **Traffic Shaping:** Implementing traffic shaping techniques helps to regulate the data flow on the network, preventing bottlenecks. ZeroMQ's high water mark settings (ZMQ_SNDHWM and ZMQ_RCVHWM) serve as essential controls in shaping traffic by limiting the number of outstanding messages allowed in the network buffer.

```
int hwm = 100;
zmq_setsockopt(socket, ZMQ_SNDHWM, &hwm, sizeof(hwm));
zmq_setsockopt(socket, ZMQ_RCVHWM, &hwm, sizeof(hwm));
```

- **Compression:** Considering message compression (where applicable) reduces bandwidth usage, particularly helpful in scenarios dealing with large data volumes, though careful balance is needed to prevent increased CPU overhead and associated latency.

- **Network Load Balancers:** Deploying load balancers in front of ZeroMQ nodes spreads incoming connections across servers, ensuring no single server is overwhelmed. These can be hardware-based or implemented as a software layer within the network.

Network Interface and Hardware Considerations: The physical network hardware plays a foundational role in achieving high performance.

1. **Network Interface Cards (NICs):** Utilizing high-capacity NICs supporting increased port speed (e.g., 10GbE or 40GbE) provides more bandwidth, ensuring that network traffic does not become a bottleneck. NIC features such as Receive Side Scaling (RSS) or Receive Flow Steering (RFS) also aid in optimizing packet throughput by distributing incoming traffic across CPU cores.

2. **Offloading Features:** Leveraging NIC features like TCP offload engines potentially reduces CPU utilization, offloading networking tasks to hardware, allowing additional CPU cycles to focus on application logic.

3. **Direct Memory Access (DMA):** Maintaining standard practices like utilizing DMA can lessen CPU overhead, especially for applications requiring high throughput network operations. DMA facilitates faster data exchange between the NIC and system memory, bypassing CPU processing.

4. **Upgrading Infrastructure:** Regularly upgrading network infrastructure to cater to increased application demands is vital. Investing in modern routers, switches, and optimized connection paths ensures that high data rates can be maintained effectively without degradation.

Concurrency and Scalability Considerations: Network designs optimizing performance should consider concurrent message handling capabilities and how the setup scales:

- **Concurrency Handling:** Designing applications that can handle numerous simultaneous message streams efficiently enables higher throughput. This involves optimizing ZeroMQ's thread affinity and setting an adequate number of context I/O threads through zmq_ctx_set.

- **Architectural Scalability:** Building architectures that can scale elastically ensures applications adjust to fluctuating demands. Techniques like worker pool scaling, where the number of active workers adjusts dynamically with the load, exemplify efficient scalability management.

```
void *dispatcher = zmq_socket(context, ZMQ_PULL);
zmq_bind(dispatcher, "tcp://*:6000");

// Pool management logic
while (active_workers < MAX_WORKERS && load_detected()) {
    spawn_worker(dispatcher);
    active_workers++;
}
```

Effective network management encompassing these considerations addresses varied performance challenges, ensuring the deployment of robust ZeroMQ solutions. By implementing these strategies and continuously monitoring and upgrading the network infrastructure, applications achieve and maintain the high performance required for tackling demanding, distributed workloads.

8.4 Improving Scalability with ZeroMQ

In distributed computing, scalability is a critical attribute, allowing systems to accommodate increasing workloads seamlessly. ZeroMQ, a high-performance asynchronous messaging library, provides robust mechanisms to enhance the scalability of applications. By offering a range of flexible communication patterns and socket types, ZeroMQ

8.4. IMPROVING SCALABILITY WITH ZEROMQ

enables developers to design scalable distributed systems capable of adapting to varying operational demands.

Scalability in ZeroMQ is influenced by multiple factors including messaging patterns, architecture design, load distribution, and horizontal scaling capabilities. This section will explore strategies to enhance scalability in ZeroMQ applications, emphasizing pattern selection, architecture design, and the application of best practices.

Selecting the Right Messaging Pattern: The choice of messaging pattern in ZeroMQ projects greatly impacts the scalability of an application. ZeroMQ offers several patterns that cater to different use case scenarios:

- **Request-Reply (REQ/REP) Pattern:** This synchronous pattern is suitable for client-server architectures where a client sends a request, and a server processes and returns a reply. To enhance scalability, this pattern can be extended into an asynchronous variant using ROUTER-DEALER socket pairs, allowing multiple concurrent requests without blocking any client or server.

- **Publish-Subscribe (PUB/SUB) Pattern:** Ideal for message broadcasting scenarios, this pattern efficiently disseminates information to multiple subscribers simultaneously. The challenge of scalability lies in managing and distributing topic subscriptions effectively, which ZeroMQ addresses by providing automatic topic filtering at the subscriber side.

- **Pipeline (PUSH/PULL) Pattern:** Primarily utilized for task distribution, this pattern allows for load balancing across a pool of worker nodes. The PUSH socket distributes tasks evenly by dispatching messages to available PULL sockets, making it well-suited for parallel processing of independent tasks.

Designing Scalable Architectures: The architecture of a ZeroMQ-based system fundamentally influences its scalability. Leveraging ZeroMQ's ability to interconnect diverse socket types, developers can construct modular, flexible architectures. The following design strategies are critical for scalability:

- **Broker-Based Architectures:** A broker architecture serves as an intermediary message router between producers and consumers. This design centralizes message routing and load balancing, simplifying scalability as brokers can be scaled independently to manage increasing demands. The broker utilizes ZeroMQ's ROUTER-DEALER pattern to maintain asynchronous communication and high availability.

```
void *context = zmq_ctx_new();
void *frontend = zmq_socket(context, ZMQ_ROUTER);
void *backend = zmq_socket(context, ZMQ_DEALER);

zmq_bind(frontend, "tcp://*:5559");
zmq_bind(backend, "tcp://*:5560");

zmq_proxy(frontend, backend, NULL);

zmq_close(frontend);
zmq_close(backend);
zmq_ctx_term(context);
```

- **Service-Oriented Architectures (SOA):** In an SOA setup, hierarchical services encapsulate discrete functionalities, with ZeroMQ facilitating communication between services through its flexible socket types. This modular approach maximizes scalability, allowing services to be developed, deployed, and scaled independently, effectively handling workloads and maintaining system coherence.

Implementing Load Balancing and Fault Tolerance: Effective load balancing and implementing fault-tolerant mechanisms ensure a scalable environment under varying load conditions and potential failures.

- **Load Balancing:** ZeroMQ inherently supports workload distribution across multiple nodes through its PUSH/PULL pattern. Further, external load balancers can be employed to manage connections and distribute traffic efficiently, ensuring no single node becomes a bottleneck.

- **Redundancy:** Introducing redundancy is essential for fault tolerance, enabling the system to continue operation despite component failures. This can be achieved by deploying redundant brokers and leveraging ZeroMQ's features like ZMQ_ROUTER_-MANDATORY for reliable message delivery even during network partitions or node failures.

- **Heartbeat Mechanisms:** To maintain the consistency of connections and detect potential failures swiftly, implementing heartbeat signals between components ensures that nodes remain in sync. A loss of heartbeat signals triggers failovers or reconnection attempts, minimizing downtime and enhancing system resilience.

Optimizing Resource Utilization for Scalability: Resource optimization plays a pivotal role in maximizing the scalability potential of ZeroMQ applications.

- **Asynchronous I/O:** Employing asynchronous I/O operations minimizes blocking, enabling the application to handle multiple connections efficiently. ZeroMQ's non-blocking I/O capabilities allow developers to design applications that remain responsive under high concurrency.

- **Thread Pool Management:** Establishing an effective thread pool management strategy ensures that no single thread becomes a chokepoint. Developers configure the number of I/O threads in ZeroMQ's context according to the number of CPU cores available, facilitating efficient parallel processing.

```
void *context = zmq_ctx_new();
zmq_ctx_set(context, ZMQ_IO_THREADS, 4);
```

- **Message Queuing and Batch Processing:** Designing applications to queue and batch messages can reduce overhead and improve throughput. ZeroMQ enables message queuing through high-water mark settings, managing flow control efficiently.

Scaling Horizontally with ZeroMQ: Horizontal scaling involves adding more nodes to the network to handle additional load. ZeroMQ facilitates horizontal scaling seamlessly through flexible network topologies and socket types, enabling dynamic node addition without disrupting existing workloads.

- **Dynamic Node Addition:** In distributed systems employing ZeroMQ, new nodes can be seamlessly integrated into the existing network topology. ZeroMQ's socket abstraction handles the registration and de-registration of nodes efficiently, ensuring continuity of service.

- **Resilient Distributed Setups:** Employing technologies such as cloud orchestration tools and containerization solutions like Docker enables the dynamic scaling of ZeroMQ applications. These platforms provide frameworks for automating node management, resource allocation, and configuration, allowing ZeroMQ applications to scale efficiently in heterogeneous environments.

Monitoring and Adjustments for Scalability: Continuously monitoring system performance aids in identifying bottlenecks and areas for improvement, ensuring sustainable scalability.

- **Metrics Collection and Analysis:** Implementing monitoring solutions that capture system metrics, such as message traffic, latency, and resource utilization, provides invaluable insights into system performance. These insights guide parameter adjustments and structural redesigns to accommodate evolving demands.

- **Profiling and Benchmarking:** Regular profiling and benchmarking of ZeroMQ applications reveal performance barriers, suggesting potential optimization areas. Adapting configurations and optimizing application logic based on insightful analytics ensures the system remains optimized for future scalability.

Scalability in ZeroMQ can be realized through careful pattern selection, effective architecture design, and strategic resource optimization. By focusing on these elements and continuously monitoring system performance, developers can build scalable, high-throughput ZeroMQ applications capable of adapting to diverse operational requirements.

8.5 Monitoring and Profiling ZeroMQ Applications

Effective monitoring and profiling are pivotal in maintaining optimal performance in ZeroMQ applications. These processes allow developers to track application behavior, diagnose potential bottlenecks, and ensure system reliability. This section delves into the methodologies and tools available for monitoring and profiling ZeroMQ applications, covering metrics collection, performance analysis, and profiling techniques.

Monitoring provides insights into the health and performance of an application. It involves continuous observation of the application's operational parameters to capture vital metrics such as message throughput, latency, error rates, and resource utilization. In contrast, profiling offers a granular analysis of application performance, aiming to identify inefficiencies and optimize resource usage.

Metrics Collection and Monitoring Systems: Capturing accurate and timely metrics is fundamental for effective monitoring. ZeroMQ, being a socket-driven messaging library, requires monitoring systems that can track both network and application-level metrics.

- **Network Metrics:** Monitoring network metrics such as bandwidth utilization, latency, and packet loss informs developers about the network condition. Tools like wireshark and nload provide protocol analysis and bandwidth tracking to diagnose network-related performance issues.

- **Application Metrics:** At the application level, measuring the number of messages sent/received, message drops, and socket creation/destruction offers insights into the application's workload and efficiency. ZeroMQ provides the zmq_socket_monitor API to track these activities. By attaching a monitor listening socket, developers receive notifications about important socket events.

```
void *context = zmq_ctx_new();
void *socket = zmq_socket(context, ZMQ_DEALER);

zmq_connect(socket, "tcp://example.com:5555");
```

```
int rc = zmq_socket_monitor(socket, "inproc://monitor",
    ZMQ_EVENT_ALL);
assert(rc == 0);

void *monitor = zmq_socket(context, ZMQ_PAIR);
zmq_connect(monitor, "inproc://monitor");

zmq_msg_t msg;
while (1) {
    zmq_msg_init(&msg);
    zmq_msg_recv(&msg, monitor, 0);
    // Handle monitoring event here
    zmq_msg_close(&msg);
}

zmq_close(socket);
zmq_close(monitor);
zmq_ctx_destroy(context);
```

- **Resource Utilization Metrics:** Monitoring CPU, memory, and disk usage is essential in identifying inefficient resource utilization which may affect application performance. System monitoring tools such as Prometheus, Grafana, or Nagios provide comprehensive dashboards for tracking these metrics, facilitating proactive resource management.

Advanced Monitoring Techniques: Beyond basic metric collection, advanced monitoring techniques enhance the robustness of ZeroMQ application observation.

- **Distributed Tracing:** Implementing distributed tracing tracks message paths across multiple nodes in a system, identifying latency sources and failures in end-to-end communication. Tracing tools like Jaeger or OpenTelemetry integrate seamlessly with ZeroMQ, providing insightful overlays of message flows.

- **Alerting Systems:** Incorporating real-time alerting frameworks helps to ensure prompt responses to performance anomalies. Configuring alert thresholds on critical metrics allows teams to address issues before they escalate. Alerts can be dispatched via email, SMS, or centralized logging services, improving response efficiency.

Profiling ZeroMQ Applications: Profiling delves into the depths

8.5. MONITORING AND PROFILING ZEROMQ APPLICATIONS

of the application to uncover inefficiencies. It involves analyzing runtime performance to identify hotspots, memory leaks, and CPU-bound operations.

- **CPU Profiling:** Detecting CPU bottlenecks suggests optimization areas where computation may be offloaded or parallelized. Tools like gprof or modern profilers such as perf provide detailed call graph analysis, informing developers about function call frequencies and duration.

- **Memory Profiling:** Memory management in ZeroMQ is automatic, yet profiling tools such as valgrind and heaptrack help identify leaks and over-usage. Efficient memory utilization is critical, particularly in high-throughput scenarios.

```
valgrind --leak-check=full --track-origins=yes --show-leak-kinds=all ./
         my_zeromq_application
```

- **I/O Profiling:** ZeroMQ's performance is closely tied to I/O operations. Profiling tools like strace provide insights into system calls, aiding developers in identifying disk or network I/O bottlenecks and prompting the optimization of data throughput operations.

Performance Tuning Based on Profiling Insights: The insights obtained from profiling are vital for performance tuning and optimization. They indicate where and how the application's efficiency can be enhanced.

- **Reducing Hotspot Impact:** Profiling uncovers areas in code (hotspots) that consume excessive CPU time. Optimization might involve recalibrating computation or parallelizing tasks using ZeroMQ's asynchronous capabilities.

- **Optimizing Serialization:** Profiling uncovers serialization inefficiencies which can be mitigated by switching to more performant data formats or optimizing serialization strategies.

- **Network Optimizations:** Network transport adjustments guided by profiling insights can involve adopting faster transport protocols (like switching from TCP to IPC where feasible) or reducing latency via direct connections.

Integrating Best Practices for Monitoring and Profiling: Combining tooling with best practices completes comprehensive performance management. This integration includes:

- **Automated CI/CD Pipelines:** Incorporating monitoring and profiling routines into continuous integration/continuous deployment (CI/CD) pipelines automates performance assessments, ensuring applications remain performant across iterations. ZeroMQ's automated test utilities can play a key role in these pipelines.

- **Regular Audits and Reviews:** Establishing systematic reviews of profiling data reinforces a culture of continual improvement within the development lifecycle. These reviews allow teams to adapt quickly to evolving performance challenges.

- **Documentation and Knowledge Sharing:** Detailed records of monitoring and profiling configurations along with resultant insights empower entire teams to remain informed about current performance states and anticipate future challenges.

Monitoring and profiling ZeroMQ applications are integral for maintaining high performance and reliability. Systematic observation, coupled with strategic profiling, ensures that applications meet operational demands effectively. Employing these techniques allows developers to preemptively identify and resolve performance bottlenecks, guaranteeing robust and scalable ZeroMQ-based solutions.

8.6 Best Practices for Robust ZeroMQ Solutions

Developing robust and reliable ZeroMQ solutions requires adherence to best practices that optimize performance, enhance reliability, and ensure maintainability. ZeroMQ, a robust messaging library used for

8.6. BEST PRACTICES FOR ROBUST ZEROMQ SOLUTIONS

building distributed applications, offers a variety of configuration options and patterns. Implementing best practices ensures that systems are both scalable and resilient to changing operational demands.

This section explores several best practices crucial for crafting robust ZeroMQ solutions, focusing on architectural design, error handling, performance optimization, and maintainability.

Architectural Design Principles: The architecture of a ZeroMQ application determines its ability to scale and handle failures efficiently.

- **Modular Architecture:** Developing applications with a modular design allows individual components to be developed, tested, and deployed independently. This reduces complexity and facilitates targeted performance enhancements.

- **Layered Architecture:** Incorporating a layered architecture segregates communication, processing, and storage concerns. Such separation simplifies component upgrades and optimizes inter-component communication.

- **Microservices Orientation:** Employing microservices for ZeroMQ applications encourages scalability and rapid deployment. ZeroMQ's inherent flexibility supports independently deployable services, enabling applications to handle diverse operational loads effectively.

Effective Error Handling Mechanisms: Implementing robust error handling improves an application's resilience against runtime failures.

- **Graceful Degradation:** Design systems to degrade gracefully under stress. Implement fallback methods when primary operations fail, ensuring partial service availability despite component failures.

- **Logging and Monitoring:** Comprehensive logging provides insights into system operations and uncovers error sources. Integrating structured logging with log aggregation tools (e.g., ELK stack) allows teams to monitor application health effectively.

CHAPTER 8. PERFORMANCE TUNING AND BEST PRACTICES

```c
#include <stdio.h>
#include <zmq.h>

void log_error(const char *error_message) {
    fprintf(stderr, "Error: %s\n", error_message);
}

int main() {
    void *context = zmq_ctx_new();
    void *socket = zmq_socket(context, ZMQ_REQ);

    if (zmq_connect(socket, "tcp://example.com:5555") != 0) {
        log_error("Failed to connect to server");
    }

    zmq_close(socket);
    zmq_ctx_destroy(context);
    return 0;
}
```

- **Exception Handling:** Ensure proper exception handling within application logic to manage anticipated and unexpected conditions, preventing system crashes.

Security Practices: Ensuring security in ZeroMQ applications is crucial for protecting data integrity and preventing unauthorized access.

- **Message Encryption:** Use ZeroMQ's built-in CURVE encryption mechanism to secure data transmission. By requiring authentication at the socket level, CURVE helps prevent interception and impersonation attacks.

  ```
  zmq_setsockopt(socket, ZMQ_CURVE_SERVER, &curve_enabled, sizeof(
      curve_enabled));
  zmq_setsockopt(socket, ZMQ_CURVE_PUBLICKEY, public_key, 40);
  zmq_setsockopt(socket, ZMQ_CURVE_SECRETKEY, secret_key, 40);
  zmq_setsockopt(socket, ZMQ_CURVE_SERVERKEY, client_public_key, 40);
  ```

- **Access Control:** Implement strong access control measures to restrict network access to trusted entities. Network-level controls—like firewalls and VPNs—safeguard communication channels against unauthorized intrusions.

- **Regular Security Audits:** Conduct periodic security audits to detect vulnerabilities and ensure compliance with industry standards. This involves reviewing encryption keys, secure communication protocols, and access controls.

8.6. BEST PRACTICES FOR ROBUST ZEROMQ SOLUTIONS

Performance Optimization Techniques: Performance tuning enhances the efficiency of ZeroMQ applications, reducing overhead and improving response times.

- **Efficient Socket Management:** Reuse sockets where possible to minimize the overhead associated with socket initialization and teardown. Implement connection pooling for frequently used services.

- **Batch Processing for High Throughput:** Implement message batching strategies to reduce the round-trip time required for each message. Batch processing improves throughput by minimizing transmission overhead.

```
void send_batch(void *socket, char *batch[], int count) {
    for (int i = 0; i < count; ++i) {
        zmq_send(socket, batch[i], strlen(batch[i]), (i < count - 1) ?
            ZMQ_SNDMORE : 0);
    }
}
```

- **Latency Reduction Techniques:** Optimize data serialization and transport routing to lower latency. Use appropriate network protocols and topologies to reduce the number of hops between communicating entities.

- **Resource Management:** Monitor and optimize resource utilization, ensuring that CPU, memory, and network resources are used efficiently. Employ monitoring tools to detect potential bottlenecks and address them proactively.

Adopting Continuous Integration and Deployment (CI/CD): Leveraging CI/CD pipelines facilitates rapid iteration and deployment, ensuring that ZeroMQ applications are continuously improved.

- **Automated Testing:** Incorporate automated testing frameworks within the CI pipeline to validate new changes and maintain system integrity. Testing across different environments reduces the likelihood of runtime failures.

- **Continuous Feedback Loop:** Maintain a continuous feedback loop to enhance responsiveness to system changes and performance issues. Integrate monitoring and alerts into CI/CD pipelines to provide timely insights into system health.

- **Version Control and Rollbacks:** Implement comprehensive version control and rollback mechanisms to mitigate issues arising from faulty deployments. Utilizing Git-based solutions (e.g., GitHub Actions) for orchestration simplifies version management.

Ensuring Maintainability and Flexibility: Maintainability and flexibility in ZeroMQ solutions allow systems to adapt to evolving requirements with minimal disruption.

- **Documentation and Standards:** Maintain thorough and up-to-date documentation. Adopt standardized coding practices to ensure consistency and clarity across development teams.

- **Decoupled Components:** Design systems with loosely coupled components to simplify maintainability. Decoupling enhances flexibility, allowing components to be modified, replaced, or scaled independently.

- **Scalability Planning:** Plan for scalability at early stages of development, enabling systems to scale seamlessly in response to increased demand. Anticipate future growth to minimize architectural redesigns.

Incorporating these best practices into ZeroMQ solutions ensures they perform efficiently and remain resilient against operational challenges. By following these guidelines, developers can build foolproof systems that adhere to optimal standards of reliability, scalability, and maintainability.

Chapter 9

ZeroMQ with Distributed Systems

ZeroMQ plays a critical role in enhancing communication within distributed systems, offering tools to create flexible and efficient messaging architectures. Its capabilities allow for the implementation of fault-tolerant and real-time data processing solutions, addressing the challenges of synchronization and coordination across distributed components. This chapter explores ZeroMQ's application in multicloud and hybrid environments, ensuring seamless data flows and interoperability. By examining real-world case studies, it provides insights into successfully deploying ZeroMQ within large-scale systems, highlighting its effectiveness in facilitating reliable and scalable distributed communication.

9.1 Role of ZeroMQ in Distributed Architectures

ZeroMQ, known for its simplicity and efficiency, becomes an invaluable asset in constructing distributed architectures. In distributed systems, communication is a fundamental component that determines scalability, fault tolerance, and overall reliability. ZeroMQ, as a high-performance asynchronous messaging library, equips developers with the tools necessary to meet these requirements, providing a low-level messaging API that hides complexities while maintaining robust functionality.

ZeroMQ operates as a concurrency framework, freeing developers from dealing with threading and serialization intricacies. It serves as an abstraction layer over raw network sockets, offering a socket-like API. This section explores how ZeroMQ meets the demands of distributed architectures, examining its core messaging patterns, efficiency in resource utilization, and adaptability within various network topologies.

At its core, ZeroMQ is built around messaging patterns, a conceptual framework that underpins its effectiveness. The most common patterns include Request-Reply, Publish-Subscribe, Push-Pull, and Exclusive Pair. These patterns provide specific messaging behavior desired in different architectures, making ZeroMQ a versatile choice for varied use cases.

The Request-Reply pattern is fundamental for client-server architectures, useful in scenarios where synchronous communication is critical. It operates with two types of sockets: a REQ (request) socket and a REP (reply) socket. The sequence of events typically involves the client sending a request message and waiting for a response from the server. The ability to automatically retry messages in case of failure makes this pattern suitable for reliable communication. Its design supports multiple concurrent clients connected to a central server, as depicted in the following example:

```
import zmq

# Server Setup
context = zmq.Context()
socket = context.socket(zmq.REP)
socket.bind("tcp://*:5555")

while True:
    message = socket.recv()
    print(f"Received request: {message}")
    socket.send(b"World")

# Client Setup
context = zmq.Context()
```

9.1. ROLE OF ZEROMQ IN DISTRIBUTED ARCHITECTURES

```
socket = context.socket(zmq.REQ)
socket.connect("tcp://localhost:5555")

for request in range(10):
    print(f"Sending request {request} ...")
    socket.send(b"Hello")
    message = socket.recv()
    print(f"Received reply {request}: {message}")
```

The Publish-Subscribe pattern enables multicast messaging, allowing messages to be filtered and broadcasted to multiple clients. It effectively decouples publishers and subscribers, allowing a dynamic ecosystem where new subscribers can join without disrupting existing ones. The PUB socket broadcasts messages to all connected SUB sockets, which can subscribe to specific topics, filtering out unwanted data. This pattern is illustrated below:

```
import zmq

# Publisher Setup
context = zmq.Context()
socket = context.socket(zmq.PUB)
socket.bind("tcp://*:5556")

while True:
    topic = "TopicA"
    message = "Data for A"
    socket.send_string(f"{topic} {message}")

# Subscriber Setup
context = zmq.Context()
socket = context.socket(zmq.SUB)

# Connect and subscribe to TopicA
socket.connect("tcp://localhost:5556")
socket.setsockopt_string(zmq.SUBSCRIBE, "TopicA")

while True:
    message = socket.recv_string()
    print(f"Received: {message}")
```

In distributed architectures where work must be executed concurrently across various nodes, the Push-Pull pattern shines. The PUSH socket distributes work among several workers implementing the PULL socket. By managing backpressure, ZeroMQ automatically distributes workload based on the availability and capability of workers, ensuring an efficient processing pipeline. This pattern facilitates scalability and parallel processing.

```
import zmq
```

```python
# Ventilator (PUSH)
context = zmq.Context()
sender = context.socket(zmq.PUSH)
sender.bind("tcp://*:5557")

for num in range(100):
    sender.send_string(str(num))

# Worker (PULL)
context = zmq.Context()
receiver = context.socket(zmq.PULL)
receiver.connect("tcp://localhost:5557")

while True:
    message = receiver.recv_string()
    print(f"Processed: {message}")
```

Lastly, the Exclusive Pair pattern is used for point-to-point communication between two peers within a local setup. It is characterized by bidirectional communication between a PAIR of sockets, where each socket can send or receive messages. Whereas this pattern's practical applications in distributed environments are limited due to its tight coupling, it is nonetheless useful for establishing direct and exclusive channels.

ZeroMQ's adaptability and high-level abstraction are best appreciated when comparing resource utilization and performance metrics. Its internal polling mechanism and asynchrony introduce mechanisms that limit blocking calls, reducing idle times and optimizing for high throughput. The following C++ example using ZeroMQ's Poller mechanism demonstrates its non-blocking capabilities:

```cpp
#include <zmq.hpp>
#include <iostream>

int main() {
    zmq::context_t context{1};
    zmq::socket_t socket{context, zmq::socket_type::req};
    socket.connect("tcp://localhost:5555");

    zmq::pollitem_t item{socket.handle(), 0, ZMQ_POLLIN, 0};

    for (int request_num = 0; request_num < 10; ++request_num) {
        socket.send(zmq::buffer("Hello"), zmq::send_flags::none);

        zmq::poll(&item, 1, std::chrono::seconds{2});

        if (item.revents & ZMQ_POLLIN) {
            zmq::message_t reply{};
            socket.recv(reply, zmq::recv_flags::none);
```

```
            std::cout << "Received " << reply.to_string() << std::endl;
        }
        else {
            std::cout << "No response from server" << std::endl;
        }
    }
}
```

Beyond the intrinsic features inherent in its messaging patterns, ZeroMQ excels by operating effectively within diverse network topologies. Nodes in distributed systems may be situated across varied geographies, each operating under different constraints imposed by network latencies, bandwidth, and security policies. ZeroMQ's ability to operate over multiple transport layers — TCP, IPC, INPROC, and more — ensures it meets specific requirements.

In a network where latency plays a critical role, ZeroMQ's IPC (Inter-process Communication) and INPROC (Inter-thread Communication) protocols offer reduced overhead by avoiding the network stack. These are instrumental in intra-node communications, maximizing data transmission rates and minimizing latency.

The argument for ZeroMQ is not without nuances. For instance, it exhibits middleware characteristics, yet it does not conform to traditional message broker roles, since ZeroMQ lacks built-in message queue persistence. Routers or dedicated brokers (like in an AMQP ecosystem) often extend its capabilities, and developers may need to handle message persistence manually, particularly in systems with strict data integrity requirements.

Moreover, ZeroMQ's focus on performance might impose limitations on complex transactional systems where message delivery guarantees are mandated. However, when trade-offs between speed and reliability are assessed, ZeroMQ is ideally suited for systems requiring rapid message exchange with minimal supervision.

ZeroMQ thrives in microservices architectures, IoT frameworks, real-time analytics, and other domains requiring scalable and flexible messaging infrastructure. Its dynamic socket creation and connection abstraction simplify microservices-based design, allowing for seamless integration and deployment across cloud services. The following example demonstrates microservice communication over a multi-node ZeroMQ network:

```python
from zmq import Context, ROUTER, DEALER

# Router/Dealer Pattern to simulate microservice interactions
context = Context()

# Frontend Router
frontend = context.socket(ROUTER)
frontend.bind("tcp://*:5559")

# Backend Dealer (worker)
backend = context.socket(DEALER)
backend.bind("tcp://*:5560")

while True:
    # Relay messages between the sockets
    zmq.proxy(frontend, backend)
```

The example above demonstrates how integration of ZeroMQ in distributed systems can lead to simplified networking logic amongst components, handling all protocol-specific handshakes and message distributions effectively.

ZeroMQ offers strategic advantages in distributed architectures by empowering developers with tools to implement effective messaging solutions. Its low overhead, adaptability to different network transports, and support for asynchronous communication make it a compelling choice for scalable, efficient, and robust infrastructures. Yet, understanding its optimal usage, patterns, and possible trade-offs is vital to successfully leverage its full potential in achieving truly distributed, resilient, and high-performance systems.

9.2 Implementing Fault Tolerance with ZeroMQ

Fault tolerance is a fundamental requirement in distributed systems, essential for maintaining system reliability and availability even in the face of component failures. In this context, ZeroMQ offers various features and patterns that can be utilized to build robust systems capable of handling faults effectively. This section explores mechanisms for achieving fault tolerance using ZeroMQ's capabilities, examining patterns, architectural strategies, and practical coding examples.

9.2. IMPLEMENTING FAULT TOLERANCE WITH ZEROMQ

Fault tolerance in distributed systems often involves detecting errors, maintaining system state, and ensuring continuity of operations. ZeroMQ contributes to this through its versatile messaging patterns and support for resilient topologies. Below are the key strategies that leverage ZeroMQ for implementing fault-tolerant systems:

Resilient Communication Patterns

Certain built-in messaging patterns in ZeroMQ, such as Request-Reply, are designed to handle network uncertainties. A common strategy includes implementing retry logic and load balancing over multiple sockets or across multiple nodes. For example, in the Request-Reply pattern, the client can be programmed to retry a request multiple times until a response is received, thus providing basic fault tolerance to transient network failures or unresponsive servers.

```
import zmq
import time

context = zmq.Context()

# Client with retry logic
socket = context.socket(zmq.REQ)
socket.connect("tcp://localhost:5555")

for request in range(10):
    try:
        socket.send(b"Hello")
        message = socket.recv(flags=zmq.NOBLOCK)
        print(f"Received reply {request}: {message}")
    except zmq.Again:
        print("No response from server, retrying...")
        time.sleep(1)
        socket.send(b"Hello")
        message = socket.recv()
```

The code snippet above demonstrates a simple retry mechanism using a non-blocking socket operation for fault detection. This logic identifies failed requests and re-attempts communication.

Dealer-Router Pattern for Load Balancing

The Dealer-Router pattern provided by ZeroMQ is inherently flexible and can be extended to provide a load-balanced architecture. It includes an intermediary component (router) that distributes client requests to a pool of worker nodes (dealers). This inherently balances loads based on the availability of worker nodes and contributes to fault tolerance as workloads are redistributed from failing nodes to operational ones.

```
import zmq

context = zmq.Context()

# Front-End Router
frontend = context.socket(zmq.ROUTER)
frontend.bind("tcp://*:5559")

# Back-End Dealer
backend = context.socket(zmq.DEALER)
backend.bind("tcp://*:5560")

zmq.proxy(frontend, backend)
```

In the above code, the 'zmq.proxy' mechanism relays messages between the front-end (client-facing) and back-end (worker-facing) sockets seamlessly, supporting runtime additions and removals of worker nodes without affecting system performance.

Heartbeat and Monitoring

Fault detection is augmented by heartbeats, enabling systems to monitor the activity and responsiveness of nodes. This provides a systematic solution to identify and isolate failing nodes swiftly. ZeroMQ doesn't provide a built-in heartbeat mechanism, but it can be implemented using the 'PUB-SUB' or 'PING-PONG' model for notifying the system about node statuses.

```
import zmq
import time

context = zmq.Context()

# Heartbeat (PING server)
heartbeat_pub = context.socket(zmq.PUB)
heartbeat_pub.bind("tcp://*:5557")

while True:
    heartbeat_pub.send_string("PING")
    time.sleep(1)
```

```
import zmq

context = zmq.Context()

# Heartbeat (PONG client)
heartbeat_sub = context.socket(zmq.SUB)
heartbeat_sub.connect("tcp://localhost:5557")
heartbeat_sub.setsockopt_string(zmq.SUBSCRIBE, "")
```

9.2. IMPLEMENTING FAULT TOLERANCE WITH ZEROMQ

```
while True:
    try:
        message = heartbeat_sub.recv(flags=zmq.NOBLOCK)
        print(f"Received: {message}")
    except zmq.Again:
        print("No heartbeat received")
```

The above setup illustrates a simple heartbeat mechanism ensuring that nodes are checked periodically for presence and responsiveness.

Persistent Queues and Data Durability

ZeroMQ's default in-memory messaging can be limiting for systems where message persistence and durability are essential. However, ZeroMQ can be integrated with persistent storage layers, such as databases or file systems, to log messages and states. This creates robust systems where data integrity is maintained despite failures.

Replication and Redundancy

Achieving fault tolerance often necessitates the inclusion of replication strategies. This involves running multiple instances of a service to ensure that even if one instance fails, another can seamlessly take over. ZeroMQ assists in developing active-active configurations where multiple service instances run concurrently, distributing workloads and ensuring high availability.

For instance, in a distributed environment, ZeroMQ can be paired with a distributor that manages replicated service instances, redirecting traffic from unresponsive instances to active ones. This requires careful design and implementation, yet it is a proven strategy for fault tolerance.

Multi-Node Synchronization

The synchronization pattern in distributed systems often involves updating and maintaining consistency across different nodes in real-time. ZeroMQ's Pub-Sub model facilitates synchronization communication streams to ensure state consistency. For example, consider a distributed system where configuration changes should propagate to all nodes immediately. A central publisher node broadcasts state changes to all subscribers, thus ensuring synchronization.

```
import zmq

context = zmq.Context()
```

```
# Configuration publisher
config_pub = context.socket(zmq.PUB)
config_pub.bind("tcp://*:5588")

# Send configuration update
config_update = { 'version': 'v1.0', 'setting': 'enabled' }
config_pub.send_json(config_update)
```

```
import zmq

context = zmq.Context()
# Configuration subscriber
config_sub = context.socket(zmq.SUB)
config_sub.connect("tcp://localhost:5588")
config_sub.setsockopt_string(zmq.SUBSCRIBE, "")

while True:
    config_update = config_sub.recv_json()
    print(f"Config updated: {config_update}")
```

In this setup, the publisher broadcasts configuration updates while subscribers react by reconfiguring themselves accordingly, achieving synchrony across distributed nodes.

Architectural Considerations

Beyond technical patterns and code implementations, several architectural considerations are pivotal in implementing fault tolerance with ZeroMQ.

- **Decentralization**: Where possible, designing from a decentralized perspective eliminates single points of failure. Leveraging ZeroMQ's capabilities requires creating autonomous services communicating peer-to-peer, reducing centralized bottlenecks.

- **Granularity of Services**: Developing microservices ensures independent scalability and fault isolation. When a fault occurs, the architecture circumvents it without affecting the whole system.

- **Statelessness**: Stateless components resist faults better, allowing re-instantiation without complex state management. ZeroMQ communicates state changes effectively when systems make transitions between states.

- **Isolation of Failures**: Isolating failures mitigates the impact on the broader architecture. Utilizing circuit-breaker patterns in ZeroMQ, managing failed nodes without propagating faults is feasible.

Programming Considerations

While working with ZeroMQ in a fault-tolerant context, the following programming considerations enhance effectiveness:

- **Idempotency**: Ensure operations are idempotent, allowing repeated attempts without adverse effects.
- **Timeouts**: Implementing appropriate timeouts for receiving messages prevents indefinite waits.
- **Error Handling**: Effective error handling logic helps distinguish between transient and persistent errors.
- **Failover Mechanisms**: Design fallback routines where critical operations can switch to backup routes or alternative protocols.

Implementing fault tolerance with ZeroMQ involves considering both its architectural patterns and practical programming techniques. Given its flexible nature, ZeroMQ acts as both the conduit for resilient network designs and the toolkit for building systems robust against multiple failure scenarios. Entailing meticulous design and strategic deployment, ZeroMQ empowers developers to craft systems capable of maintaining operational stability amidst inevitable failures in distributed environments.

9.3 ZeroMQ for Real-time Data Pipelines

In modern computing, real-time data pipelines play a pivotal role in systems that require continuous ingestion, processing, and delivery of data with minimal latency. ZeroMQ, with its high throughput and efficient message handling capabilities, provides a powerful framework for building such pipelines in distributed systems. This section examines the strategies and methodologies for utilizing ZeroMQ to construct robust real-time data pipelines, emphasizing its patterns, integration potential, and practical examples.

A real-time data pipeline involves several stages, typically including data ingestion, transformation, and delivery. ZeroMQ facilitates each of these stages through its asynchronous and non-blocking I/O features, enabling seamless data flow across distributed nodes. By leveraging ZeroMQ, developers can create scalable pipelines capable of handling high-velocity data streams, essential for applications like financial trading systems, monitoring solutions, and data analytics platforms.

Data Ingestion

Ingesting data in real-time is the first step of a data pipeline. Typically, data originates from various sources, ranging from sensors and log files to APIs. ZeroMQ's Publish-Subscribe pattern is especially suited for data ingestion, allowing multiple data sources to publish data simultaneously to the pipeline, which can be dynamically scaled to accommodate an increasing number of publishers and subscribers.

```
import zmq

context = zmq.Context()

# Publisher for Data Ingestion
data_source = context.socket(zmq.PUB)
data_source.bind("tcp://*:5558")

# Send a data point
while True:
    topic = "data_source"
    data_point = "sensor_reading:100"
    data_source.send_string(f"{topic} {data_point}")
```

In the example above, the data source continuously sends data points that subscribers, part of the pipeline, ingest in real time. Subscribers can apply filtering based on topics to focus on relevant data streams.

Data Transformation

After ingestion, data must be transformed to a format suitable for analysis or storage. This stage often involves enrichment, aggregation, or windowed computations. ZeroMQ's Push-Pull pattern offers an optimal solution for distributing transformation tasks across several worker nodes, capable of scaling horizontally and processing data in

9.3. ZEROMQ FOR REAL-TIME DATA PIPELINES

parallel to minimize latency.

```
import zmq

# Context and Socket setup for Worker (Pull)
context = zmq.Context()
receiver = context.socket(zmq.PULL)
receiver.connect("tcp://localhost:5558")

# Push transformed data to next stage
sender = context.socket(zmq.PUSH)
sender.connect("tcp://localhost:5560")

# Receive and transform data
while True:
    raw_data = receiver.recv_string()
    transformed_data = raw_data.upper() # Example transformation
    sender.send_string(transformed_data)
```

This code demonstrates a transformation node receiving data, applying a transformation, and forwarding the results. The flexibility of ZeroMQ allows developers to implement complex transformation operations as needed.

Next to transformation, a crucial aspect involves ensuring data quality, which necessitates validation and filtration mechanisms that can be implemented within these worker nodes. Workers can validate data to remove duplicates, correct anomalies, and enforce schema consistency.

Data Delivery and Aggregation

Data delivery forms the final stage, where transformed data is sent to storage systems, dashboards, or other integrative systems for persistence and visualization. In real-time data pipelines, low-latency communication to external systems is crucial. ZeroMQ's Dealer-Router pattern enhances robustness in such scenarios, as demonstrated below:

```
import zmq

context = zmq.Context()

# Router for data aggregation
aggregator = context.socket(zmq.ROUTER)
aggregator.bind("tcp://*:5560")

# Dealer nodes processing aggregated data
dealer = context.socket(zmq.DEALER)
dealer.bind("tcp://*:5561")

while True:
```

```
# Relay transformed data to persistent storage or visualization tools
zmq.proxy(aggregator, dealer)
```

In this example, an aggregator node collects data from various processing units before dispatching it using ZeroMQ's internal proxy functionality to suitable endpoints for further action.

Integration with External Systems

A real-time data pipeline must often interact with external systems for tasks such as persisting data into databases or invoking external APIs for further processing. ZeroMQ supports integration with systems like Kafka, Hadoop, or SQL databases by bridging the communication gap.

For instance, consider a scenario where the pipeline involves a Kafka broker receiving data from a ZeroMQ endpoint. You can use connectors that consume the output of a ZeroMQ endpoint and produce it to a Kafka topic. Python provides libraries like confluent_kafka for such integrations.

```
from confluent_kafka import Producer

# Setup Producer for Kafka
conf = {'bootstrap.servers': "server1"}
producer = Producer(**conf)

# Callback
def delivery_report(err, msg):
    if err is not None:
        print(f"Delivery failed for {msg.key()}: {err}")
    else:
        print(f"Message delivered to {msg.topic()} [{msg.partition()}]")

# Send transformed data to Kafka
transformed_data = "transformed_message"
producer.produce('my_topic', transformed_data, callback=delivery_report)
producer.flush()
```

This setup extracts messages from ZeroMQ and forwards them to Kafka for downstream processing by connecting consumed messages from the ZeroMQ pipeline to Kafka's highly reliable storage system.

Scaling the Pipeline

Scalability is an inherent requirement of real-time data pipelines, where ZeroMQ's architecture allows easy expansion of nodes. New nodes can be dynamically added to accommodate increased workloads without downtime or reconfiguration of existing components.

9.3. ZEROMQ FOR REAL-TIME DATA PIPELINES

Integration with orchestration tools like Docker Swarm or Kubernetes further augments scalability, ensuring seamless deployment and management of ZeroMQ nodes.

A typical deployment involves containerizing each unit (Pub, Sub, Transform, etc.). Orchestrators manage node redundancy and auto-scaling based on metrics or defined policies, ensuring that the pipeline is continuously optimized for performance.

Monitoring and Maintenance

Comprehensive monitoring is vital to ensure performance and identify bottlenecks within the pipeline. ZeroMQ does not directly provide monitoring tools, but it can be paired with tools such as Prometheus or Grafana which monitor messages via intermediaries or custom-built exporters.

Maintenance further involves ensuring messages are handled idempotently, facilitating recomputation or resending without errors impacting data consistency. Furthermore, implementing adaptive timeouts on message reception helps prevent conditions where sluggish components block the pipeline.

Security Considerations

Data pipelines inherently process sensitive information, necessitating secure communication channels. ZeroMQ supports encryption via CurveZMQ, securing data transit through authentication and encryption of full network paths.

```
import zmq.auth
from zmq.auth.thread import ThreadAuthenticator

context = zmq.Context.instance()

# Start an authenticator
auth = ThreadAuthenticator(context)
auth.start()
auth.allow('127.0.0.1')
auth.configure_curve(domain='*', location=zmq.auth.CURVE_ALLOW_ANY)

# CurveZMQ Security setup
server = context.socket(zmq.ROUTER)
server_secret_file = 'server.key_secret'
server.curve_secretkey, server.curve_publickey = zmq.auth.load_certificate(
    server_secret_file)
server.curve_server = True
server.bind('tcp://*:5562')
```

The above code sets up a secure server communication path using CurveZMQ, crucial for ensuring data integrity and confidentiality during transmission.

Efficient security management involves continuously updating security keys and closely monitoring inexplicable connection attempts through network intrusion detection systems.

ZeroMQ emerges as a formidable player in constructing real-time data pipelines, offering performance-efficacious messaging infrastructure that scales with demand. Its adaptability, comprehensive pattern catalog, and seamless integration make it highly effective for data-intensive applications, allowing developers to create interactive data streams, transformations, and synchronizations in high-throughput scenarios. By incorporating best practices around ZeroMQ's architecture, security, and integration potential, developers can build powerful, fault-resilient real-time pipelines aligned with business and technical requirements.

9.4 Synchronizing Distributed Components

Synchronization is a critical aspect of distributed systems, crucial for maintaining consistency and coordination among components operating in parallel across different nodes. ZeroMQ provides mechanisms for synchronizing distributed components, ensuring that operations proceed coherently, leveraging its asynchronous communication capabilities and efficient messaging patterns. This section discusses strategies, techniques, and examples of achieving synchronization in distributed systems using ZeroMQ.

Understanding Synchronization Requirements

Synchronization involves coordinating tasks and ensuring that multiple components of a distributed system operate in harmony, whether processing shared data, following distributed algorithms, or adhering to a coherent system state. It addresses challenges such as:

1. **Consistency**: Maintaining uniform data views across distributed components. 2. **Coordination**: Orchestrating task execution order

9.4. SYNCHRONIZING DISTRIBUTED COMPONENTS

or dependencies. 3. **Consensus**: Achieving agreement among distributed components on shared state or values.

ZeroMQ aids these challenges through its rich pattern ecosystem and focus on asynchronous, non-blocking communication, allowing components to exchange synchronization signals and states effectively.

Barrier Synchronization Using ZeroMQ

Barrier synchronization ensures that a set of distributed processes reaches a certain point in execution before continuing. A common approach involves developing a coordinator node overseeing when all nodes have reached the synchronization point.

```
import zmq
import time

# Coordinator
context = zmq.Context()
sync_service = context.socket(zmq.REP)
sync_service.bind("tcp://*:5555")

sync_count = 0
total_nodes = 5

while sync_count < total_nodes:
    message = sync_service.recv()
    print(f"Received synchronization from: {message}")
    sync_count += 1
    sync_service.send(b"ACK")

print("All nodes synchronized, continuing processing...")
```

Each participating node sends a synchronization signal to the coordinator:

```
import zmq

context = zmq.Context()
sync_client = context.socket(zmq.REQ)
sync_client.connect("tcp://localhost:5555")

# Notify Coordinator
sync_client.send_string("Node has synchronized")
sync_client.recv()
```

The coordinator waits until all nodes reach the barrier before issuing acknowledgements, ensuring systematic progression across nodes.

Using the PUB-SUB Pattern for State Dissemination

The Publish-Subscribe pattern is instrumental in broadcasting state changes from a master node to all subscribed nodes, ensuring updates are simultaneously disseminated. This is especially useful for configuration management or distributing consensus state among nodes.

```
import zmq

context = zmq.Context()

# Publisher
state_pub = context.socket(zmq.PUB)
state_pub.bind("tcp://*:5560")

state = {"node1": "updated", "node2": "outdated"}

for node, status in state.items():
    state_pub.send_string(f"{node} state:{status}")
```

```
import zmq

context = zmq.Context()

# Subscriber
state_sub = context.socket(zmq.SUB)
state_sub.connect("tcp://localhost:5560")
state_sub.setsockopt_string(zmq.SUBSCRIBE, "node1")

while True:
    message = state_sub.recv_string()
    print(f"Received state update: {message}")
```

In this implementation, the publisher broadcasts each node's state, while subscribers listen for relevant updates, enabling synchronized state management.

Leader Election and Consensus Algorithms

Leader election is a process that selects a node to act as a coordinator for synchronization tasks, typically used in consensus algorithms. Though ZeroMQ doesn't intrinsically offer leader election, it facilitates its development through custom protocols.

Consider implementing an election where nodes exchange heartbeats to maintain connection status. If heartbeat interruptions occur, nodes can initiate a leader re-election process through pre-defined logic.

```
import zmq
import threading
import time

context = zmq.Context()
```

9.4. SYNCHRONIZING DISTRIBUTED COMPONENTS

```
# Node
heartbeat_socket = context.socket(zmq.PUB)
heartbeat_socket.bind("tcp://*:5565")

def send_heartbeat():
    while True:
        heartbeat_socket.send_string("Node Heartbeat")
        time.sleep(1)

threading.Thread(target=send_heartbeat).start()
```

Parallel processes in distributed systems can collect heartbeats and initiate election protocols during heartbeat absence. This logic forms the basis of consensus protocols and can cohesively integrate with modules like RAFT or Paxos using ZeroMQ as the communication substrate.

Distributed Lock Management

Locks are fundamental primitives critical for mutual exclusion and concurrency control in distributed scenarios. Creating a distributed lock manager involves ensuring that only a single node at a time can gain access to a shared resource.

One approach involves leveraging ZeroMQ's Request-Reply pattern, creating a lock server that grants locks to requesting nodes.

```
import zmq

context = zmq.Context()

# Lock Server
lock_service = context.socket(zmq.REP)
lock_service.bind("tcp://*:5570")

lock_owner = None

while True:
    requester = lock_service.recv_string()
    if not lock_owner:
        lock_owner = requester
        lock_service.send_string(f"Lock granted to {lock_owner}")
    elif lock_owner == requester:
        lock_owner = None
        lock_service.send_string(f"Lock released from {requester}")
    else:
        lock_service.send_string(f"Lock already held by {lock_owner}")
```

```
import zmq

context = zmq.Context()
```

CHAPTER 9. ZEROMQ WITH DISTRIBUTED SYSTEMS

```
# Requester
lock_client = context.socket(zmq.REQ)
lock_client.connect("tcp://localhost:5570")

# Request Lock
lock_client.send_string("Node requesting lock")
reply = lock_client.recv_string()
print(reply)
```

Nodes request lock ownership, and the lock server orchestrates access approvals, ensuring serialized access to resources across distributed systems.

Vector Clocks for Event Ordering

Vector clocks are a method for ordering events in distributed systems, helpful for casual dependency tracking. ZeroMQ communicates vector clock updates across nodes, promoting consistent views of system states.

Nodes maintaining vector clocks send updates alongside messages during interactions, allowing global system state resolution and causality maintenance.

Synchronization through Workflow Orchestration

Beyond manual synchronization, external orchestration frameworks optimizing ZeroMQ handling augment component coordination. Systems like Apache Airflow or Celery use ZeroMQ for task delegation, state management, and workflow executions.

Configured to interconnect and scheduling distributed tasks efficiently, orchestrators enhance reproduction and precision within automated processes, maintaining consistent communication and synchronization through well-defined scheduler-executor interfaces.

Collectively, ZeroMQ's patterns and capabilities form a foundation for synchronizing distributed components, promoting systems where operations align across different levels and scenarios. Capitalizing on asynchrony, decentralized design principles, and fault-tolerance, and modular framework integration, ZeroMQ facilitates coordinated and synchronized distributed systems sustainably developed for contemporary high-scalability demands.

9.5 ZeroMQ in Multicloud and Hybrid Environments

The increasing complexity of distributed systems has led to the adoption of multicloud and hybrid environments, where infrastructure spans across different cloud providers and on-premises data centers. ZeroMQ, with its advanced messaging capabilities, is well-suited for facilitating efficient communication in such diverse setups. This section explores how ZeroMQ can be strategically implemented in multicloud and hybrid environments to achieve seamless interoperability and robust performance, providing insight through detailed strategies, architectural patterns, and coding practices.

Understanding Multicloud and Hybrid Environments

Multicloud environments utilize services from multiple cloud providers, such as AWS, Azure, and Google Cloud, to leverage unique offerings or reduce reliance on a single vendor. Hybrid environments, on the other hand, integrate on-premises resources with cloud-based resources to meet specific data or computation requirements. These architectures demand high adaptability and reduced latency across platforms, necessitating an effective messaging layer like ZeroMQ.

Architectural Components of ZeroMQ in Hybrid Systems

When deploying ZeroMQ within these environments, several architectural components must be considered:

- **Interoperability**: ZeroMQ must function seamlessly across heterogeneous systems and manage varied data formats, protocols, and security models inherited from each cloud provider and on-premises configuration.

- **Scalability**: The architecture must support dynamic scaling, capable of flexibly allocating resources based on demand, and incorporating new nodes or removing existing ones without disruption.

- **Latency Reduction**: Considering data moving across different geographic locations, the system must optimize paths and transfer protocols to minimize latency, maintaining efficiency in data delivery.

- **Security**: Environments must ensure secure data transfer between nodes in different security domains, protecting sensitive information through encryption and secure authentication.

Pattern Deployment and Network Configuration

Optimal pattern selection is pivotal for efficient cross-environment communication.

Cross-cloud Communication with PUSH-PULL

The Push-Pull pattern is instrumental for distributing workloads across nodes positioned in different cloud environments. It establishes a modular topology where work producers can disseminate tasks to various consumers, which may reside on vastly different networks.

```
import zmq
# Cloud Worker (PULL)
context = zmq.Context()
cloud_receiver = context.socket(zmq.PULL)
cloud_receiver.connect("tcp://<Cloud-IP>:5559")

while True:
    task = cloud_receiver.recv_string()
    print(f"Processing task: {task}")
```

```
import zmq
# On-premises Client (PUSH)
context = zmq.Context()
task_sender = context.socket(zmq.PUSH)
task_sender.bind("tcp://*:5559")

tasks = ["task1", "task2", "task3"]
for task in tasks:
    task_sender.send_string(task)
```

In the provided code, tasks generated at on-premises nodes are efficiently distributed to cloud-based workers, allowing task parallelism and availability across geographic distribution.

Load Balancing Across Clouds Using DEALER-ROUTER

Load balancing is essential in multicloud setups to ensure even distribution of tasks. The Dealer-Router pattern effectively organizes workloads among distributed resources and decouples message exchange

9.5. ZEROMQ IN MULTICLOUD AND HYBRID ENVIRONMENTS

from endpoint control. This pattern allows ZeroMQ to dynamically adjust to node availability, offering resilience against node failures and improving resource utilization.

```
import zmq

# Central Router
context = zmq.Context()
router = context.socket(zmq.ROUTER)
router.bind("tcp://*:5560")

# Backend deals with cloud-specific data processing
backend = context.socket(zmq.DEALER)
backend.bind("tcp://*:5561")

zmq.proxy(router, backend)
```

Implementing Secure Communication Channels

Security is paramount in multicloud and hybrid frameworks. ZeroMQ supports encryption using CurveZMQ, a robust library ensuring secure transmission across nodes with diverse security policies.

```
import zmq
import zmq.auth

context = zmq.Context()

# Setup authentication
auth = zmq.auth.ThreadAuthenticator(context)
auth.start()
auth.allow('127.0.0.1')
auth.configure_curve(domain='*', location=zmq.auth.CURVE_ALLOW_ANY)

# Secure ROUTER with CurveZMQ
secure_router = context.socket(zmq.ROUTER)
server_public, server_secret = zmq.auth.create_certificates('.', 'server')
secure_router.curve_secretkey, secure_router.curve_publickey = server_secret,
    server_public
secure_router.curve_server = True
secure_router.bind("tcp://*:5560")
```

This example ensures secure, authenticated communication channels between nodes, adhering to hybrid environment security standards.

Network Latency and Data Locality

Latency poses significant challenges in multicloud and hybrid environments due to varying data transfer speeds across networks. ZeroMQ's ability to select and adapt to optimal transport protocols can efficiently minimize latency. A common approach involves implementing local caches or edge servers to handle data close to the source, reducing transit paths.

Moreover, network topology awareness is essential. ZeroMQ's flexibility to switch between TCP, IPC, and other transports allows custom routing strategies to align with network infrastructure, choosing the fastest available path for data exchange.

Resilience through Redundancy and Failover

ZeroMQ brings redundancy at multiple architecture layers, enabling resilient service against outages. Deploying redundant ZeroMQ brokers on different clouds ensures that failure in one provider does not impact the overarching communication fabric, orchestrating automatic failover. Integration with monitoring solutions like Prometheus or Grafana offers invaluable insights into broker health-examining metrics like message processing rates or error rates, preemptively managing potential disruptions.

Centralized Configuration Management

Real-time configuration management is key in maintaining coherent state across distributed systems. ZeroMQ-based configuration distribution via Pub-Sub maximizes this process, ensuring consistent setting across varied nodes.

```
import zmq

context = zmq.Context()

# Publish configuration updates
config_publisher = context.socket(zmq.PUB)
config_publisher.bind("tcp://*:5562")
config = {"key": "value"}

while True:
    config_publisher.send_json(config)
    time.sleep(10)
```

Subscribing nodes dynamically react to new configuration sets, preserving homogeneous environment states even during live system updates.

Resource-Oriented Cost Efficiency

Beyond technical alignment, adopting a ZeroMQ-based architecture in cloud implementations efficiently interpolates resource usage against cost. Effectively balancing workloads, dynamically provisioning and de-provisioning instances limits costs associated with constant uptime of cloud resources, achieving significant financial efficiency while guaranteeing service availability.

Integration with Cloud-Native Services

ZeroMQ excellently combines with existing cloud-native services. Synchronizing with cloud-specific messaging platforms like AWS SNS or Google Cloud Pub/Sub creates hybrid systems with harmonized communication paths. Patterns such as transforming ZeroMQ messages for other service consumptions or embedding ZeroMQ's security and protocol features into proprietary workflows parallelly elevate the system's overall latency and responsiveness.

Use Case Highlight: Global Data Distribution Network

Consider a global retail company deploying in multiple regions with real-time inventory updates and analytics dictated across various nodes hosted on different cloud services. Implementing a ZeroMQ multicloud network allows efficient hierarchical coordination of transactional data triggered by POS systems, leveraging ZeroMQ's diverse patterns from edge controllers to backend analytic computation clusters.

ZeroMQ forms the foundational layer, ensuring that data ingest, event processing, and distributed storage stay coordinated under contemporary multicloud paradigms. By providing secure, low-latency communication, and ensuring orchestration within the logically unified network, ZeroMQ caters towards both immediate enterprise needs as well as aligned future scalability endeavors.

In summation, utilizing ZeroMQ in multicloud and hybrid environments equips distributed systems with enhanced communication efficiencies. The ability to adeptly extend across diverse environments, support modular growth, and focus on enriched security measures cements ZeroMQ's position as an indispensable strategic component for modern architectural designs that embed core service assurances while embracing transformative technological advancements.

9.6 Case Studies: ZeroMQ in Large-Scale Systems

ZeroMQ's versatility as an efficient messaging library makes it highly suitable for deployment within large-scale distributed systems. This section presents detailed case studies that explore practical applications of ZeroMQ, illustrating how its features have been leveraged to solve complex communication challenges across various domains. By examining these implementations, readers can gain insights into the effective application of ZeroMQ in demanding environments.

Case Study 1: High-Frequency Trading Platform

In high-frequency trading (HFT), systems often require microsecond-level transaction capabilities. These platforms depend on rapid data dissemination, low-latency order processing, and real-time analytics. A trading firm can employ ZeroMQ to meet these stringent requirements by handling data stream management, order execution, and market data distribution efficiently.

Architecture and Implementation

- **Data Ingestion and Market Data Feed**: A Publish-Subscribe pattern allows the streaming of market data feeds to multiple trading engines, each processing data independently to identify trading opportunities.

    ```
    import zmq

    context = zmq.Context()

    # Market Data Publisher
    data_pub = context.socket(zmq.PUB)
    data_pub.bind("tcp://*:5550")

    data_feeds = [("stock1", "price:100"), ("stock2", "price:50")]

    # Publish market data
    for feed in data_feeds:
        data_pub.send_string(f"{feed[0]} {feed[1]}")
    ```

Traders employ subscribers with filters to receive relevant stock updates, allowing for responsive and high-speed analysis and trading decisions.

- **Order Execution and Confirmation**: Using a Dealer-Router pattern facilitates multiple clients' communication with the execution broker, enabling concurrent order submissions and confirmations to multiple exchange endpoints.

```
import zmq

context = zmq.Context()

# Execution Broker (Router)
broker = context.socket(zmq.ROUTER)
broker.bind("tcp://*:5551")

# Handling multiple clients
while True:
    # Process order messages and send confirmation
    client_id, order = broker.recv_multipart()
    print(f"Received order: {order} from {client_id}")
    broker.send_multipart([client_id, b"order confirmed"])
```

Here, the Dealer-Router pattern allows for effective load distribution and immediate response handling, supporting the concurrent high-speed execution of trade orders.

Benefits Realized

- **Low Latency**: ZeroMQ's asynchronous I/O and compact message serialization contributed to microsecond latencies in data handling and trading decision workflows.

- **Scalability**: The architecture supports high concurrency levels, processing millions of market data updates and trade transactions simultaneously.

Case Study 2: Distributed Logging System

A corporation deploying a distributed logging system to aggregate logs from various data centers globally enhances operational insight and incident response by utilizing ZeroMQ to streamline and manage log data flows.

System Overview and Implementation

- **Log Collection**: Agents deployed on servers collect log data and communicate this data to regional log collectors via a Push-Pull pattern, optimized for continuous data flow and backpressure handling.

```
import zmq

context = zmq.Context()

# Log Collector (PULL)
log_collector = context.socket(zmq.PULL)
log_collector.bind("tcp://*:5552")

# Receive logs
while True:
    log = log_collector.recv_string()
    print(f"Log received: {log}")
```

- **Log Aggregation and Storage**: Centralized log aggregators collect data from regional collectors. Using a Publisher for redundancy and scalable data relay, ZeroMQ ensures efficient data consolidation in a globally accessible log storage system.

```
import zmq

context = zmq.Context()

# Aggregating logs
log_aggregator = context.socket(zmq.PUB)
log_aggregator.bind("tcp://*:5553")

log_entries = ["error at server1", "access at server2"]

for entry in log_entries:
    log_aggregator.send_string(f"log_message {entry}")
```

Benefits and Outcomes

- **Centralized Monitoring**: The system's ability to aggregate logs centrally allowed quicker troubleshooting and mapping of incident patterns across geographical regions.

- **Reduction in Overhead**: ZeroMQ's efficient message dispatching and smart queuing improved system responsiveness and lowered bandwidth use across long-distance data travels.

Case Study 3: IoT Sensor Network

A city-wide sensor network designed to optimize urban traffic and environmental monitoring adopts ZeroMQ to manage sensory data trans-

9.6. CASE STUDIES: ZEROMQ IN LARGE-SCALE SYSTEMS

mission from thousands of devices distributed across metropolitan areas.

Configuration and Operation

- **Sensor Data Transmission**: Sensors embedded in infrastructure elements like traffic lights and environmental stations use the Pub-Sub model to send metrics to dedicated monitoring systems, characterized by multicast efficiencies.

```
import zmq

context = zmq.Context()

# Sensor (Publisher)
sensor_pub = context.socket(zmq.PUB)
sensor_pub.bind("tcp://*:5554")

sensor_data = [("traffic", "busy"), ("pollution", "high")]

for data in sensor_data:
    sensor_pub.send_string(f"{data[0]} level:{data[1]}")
```

Subscribed to sensor broadcasts, real-time monitoring applications react dynamically – ensuring swift responses to acute conditions, such as controlling traffic light timings to alleviate congestion.

- **Data Processing Hub**: Hierarchical layer design facilitates data processing and feeds collated sensor data to central data centers for big data analytics and reactive measures.

Benefits and Achievements

- **Real-time Monitoring**: By relaying live sensor updates, municipal bodies experienced improved condition awareness and real-time issue response capabilities.

- **Enhanced Network Efficiency**: The asynchronous model employed in ZeroMQ minimized chokepoints, facilitating notable data throughput and reliability improvements despite considerable sensor traffic scale.

Case Study 4: Remote Telemetry in Aerospace

Implementing telemetry systems for aerospace platforms requires systems capable of robust telemetry data acquisition and command dissemination, maintaining integrity and timeliness throughout extensive deployments. ZeroMQ facilitates these imperatives.

Architecture Components and Strategies

- **Telemetry Data Acquisition**: Utilizing a hierarchical series of pub-sub nodes, telemetry is gathered from airborne systems, enabling ground systems to continuously monitor and adapt mission parameters.

```
import zmq

context = zmq.Context()

# Telemetry Publisher
telemetry_pub = context.socket(zmq.PUB)
telemetry_pub.bind("tcp://*:5555")

telemetry_data = [("altitude", "35000"), ("speed", "450kn")]

for data in telemetry_data:
    telemetry_pub.send_string(f"{data[0]} value:{data[1]}")
```

- **Command and Control**: Using a combination of request-reply and pub-sub patterns, command-and-control messages are sent assuring point-to-multipoint fluidity, orchestrating controlled operations across distributed flight components.

Realizations and Success Metrics

- **Seamless Data Handling**: Coordinated telemetry collection and dissemination ensured effective mission control and enhanced aerospace multi-node system cohesion.

- **Operational Resilience**: ZeroMQ's decentralized logical topology allowed continued safe operation despite intermittent node losses, enhancing mission reliability.

Summary Observations

Across these diverse applications, ZeroMQ proves to be invaluable in synchronizing operations under demanding conditions, offering ro-

9.6. CASE STUDIES: ZEROMQ IN LARGE-SCALE SYSTEMS

bust, scalable, and high-performance communication solutions. These case studies highlight core advantages such as:

- **Flexibility and Scalability**: ZeroMQ's seamless adaptability across organizations' distributed architecture fosters efficient use of heterogeneous systems.

- **Latency Optimization**: Asynchronous processing ensures swift data passage, reducing latency and increasing throughput in time-sensitive applications.

- **Reliability and Fault Tolerance**: Through architectural constructs such as dealer-router and pub-sub, ZeroMQ offers inherent resilience against individual node failures.

ZeroMQ continues to facilitate innovation in distributed computing frameworks, becoming integral to large-scale systems striving for enhanced communication efficiency and resiliency in volatile environments. These implementations often see significant improvements in task parallelism, workload adaptability, and overall system responsiveness, serving as testaments to ZeroMQ's capability in fulfilling contemporary distributed system requirements.

Chapter 10

Exploring Real-world Applications of ZeroMQ

ZeroMQ's versatility is demonstrated through its application across various industries, including financial services, IoT, media, healthcare, and telecommunications. In financial services, ZeroMQ supports high-frequency trading platforms with low-latency messaging. It enhances IoT systems by enabling efficient data aggregation and communication among devices. Media streaming and content delivery networks benefit from ZeroMQ's reliable data flow capabilities. In healthcare, it facilitates secure data exchanges between medical systems. Additionally, ZeroMQ plays a significant role in telecommunications for real-time messaging and collaborative software development environments, streamlining team communication and coordination. This chapter explores these real-world applications, showcasing ZeroMQ's adaptability and effectiveness.

10.1 Financial Services and Trading Platforms

In financial services and trading platforms, the ability to process transactions with high-frequency and low-latency is not only advantageous but a prerequisite for operational success and competitiveness. ZeroMQ is increasingly prevalent in this domain due to its capabilities that meet these exacting demands. By providing a flexible, asynchronous messaging infrastructure compatible with various languages and systems, ZeroMQ facilitates the seamless transmission of critical financial data under stringent time constraints.

The implementation of ZeroMQ in financial markets primarily revolves around its capacity to optimize message-passing frameworks, enhance data throughput, and support sophisticated trading algorithms. This is crucial in environments where nanoseconds can equate to significant financial gain or loss.

High-Frequency Trading (HFT) Requirements

High-frequency trading systems hinge on low-latency communications to disseminate trading signals, execute trades, and manage numerous market interactions in real time. ZeroMQ presents several features that align well with the requirements of HFT systems:

- **Non-blocking I/O**: ZeroMQ employs non-blocking input/output operations to ensure continuous message flow without interruption, crucial for minimizing latency.

- **Load Balancing**: Through efficient load balancing, ZeroMQ can handle multiple data streams concurrently, ensuring that the message queue remains unimpeded.

- **Scalability**: The inherent scalability of ZeroMQ allows for augmented processing capabilities when handling surges in market data or an increased number of transactions.

Here is a simple model code snippet to illustrate a basic ZeroMQ publisher and subscriber model, tailored for real-time financial data dissemination:

10.1. FINANCIAL SERVICES AND TRADING PLATFORMS

```
import zmq
import time
import json

context = zmq.Context()

# Socket to send messages on
publisher = context.socket(zmq.PUB)
publisher.bind("tcp://*:5556")

while True:
    # Simulated trading data
    trade_data = {
        'symbol': 'AAPL',
        'price': 150.27,
        'volume': 1000
    }
    publisher.send_string("%s %s" % (trade_data['symbol'], json.dumps(trade_data)))
    print("Published: ", trade_data)
    time.sleep(0.01)
```

In the above example, a ZeroMQ publisher is configured to emit simulated trading data regarding stock trades at ten-millisecond intervals. This simulation underscores the principle of rapid data dissemination essential in financial contexts.

Latency Reduction Techniques

To achieve optimal performance, financial institutions often pair ZeroMQ's capabilities with advanced techniques to minimize latency further. Techniques include:

- **Using In-Memory Queues**: By avoiding disk I/O, ZeroMQ minimizes time delays inherent in writing to and reading from physical storage.

- **Affinity Settings**: Configuring CPU affinity for threads handling ZeroMQ ensures that these threads remain on specific cores, improving cache efficiency and reducing context-switching overhead.

- **Persistent Connections**: Retaining sustained, always-on TCP connections between nodes diminishes the latency arising from repeatedly establishing and tearing down network connections.

Fault Tolerance and Reliability

In trading platforms, reliability and fault tolerance are necessary due to the potential for losses caused by missed or incorrect data transmission. ZeroMQ addresses these concerns through:

- **Message Persistence**: While ZeroMQ itself is designed for throughput over delivery guarantees, it can be paired with external libraries or frameworks, such as Apache Kafka, to persist and recover messages.

- **High Availability (HA)**: Architectures utilizing ZeroMQ can be designed to support high-availability configurations, with failover mechanisms to alternate nodes or systems if a failure occurs.

- **Back-pressure Handling**: Through mechanisms like the high-water mark settings, ZeroMQ prevents buffer overflow situations, ensuring system stability during message spurts.

This snippet demonstrates how multiple ZeroMQ components can interoperate to manifest a high-reliability system:

```
import zmq

context = zmq.Context()

# Socket to receive messages
receiver = context.socket(zmq.PULL)
receiver.connect("tcp://dataserver:5558")

# Socket to send processed messages forward or log
forwarder = context.socket(zmq.PUSH)
forwarder.bind("tcp://*:5559")

while True:
    try:
        # Receive trade signal
        message = receiver.recv_json()
        process_trade(message)
        forwarder.send_json(message)
    except zmq.ZMQError as e:
        # Implement logging and error handling
        handle_error(e)
```

The above model references a simple PULL-PUSH pattern that pulls data from a primary data server and safely forwards it post-processing. The logic allows for intermediary logging or transformation, ensuring rendition of financial data with reliability.

10.1. FINANCIAL SERVICES AND TRADING PLATFORMS

Market Data Feed Handlers

The nature and characteristics of financial data, characterized by its colossal volume and velocity, mandate systems that can parse and disseminate this data effectively. ZeroMQ offers the flexibility and speed necessary to handle market data feeds by:

- **Subscribing to Specific Assets**: ZeroMQ's capability to filter messages at the server level ensures that only relevant data, such as specific stock tickers or asset classes, is transmitted.

- **Concurrent Processing Streams**: By leveraging ZeroMQ's built-in support for message patterns and control of execution steps, processes can be arranged to run concurrently, maximizing data handling efficiency.

- **Customizable Data Formatters**: Employing custom serialization methods alongside ZeroMQ can optimize the speed of real-time data feed parsing.

```
import zmq

context = zmq.Context()
socket = context.socket(zmq.SUB)

# Connect to the market data feed server
socket.connect("tcp://markets:5500")

# Subscribe to particular stock symbols
socket.setsockopt_string(zmq.SUBSCRIBE, 'AAPL')
socket.setsockopt_string(zmq.SUBSCRIBE, 'GOOG')

while True:
    string = socket.recv_string()
    print("Received update: ", string)
```

This code highlights how a subscriber identifies specific stock symbols for interest, demonstrating the efficiency and power of filtering capabilities possible with ZeroMQ's messaging model.

The architecture utilizing ZeroMQ in trading platforms has been transformative, offering the advantages of flexibility and speed along with a design that encourages reliability and extends scalability. These characteristics are essential for reducing latency, increasing throughput, and maintaining financial data integrity under varied and arduous market conditions. By facilitating the real-time dissemination and processing of large volumes of trade data, ZeroMQ fortifies the infrastructure that supports modern high-frequency trading systems and financial services.

10.2 ZeroMQ in IoT and Sensor Networks

The Internet of Things (IoT) and sensor networks represent a significant area where the deployment of efficient and reliable communication frameworks is vital. ZeroMQ's lightweight messaging library is well-suited to address the specific needs of IoT environments, characterized by numerous devices generating continuous streams of data. By facilitating low-latency and resilient communication across diverse devices, ZeroMQ enhances data aggregation, processing, and dissemination within the IoT ecosystem.

IoT Requirements: Connectivity and Interoperability

IoT implementations necessitate a robust communication layer that bridges a variety of devices, platforms, and protocols. Key requirements include:

- **Heterogeneous Device Communication**: IoT environments consist of myriad devices with varying communication capabilities, from low-power sensors to powerful edge computing nodes.

- **Scalability and Flexibility**: As IoT networks expand, communication frameworks must adapt seamlessly to an increasing number of devices and communications patterns.

- **Microsecond Response Times**: Many IoT applications, such as industrial automation or autonomous driving, demand rapid response times.

ZeroMQ fulfills these requirements, offering a bidirectional, asynchronous messaging pattern that encompasses pub/sub, push/pull, and request/reply models.

10.2. ZEROMQ IN IOT AND SENSOR NETWORKS

Data Aggregation and Distribution

In IoT networks, sensor nodes produce data that must be aggregated for analytics and decision-making. ZeroMQ facilitates the following data processes:

- **Efficient Data Collection**: Sensor nodes transmit data to data collectors, which are configured to collect at various network points.
- **Real-Time Data Dissemination**: Aggregated data must be distributed to processing units or storage solutions efficiently.
- **Node-to-Node Communication**: Actuating devices may require a command-response architecture with other nodes.

Here is an example of a simple ZeroMQ setup utilizing the pub/sub model that enables a sensor node to broadcast data, illustrating foundational IoT data handling:

```
import zmq
import time
import random

context = zmq.Context()

# Socket to send messages on
sensor_node = context.socket(zmq.PUB)
sensor_node.bind("tcp://*:5556")

while True:
    # Generate mock sensor data
    temperature = random.uniform(20.0, 30.0)
    humidity = random.uniform(30.0, 60.0)

    data = f"Temperature: {temperature:.2f}, Humidity: {humidity:.2f}"
    sensor_node.send_string(data)
    print("Published: ", data)
    time.sleep(1)
```

This code simulates a sensor node broadcasting temperature and humidity readings. The flexibility of ZeroMQ's pub/sub model is evidenced through its simple setup process, essential for sensor networks where multiple nodes publish and consume data.

Sensor Network Topologies

Various topologies can be effectively implemented using ZeroMQ, each providing unique benefits:

CHAPTER 10.   EXPLORING REAL-WORLD APPLICATIONS OF ZEROMQ

- **Star Topology**: Central nodes collect and control data emission and reception, suitable for networks with centralized control systems.

- **Mesh Topology**: Provides redundancy and reliability, where each node can communicate with multiple nodes, ideal for self-healing networks.

- **Hybrid Topology**: Combines both star and mesh systems allowing more complex network designs conducive to scalable IoT scenarios.

ZeroMQ's agnostic design regarding network topology allows developers to craft numerous communication patterns that can evolve with the network's size and reliability requirements.

Integration with Edge and Cloud Computing

For IoT scenarios requiring advanced data-processing capabilities, edge and cloud computing infrastructures often accompany traditional device processing. ZeroMQ's seamless integration capabilities are well-suited for these hybrid environments:

- **Edge Processing**: By transmitting data to edge nodes, ZeroMQ can help process massive concurrent data streams at the data source, reducing overall latency.

- **Cloud Coordination**: Cloud services facilitate additional computation-intensive tasks, such as machine learning model training and data analytics, aided by ZeroMQ's ability to voxelize and transport large data sets efficiently.

ZeroMQ's modular design and language-agnostic protocol provide seamless compatibility with various cloud services and edge devices.

Security Considerations

Security is an ever-present concern in IoT networks. ZeroMQ facilitates safe transmission of data through the following methods:

- **Encryption Protocols**: Leveraging CurveZMQ, ZeroMQ can encrypt messages between nodes using modern cryptographic protocols for confidentiality and integrity.

10.2. ZEROMQ IN IOT AND SENSOR NETWORKS

- **Authentication Mechanisms**: Systems can integrate authentication to ensure only authorized entities communicate across the network.

- **Network Isolation and Segmentation**: ZeroMQ's flexible communication design supports microservice architectures where segmentation improves isolation and containment strategies.

Security practices ensure that data integrity and privacy mandates are met, reducing risk in valuable IoT ecosystems.

Handling Fault Tolerances and Network Dependencies

With device connectivity potentially unstable in IoT networks, ZeroMQ's various design patterns offer robust fault-tolerance mechanisms:

- **Retry Patterns and Back-off Strategies**: When devices fail to send data, ZeroMQ can deploy exponential back-off strategies to reestablish communications accurately.

- **Agent-based Redundancies**: Multiple data paths and messaging redundancies maintain operations automatically even when parts of the communication grid are down.

- **Message Queueing and Store-and-Forward**: Ensures data is buffered and transmitted once links are reestablished, preventing loss.

```
import zmq

context = zmq.Context()

# Main controller pulling sensor data
controller = context.socket(zmq.PULL)
controller.bind("tcp://*:5558")

while True:
    try:
        message = controller.recv_string(flags=zmq.NOBLOCK)
        process_sensor_data(message)
    except zmq.Again:
        # Implement wait or retry strategies
        print("No data received, checking again...")
```

This simple PULL socket implementation from a central controller outlines a retry pattern mechanism, showing ZeroMQ's non-blocking use case for periodic data checks in sensor networks.

ZeroMQ's adaptability and lightweight design provide a foundational building block for developing sophisticated IoT and sensor network systems. From enabling real-time communication to supporting extensive data processing workflows, ZeroMQ plays an integral role in modern-day IoT applications. Its suitable application spans from home automation to industrial IoT, providing solutions capable of scaling, securing, and dynamically enhancing IoT ecosystems.

10.3 Media and Content Delivery Networks

The media landscape has evolved remarkably over the past decade, with Content Delivery Networks (CDNs) playing a pivotal role in how media content is distributed across the globe. In this context, ZeroMQ offers capabilities that enhance CDNs, enabling efficient, reliable, and low-latency distribution of media content to diverse consumer devices. By supporting robust, scalable message-oriented communication patterns, ZeroMQ facilitates real-time streaming, effectively managing traffic spikes and ensuring high-quality content delivery.

Content Delivery Network Requirements

Modern CDNs require scalable and robust infrastructures capable of handling vast amounts of data with minimal latency. Core requirements include:

- **Low Latency Distribution**: Delivering media content quickly to minimize buffering and load times for end-users.

- **Adaptive Scalability**: Ability to handle sudden spikes in traffic, such as during live events or new content releases.

- **Geographic Reach**: Deploying content across global points of presence (PoPs) to optimize delivery paths and reduce congestion.

10.3. MEDIA AND CONTENT DELIVERY NETWORKS

ZeroMQ aligns well with these requirements due to its decentralized, peer-to-peer messaging model that supports complex distribution architectures.

Efficient Media Streaming

Real-time media streaming benefits significantly from ZeroMQ's capabilities in managing asynchronous message flows. Key implementations include:

- **Publisher-Subscriber Model**: Enables media servers to broadcast streams to multiple subscribers across varied locations, ensuring efficient one-to-many distribution.
- **Load Balancing and Fair Queuing**: Through interwoven socket patterns, ZeroMQ ensures balanced load distribution across media servers, optimizing resource utilization and minimizing delays.

Consider an example ZeroMQ setup where a media server streams video data using the pub/sub model:

```python
import zmq
import time

context = zmq.Context()

# Video server socket - Publish pattern for streaming video content
video_server = context.socket(zmq.PUB)
video_server.bind("tcp://*:5555")

# Simulate a video stream of frame updates
def video_stream():
    frame_number = 0
    while True:
        # Mock video frame data
        frame_data = f"Frame {frame_number}"

        # Publish frame
        video_server.send_string(f"video {frame_data}")
        print("Published:", frame_data)
        frame_number += 1
        time.sleep(0.033)  # 30 FPS

video_stream()
```

This code snippet demonstrates a simplistic publishing server that broadcasts frames at approximately 30 frames per second (FPS). Such a stream can be consumed and processed by clients in a CDN to construct real-time video content display.

Dynamic and Adaptive Content Distribution

ZeroMQ supports the construction of dynamic architectures that adjust content distribution strategies in real time:

- **Intelligent Traffic Management**: By implementing intelligent routing at intermediary nodes using ZeroMQ patterns, CDNs can dynamically adjust the distribution routes based on network conditions and server loads, thereby avoiding bottlenecks.

- **Peripheral Content Caching**: Edge nodes near end-users receive content pushed via ZeroMQ. This caching minimizes redundant data transmission on backbones by serving local requests directly.

The multiple sockets model illustrates how ZeroMQ can combine parallel data flows ensuring that larger network changes do not trip service quality.

Reliability and Fault Tolerance in CDNs

In high-stakes media content delivery, reliability is non-negotiable. ZeroMQ provides means to ensure continuous data delivery even amidst network failures:

- **Multi-path Communication**: By utilizing multi-part connections, ZeroMQ's message handlers offer redundancy pathways, seamlessly switching paths should an outage occur.

- **Resilient Node Configurations**: Crucial CDN nodes maintain multi-endpoint connections for guaranteed data propagation, regardless of local connection states.

- **Message Acknowledgements**: While ZeroMQ itself operates on a best-effort delivery, enhanced layers and libraries can introduce message durability, ensuring data integrity.

10.3. MEDIA AND CONTENT DELIVERY NETWORKS

```
import zmq
import sys

context = zmq.Context()

# Pull updates from media server
streaming_client = context.socket(zmq.SUB)
streaming_client.connect("tcp://videoserver:5555")

# Subscribe to video stream
streaming_client.setsockopt_string(zmq.SUBSCRIBE, 'video')

try:
    while True:
        update = streaming_client.recv_string()
        print("Received update:", update)
except KeyboardInterrupt:
    print("Streaming interrupted by user")
finally:
    streaming_client.close()
    context.term()
```

This illustrative subscriber indicates the simplicity of consuming media streams where ZeroMQ efficiently handles reconnections and message propagations behind the scenes.

Latency Optimization Techniques

To further optimize latency, CDN architectures leveraging ZeroMQ employ strategies that enhance response times:

- **Direct Path Routing**: Leveraging shortest-path analytics, content paths adaptively recalibrate ensuring data packets move with minimal hop counts.

- **Proactive Buffering Strategies**: Implementing smart buffering logic in subscribers, downstream network disturbances preemptively account for content buffering, anticipating network fluctuations.

- **Predictive Load Steering**: ZeroMQ supports real-time analytics sharing among nodes improving pre-emptive resource allocation in anticipation of traffic patterns.

Security Considerations in Media Networks

Securing media delivery involves protecting both data streams and metadata surrounding content dissemination:

- **Data Stream Encryption**: ZeroMQ can integrate CurveZMQ, encrypting media streams in transit, crucial for protecting intellectual property.

- **Authentication and Access Control**: Implementing OAuth-like mechanisms with ZeroMQ ensures restricted access to premium content.

- **Monitoring and Intrusion Detection**: Analytics integrated with ZeroMQ traffic flows can harness machine-learning algorithms to actively monitor, detect, and respond to anomalous behaviors.

ZeroMQ's open-ended approach allows the custom appetite for regulatory compliance or a focus on geographical information constraints, ensuring a global outreach with defined local configurations.

Media and Content Delivery Networks empowered by ZeroMQ stand poised at the pinnacle of contemporary solutions that address sophisticated, real-time distribution concerns. It forms a robust backbone in media transport, offering configurable, adaptive, and scalable functionalities necessary for the interactive content demands of today's digital consumer. With potential exploration continually pushing the envelope on performance improvements and security enhancements, ZeroMQ continues to be an essential component of next-generation content delivery strategies.

10.4 Healthcare Information Systems

Healthcare Information Systems (HIS) embody the intersection of medical record management, patient care, and technology. ZeroMQ plays a critical role in these systems, providing a reliable and efficient messaging infrastructure that supports the secure exchange of information among medical devices, systems, and healthcare professionals. The integration of ZeroMQ into HIS is driven by its ability to facilitate low-latency, scalable, and robust messaging patterns, essential in environments where timely and accurate information can directly impact patient outcomes.

Key Requirements for Healthcare Information Systems

Modern HIS must address numerous complex requirements to ensure they deliver value effectively and reliably:

- **Real-time Data Exchange**: Patient data must be communicated instantly across systems to facilitate immediate and informed medical interventions.

- **Interoperability and Integration**: Systems must communicate seamlessly across heterogeneous medical devices and software platforms.

- **Scalability and Adaptability**: As healthcare operations evolve, HIS must scale to include new technologies and increased patient loads without performance degradation.

- **Security and Privacy**: Protecting patient data through secure transmission methods to comply with regulations such as HIPAA.

ZeroMQ's flexible messaging system readily addresses these requirements by providing a layer of abstraction that facilitates the complex interactions inherent to healthcare environments.

Real-time Clinical Data Sharing

In healthcare facilities, diverse systems and devices generate data which must be integrated and analyzed in real time to support clinical decision-making processes. ZeroMQ simplifies this by:

- **Sending Alerts and Monitoring Data**: Critical patient-related metrics can trigger alerts sent to healthcare professionals across different departments.

- **Sharing Electronic Health Records (EHRs)**: Facilitates the distribution of EHRs across departments, ensuring all stakeholders have timely access to complete patient information.

- **Device-to-Device Communication**: Allows for efficient data exchanges directly between medical devices, critical for the operation of integrated medical equipment systems.

Consider the following example where ZeroMQ is employed to manage monitoring data:

```
import zmq
import json
import time

context = zmq.Context()

# Setup publisher for vital signs monitor
monitoring_system = context.socket(zmq.PUB)
monitoring_system.bind("tcp://*:5557")

# Simulate patient monitoring example
def monitor_patient_vital_signs():
    while True:
        # Mockup of patient vital signs data
        vital_signs = {'heart_rate': 80, 'blood_pressure': '120/80', 'temperature': 37.0}

        # Broadcast the data
        monitoring_system.send_json(vital_signs)
        print("Published vital signs:", vital_signs)
        time.sleep(1)

monitor_patient_vital_signs()
```

In this example, a vital signs monitoring system publishes data using ZeroMQ's pub/sub pattern. This model is ideal for broadcasting updates from monitors to subscribing systems, ensuring crucial patient data remains up-to-date across hospital systems.

Interoperability and System Integration

One of the significant challenges in healthcare is the integration of numerous specialized and often proprietary systems. ZeroMQ fosters interoperability in HIS by:

- **Providing Language-Agnostic Protocols**: ZeroMQ's support for various programming languages and protocols enables seamless integration across diverse systems.

- **Encapsulation through Service-Oriented Architectures (SOA)**: Facilitating communication between modular components in a healthcare system through well-defined interfaces.

- **Supporting Legacy Systems**: Helps legacy medical applications communicate with modern IT systems using message queues and bridges.

10.4. HEALTHCARE INFORMATION SYSTEMS

Here, ZeroMQ's multiplexing enables a universal envelope for messages, cooperating between older and newer technologies.

Scalability through Distributed Architectures

Healthcare institutions experience varying levels of demand, thus HIS need to be scalable:

- **Load Distribution**: ZeroMQ supports distributed architectures, ensuring message loads can scale across systems efficiently by distributing the data processing.

- **Horizontal Scalability**: Through ZeroMQ's dynamic socket connections, expanding system capacity to accommodate more stakeholders or devices can be achieved seamlessly.

- **Flexible Workload Allocation**: Facilitates the dynamic reassignment of resources, handling fluctuations in service demand effectively.

An effective use case is depicted in balancing data loads across multiple departmental queues, each processing patient data concurrently:

```
import zmq

context = zmq.Context()

# Router pattern for task balancing across hospital departments
task_router = context.socket(zmq.ROUTER)
task_router.bind("tcp://*:5558")

# Simulation of distributing tasks
while True:
    dept_id = task_router.recv_string()
    task_description = task_router.recv_string()
    # Load balance task assignment
    task_router.send_string(task_description, zmq.SNDMORE)
    task_router.send_string(f"Task assigned to department {dept_id}")
```

This example serves as a reduction of ZeroMQ using a router pattern to effectively distribute tasks across server nodes, representing departments in healthcare environments.

Robust Security and Privacy

Patient confidentiality is paramount in healthcare services. ZeroMQ equips HIS systems with:

- **Message Encryption and Authentication**: ZeroMQ supports CurveZMQ encryption to secure endpoints, providing authenticity and confidentiality assurances.

- **Secure End-to-End Communication**: Encrypted channels safeguard messages from interception and tampering, ensuring that all transmissions are protected.

- **Compliance with Healthcare Regulations**: ZeroMQ's adaptable encryption methods ensure systems comply with data protection laws like GDPR or HIPAA.

Monitoring and Maintenance

Efficient HIS demand monitoring capabilities that proactively manage and maintain system health to minimize downtimes and data inconsistencies:

- **Real-Time Analytics and Dashboards**: ZeroMQ facilitates streaming analytics, presenting real-time views into system operations, crucial for workflow optimizations.

- **System Health Checks**: Through brokerless architectures, ZeroMQ can implement distributed health probes dynamically, ensuring responsiveness and performance integrity.

- **Logging Mechanisms**: ZeroMQ's integration allows for decentralized, real-time logging solutions tracing operational history for audits and compliance checks.

Healthcare Information Systems supported by ZeroMQ frameworks endow healthcare providers with powerful communication tools, facilitating the real-time flow of information with security and reliability at its core. This ensures accelerated data exchanges that translate into timely interventions and improved patient outcomes. Through ZeroMQ's extensive flexibility, HIS becomes a robust network for dynamic environments, optimized for optimal patient care amid the demands of a continually evolving healthcare landscape.

10.5 Telecommunications and Messaging Systems

The telecommunications industry forms a complex network of services, including voice, data, and multimedia communications. In such an environment, rapid, reliable message transmission is essential, and ZeroMQ provides a messaging backbone for managing these communications effectively. Its natural support for asynchronous message patterns and scalable networks enhances telecommunications infrastructures by enabling agile, low-latency data transfer crucial for both traditional telecommunication systems and modern messaging platforms.

Core Requirements of Telecommunications Systems

To meet the demands of telecommunications, systems must ensure:

- **Reliability and Resilience**: Any delay or error in message delivery can impact service quality, making reliable and resilient messaging essential.

- **Scalability**: With an ever-growing demand for data, systems must scale to accommodate increasing user bases and data volume.

- **Low Latency**: Minimizing the delay in data transmission is critical to maintaining service integrity in real-time communications.

- **Interoperability**: Systems must interact fluidly with a wide array of devices and protocols to ensure seamless globalization of services.

ZeroMQ's design inherently fulfills these requirements, offering asynchronous communication capabilities and flexible architecture patterns, making it a natural fit for telecommunications applications.

Implementing Messaging Architectures

Telecommunications systems leverage various messaging models to ensure efficient data handling and distribution:

- **Request-Reply (REQ/REP)**: Serves as a synchronous message pattern facilitating straightforward two-way communication, critical for client-server models in telecommunications.

- **Publish-Subscribe (PUB/SUB)**: Efficient for broadcast applications like news updates or topic-based data dissemination.

- **Pipeline (PUSH/PULL)**: Ensures distributed task scheduling and load balancing across various processing nodes within the network.

An example implementation using the PUB/SUB model for broadcasting updates across a network:

```
import zmq
import time

context = zmq.Context()

# Set up a publisher to broadcast system updates
publisher = context.socket(zmq.PUB)
publisher.bind("tcp://*:5560")

def broadcast_system_updates():
    while True:
        # Example system update
        update_message = "New network encryption standards implemented"
        publisher.send_string(update_message)
        print("Broadcasted: ", update_message)
        time.sleep(2) # Interval between updates

broadcast_system_updates()
```

In this code example, a central system node broadcasts updates across the network. The model efficiently shares critical information across wide-reaching subscriber systems, pivotal for maintaining synchronized operational states.

Ensuring Scalability and Load Management

Scalability in telecommunications is crucial as the systems need to handle an ever-growing user base. ZeroMQ facilitates:

- **Dynamic Load Balancing**: Efficiently distributes work among nodes to manage system load and prevent bottlenecks.

- **Horizontal Scalability**: Accommodates increasing service de-

10.5. TELECOMMUNICATIONS AND MESSAGING SYSTEMS

mand by adding nodes to network architectures without interrupting existing services.

- **Exploration of Edge Computing**: Expands processing to network edges, reducing central system load and enhancing response times.

Below illustrates ZeroMQ handling load balancing with a PUSH/PULL architecture:

```
import zmq

context = zmq.Context()

# Setup PUSH socket to distribute tasks to workers
task_distributor = context.socket(zmq.PUSH)
task_distributor.bind("tcp://*:5559")

def distribute_load():
    task_id = 0
    while True:
        task = f"Task {task_id}"
        task_distributor.send_string(task)
        print(f"Distributed: {task}")
        task_id += 1
        time.sleep(1)  # Load distribution interval

distribute_load()
```

This model effectively balances tasks across worker nodes, demonstrating efficient resource distribution where tasks are managed dynamically, crucial for telecommunications centers with varying processing demands.

Optimizing Latency for Real-time Communication

Achieving minimal latency is vital; ZeroMQ provides several strategies:

- **Use of In-memory Queueing**: Avoids the overhead of persistent storage operations, allowing faster message transit.

- **Message Batching and Compression**: Minimizes the number of network packets by consolidating messages, reducing overhead and increasing throughput.

- **Path Optimization and Caching**: Employs shortest-path algorithms and caching to expedite data transmission across the network.

Incorporating these techniques within a ZeroMQ framework ensures real-time data processing, critical for communications requiring immediate transmissions, such as VoIP or live streaming services.

Security Protocols in Telecommunications

Given the sensitive nature of telecommunications data, ZeroMQ supports:

- **End-to-End Encryption**: Implementing secure protocols like CurveZMQ ensures data encryption from source to destination across communication channels.

- **Authentication and Authorization**: Protects against unauthorized access by ensuring only verified entities can participate in network communications.

- **Data Integrity and Verification**: Uses checksum mechanisms to ensure data consistency, alerting systems to any transmission anomalies.

By embracing ZeroMQ, telecommunications systems bolster data security and compliance with regulatory requirements, essential for maintaining user trust and safeguarding proprietary data.

Advanced Features for Modern Messaging Systems

ZeroMQ's architecture supports features innovative in modern messaging platforms:

- **Multi-protocol Support**: Integrates with existing systems utilizing different communication protocols, ensuring rich interoperability.

- **Flexibility in System Design**: ZeroMQ's brokerless model encourages custom, adaptable communication structures geared towards unique business and operational needs.

- **Service Quality Monitoring**: Implements tracking and monitoring analytics into messaging workflows, optimizing service quality and user satisfaction.

Consider the following example for a responsive messaging client utilizing ZeroMQ's REQ/REP model:

```python
import zmq
import sys

context = zmq.Context()

# Prepare socket as a client's request point
requester = context.socket(zmq.REQ)
requester.connect("tcp://server_address:5570")

def request_service():
    for i in range(10):
        message = f"Request {i}"
        print(f"Sending: {message}")
        requester.send_string(message)
        reply = requester.recv_string()
        print(f"Received reply: {reply}")

request_service()
```

This demo illustrates ZeroMQ's synchronous message exchange, ensuring robust request-response communication that is sees high use in client-server telecommunications models.

ZeroMQ's comprehensive libraries and ecosystem offer revolutionary changes in telecommunications and messaging systems, from traditional network infrastructure to cutting-edge real-time communication applications. Its versatility, combined with robust security and performance optimizations, paves the way for scalable, secure, and low-latency communications vital to the telecommunications industry's current and future needs.

10.6 Collaborative and Distributed Software Development

The world of software development is increasingly characterized by collaboration across geographically distributed teams. This paradigm necessitates robust communication and synchronization mechanisms to ensure cohesion, productivity, and the seamless integration of developmental outputs. ZeroMQ provides an essential messaging framework that supports these objectives, offering asynchronous messaging, minimal latency, and high scalability critical for collaborative and distributed software development environments.

Requirements for Collaborative Software Development

The complexities of distributed software development impose several critical requirements on systems supporting this workflow:

- **Real-time Collaboration**: Teams need to access shared resources and communicate instantly to maintain project velocity and cohesion.

- **Version Control and Integration**: Ensures consistent state across codebases, facilitating synchronization and integration of diverse project components.

- **Scalability**: Systems must cater to fluctuating team sizes and project demands without affecting performance.

- **Fault Tolerance**: Robust error handling and recovery capabilities to minimize development disruptions.

ZeroMQ's versatile communication patterns and supportive libraries make it highly suitable for implementing these requirements efficiently within development environments.

Real-time Communication and Coordination

Robust communication mechanisms are fundamental in fostering team collaboration. ZeroMQ aids in:

- **Instant Messaging and Notifications**: Facilitates instant message broadcasting among participants, keeping the team aligned on project progress and updates.

- **Task and Resource Allocation**: Allows for real-time task distribution, ensuring equitable resource usage across development teams.

- **Code Review and Feedback Loops**: Supports efficient feedback cycles with asynchronous communications like the PUB/SUB model enabling distributed code review processes.

10.6. COLLABORATIVE AND DISTRIBUTED SOFTWARE DEVELOPMENT

An example illustrating a simple pub/sub setup for broadcasting task updates:

```
import zmq
import time

context = zmq.Context()

# Publisher for task notifications
task_notifier = context.socket(zmq.PUB)
task_notifier.bind("tcp://*:5580")

def broadcast_task_updates():
    task_id = 1
    while True:
        task_message = f"Task {task_id} completed"
        task_notifier.send_string(task_message)
        print("Broadcasted: ", task_message)
        task_id += 1
        time.sleep(2) # Interval between task notifications

broadcast_task_updates()
```

In this code snippet, a task notifier system disseminates information about task completions, facilitating real-time updates to the team for better workflow and task management.

Version Control and Code Integration

Distributed teams require mechanisms to automate and streamline code synchronization and integration, critical for maintaining consistent code states:

- **Continuous Integration/Continuous Deployment (CI/CD) Pipelines**: ZeroMQ's messaging forms the backbone of communications within CI/CD pipelines, making integrations efficient.

- **Event-driven Code Syncs**: Utilizes ZeroMQ to trigger real-time synchronization processes on code changes.

- **Branch/Merge Notifications**: Supports notification systems that alert developers to branch merges or conflicts, facilitating swifter resolutions.

An effective implementation utilizes ZeroMQ to orchestrate build and deploy processes, ensuring smooth transitions from development through deployment phases.

Handling Scalability in Development Processes

As teams scale, it becomes crucial to manage resources effectively:

- **Resource Monitoring and Load Balancing**: ZeroMQ facilitates real-time monitoring of system resources, enabling balanced workload distribution.

- **Dynamic Infrastructure Scaling**: Supports the adjustment of computational and storage resources in response to project needs, assuring consistent development velocity.

- **Distributed Task Scheduling**: ZeroMQ enables effective task queues, allocating development tasks dynamically across teams to maximize efficiency.

Here is a prototype load balancer using ZeroMQ's PUSH/PULL pattern for task assignments:

```
import zmq

context = zmq.Context()

# Setup PUSH socket to distribute development tasks
task_scheduler = context.socket(zmq.PUSH)
task_scheduler.bind("tcp://*:5581")

def assign_tasks():
    task_queue = ["Develop feature A", "Bug fix #42", "Optimize module Z"]
    for task in task_queue:
        task_scheduler.send_string(task)
        print(f"Assigned: {task}")
        time.sleep(1) # Delay to simulate task distribution pace

assign_tasks()
```

This simulation outlines task distribution among developers, demonstrating efficient resource management by leveraging a queue of software development activities distributed across varying nodes through ZeroMQ's robust push/pull paradigm.

Ensuring Fault Tolerance in Development Tools

Consistently operating development environments minimize disruptions:

- **Automated Error Detection and Recovery**: ZeroMQ apps

10.6. COLLABORATIVE AND DISTRIBUTED SOFTWARE DEVELOPMENT

utilize health checks and automated failover processes to detect and correct errors rapidly.

- **Transaction Consistency**: Implements mechanisms that ensure all modifications and contributions are appropriately tracked, ensuring development integrity.
- **Data Backup and Recovery Tools**: ZeroMQ integrates with backup solutions providing failsafe data recovery options.

Consider a heartbeat monitoring system utilizing a ZeroMQ dealer/router setup to perform health checks and status validation, ensuring system resilience.

Facilitating Security and Access Control

A secure environment is critical in protecting intellectual property and sensitive project information:

- **Authentication and Encryption**: ZeroMQ integrates CurveZMQ encryption, ensuring all communications are secure, supporting authentication layers to validate users.
- **Role-based Access Control (RBAC)**: Establishes clear permission hierarchies aligning with ZeroMQ's event-driven architectures, providing controlled access.
- **Audit and Compliance Tools**: Enables logging of operations and changes, offering transparency and audit trails conducive to compliance efforts and security checks.

Such security measures embody state-of-the-art protective measures ensuring integrity and security in collaborative development.

ZeroMQ stands as a robust facilitator for distributed software development, fostering collaboration and resilience with flexible messaging capabilities. Its integration into real-time communication, collaboration, version control, and security systems manifests into an ecosystem driving productivity and innovation in distributed environments. Through ZeroMQ, collaborative software development captures the forefront of modern engineering processes, cleverly balancing throughput, security, and fluidity of operations essential to next-generation software projects.

www.ingramcontent.com/pod-product-compliance
Lightning Source LLC
Chambersburg PA
CBHW052143220526
45471CB00004B/1496